The Dragon's Pearl

Sirin Phathanothai
with James Peck

A gripping memoir by the only foreigner ever raised in the innermost world of China's powerful and reclusive leadership provides a unique portrait of the near-mythic figures who led the Communist Revolution.

In 1956, eight-year-old Sirin Phathanothai and her twelve-year-old brother were secretly sent as an offering of goodwill from Thailand's political elite to China, a "living bridge" between the two countries at a time when Thailand was publicly a determined enemy of China. Sirin became the ward of Premier Zhou Enlai, and until his death in 1976, Zhou undertook to educate her in the ways of China. She came to know the legendary founders of Communist China—Zhu De, father of the Red Army; Foreign Minister Chen Yi; and President Liu Shaoqi. Sirin observed Mao himself on many formal and informal occasions, and one of Zhou's closest aides became her "father." The leaders' children, many of whom are prominent in China today, were her friends.

In 1966, the Cultural Revolution tore her privileged world apart. She was forced to denounce her brother and father over Radio Beijing. Under attack himself, Zhou could save her only by sending her into hiding deep in the heart of rural China. There, and later in a factory in Beijing, Sirin endured a life far harsher, and far more dangerous, than she had ever imagined.

Sirin Phathanothai maintains her close ties to China's leadership. She has played a critical role in political and economic matters between China and other countries. She lives in Paris, France, with her husband, Ambassador Anton Smitsendonk of the Netherlands. James Peck is Director of the U.S.-China Book Publications Project and Executive Editor of the Culture and Civilization Project at Yale University Press.

Autobiography
6 ⅛ x 9 ¼, 320 pages
8 pages of b/w photographs. index
0-671-79546-5.

The Dragon's Pearl

by SIRIN PHATHANOTHAI

with JAMES PECK

SIMON & SCHUSTER
New York   London   Toronto   Sydney   Tokyo   Singapore

SIMON & SCHUSTER
Rockefeller Center
1230 Avenue of the Americas
New York, New York 10020

Copyright © 1994 by Sirin Phathanothai

SIMON & SCHUSTER and colophon are registered trademarks
of Simon & Schuster Inc.

Designed by TK
Manufactured in the United States of America

10 9 8 7 6 5 4 3 2 1

Library of Congress Cataloging in Publication Data
TK
ISBN: 0-671-79546-5

Acknowledgments

In the years spent working on this book I have incurred countless debts of gratitude. Its writing was a long process of understanding and making sense of myself, my family, my guardians Premier Zhou Enlai and Liao Chengzhi, and China itself. As a little girl I was thrown onto the complex political stage of China, and I grew up among its great historical figures without truly comprehending my situation. To me, as to many others, China seems a repository of myths; living in their midst, I found I could only occasionally pierce them. And without my so choosing, I was borne along on the current of tumultuous political change and struggle occurring both in China and in my native Thailand. For years, until the idea of writing a book came up, I lived in silence about that time. It was my friends Sol and Pat Adler who, in 1982, encouraged me to undertake this work. In our numerous discussions, they were invaluable, helping me as well to draft accounts of the important events of my life. Without the two of them, I might never have begun.

Since then, many other people have contributed to this book. My father strongly supported the undertaking during the years I lived in Bangkok in the 1980s, up until his death in 1986. He did so by recounting for me aspects of his past and explaining the thinking that had underlain his actions. I learned a great deal about his views on China, Thailand, and the United States and his understanding of global politics. I came to comprehend more fully why in 1956, during the height of the Cold War, he and Prime Minister Pibul Songkram of Thailand secretely agreed with Premier Zhou Enlai to send my brother Warnwai and me to be raised in China under

Zhou's auspices.

As if they were meant to recover for me something that I had lost in childhood, the seven years I spent with my mother when I returned to Thailand with my two young boys served to help heal my old wound. My mother's love and care and long years of self-sacrifice for the family were the main inspiration for this book. Even in her daily actions I sensed the strength that had pulled the family together through numerous upheavals; it was her quiet self-respect that preserved its dignity. Her happy recollections of my childhood and our family history provided me with essential background information.

My brother Warnwai has been a continued source of support and encouragement throughout, and his diary, which I draw on in this book, was crucial both in providing transcripts or detailed notes of our meetings and conversations with Zhou Enlai and in assisting me to recall innumerable specific situations and events. Warnwai particularly helped me fill in the details of our early years in China, and his own story, interwoven with mine, is very much a part of my account. We experienced our unexpected historical mission each in our own way, but we shared a closeness that has sustained me through the years. Today he remains my inseparable companion on a mission of even wider scale, both politically and economically.

When my father died, my eldest brother, Man, became head of the Phathanothai family. In him I see the political and humane qualities that shaped my father's public life, and as a member of the Thai Parliament he has the same strong determination to bring them to bear in the world around him. He furthered my understanding of my father's personality, and his great knowledge of Thai political history has enriched my own account.

With friends in China, young and old, I have discussed many of the personalities and issues in this book. Several of these people are the children of the leaders I knew as I grew up, and they reminded me of many experiences we shared. Some of them, with their sense of historical responsibility, their objective vision of China today and in the future, already have taken on, or soon will take on, the task of leading the country into the more modern world. Their analysis of their country is acute, and I have been aided by their insight into its history and problems.

Acknowledgments

In 1986 Sol Adler introduced me to James Peck, and in the years since—in Bangkok, Beijing, and Paris—we have worked together closely. Jim was a good, patient listener, sometimes taking copious notes, sometimes taping our conversations. He was also a sensitive and intuitive questioner and writer who helped me enormously to make sense of what I had gone through. Jim became my trusted friend. I often said to him, "You understand me better than I do!" and this was true in many ways. Each time we worked together, he would observe me closely—my moods, my particular way of putting something—probing to find the best means for me to tell my story in my own voice. He often succeeded in finding the right words for the right idea. In all the drafts that went back and forth, I felt I had a firm advocate for what I wanted to say. His sound knowledge of China, too, made him all the more perceptive about me and the unique circumstances that molded my experience. He was an integral part of making this book.

My editor at Simon and Schuster, Alice Mayhew, had a strong intuitive sense from our first meeting of what this book could become, and she has been helpful in innumerable ways in the course of our working on the manuscript. Her assistant, Elizabeth Stein, contributed greatly to shaping the manuscript into its final form. I am deeply grateful to Roslyn Schloss for her fine editorial work.

The completion of this book owes a great deal to my discussions with, and the help and understanding of, my husband, Anton, who served in China for five years as the ambassador of the Netherlands. He knew how to guide me without interfering, and he has been a pillar of strength and security to me.

Finally, I thank my sons, Joe and Leo, who lived with this book in their lives for so many years. They made it easier for me to go through the ordeal of finishing it. In their own ways, they too are bridges between worlds, and their own lives have been shaped profoundly by the ways Premier Zhou Enlai and my father sought greater understanding among the different countries of the world.

This book is dedicated to the memory of those who put me on this road: my parents and Premier Zhou Enlai; to my brother Warnwai, who accompanied me to China; to my husband, Anton; and to my sons, Joe and Leo, who in their own way will continue the journey.

Contents

Epigraph TK

CHAPTER 1

A Politician's Daughter

"CHILDREN, I HAVE AN INVITATION FOR YOU to go to China from my close friend Premier Zhou Enlai. What do you say?"

Father looked intently at my brother Wai and me, a letter in his hand. I stared at the strange Chinese script.

The letter had arrived some days before; for the previous few weeks I had heard even more about China and Zhou Enlai than usual. Not only had Father disappeared for his countless meetings with the prime minister, Field Marshal Pibul Songkram, but I had been brought along more frequently. I had grown up learning to amuse my father's friends by repeating the big political words and names of their world. To me, only eight years old, "China" was just another such word—a country that could have been as far away as Switzerland or as close as Burma, for all I knew. For the last week I had been happily tossing about "China" and "Premier Zhou" and finding myself more at the center of my father's world than ever. It was great fun.

Wai had not been brought into my father's world to observe or amuse. Four years older than I, he had never shared those pleasures of mine. He had others. Wai's early years had been spent with our paternal grandparents in a fishing village set at the edge of the forest. He had loved it there, and though he had come to Bangkok when he was six and gradually adjusted to big-city ways, he was not drawn to Father's political world. But he immediately sensed some of the consequences of this surprising "invitation."

"Father, I'm too young to go. I'll go when I get bigger," Wai said.

At twelve, Wai was the younger son; perhaps he hoped our older brother, Man, would be asked instead.

Father shifted his gaze toward me. "I want to go!" I cried out impulsively. Why had I said this again? In the many discussions about China between Father and his friends in the last few weeks, I'd blurted out "Let me go" before. The results had been deeply gratifying to me: attention, merriment, a bantering back and forth of those big political words that formed so much of my life with Father. I thought happily of going abroad, showing off to my classmates, a trip of a few weeks. But this time I knew something was different. His look and his words seemed so final, so ominous to me. I felt as though I were peering into a dark chasm, trying to hold myself back from it, my comfortable daily world rapidly crumbling. Never had I felt this before: I was being sent away.

Father seemed pleased by my response. He barely paused, though. The words began to pour out.

"China is one of the greatest countries in the world, and we know very little about her. She is like an unknown treasure island to be explored. Your adventures there will yield great treasures."

I blocked my conflicting feelings for a moment and started to listen. Father always had a way of making his world sound appealing and exciting. About this invitation I was anything but clear. Was it to be my first vacation away from the family? His words kept coming, but they didn't quite seem to add up to that.

"You are going on behalf of Grandpa Pibul," he said. Pibul was not my grandfather, of course, but the title, like "uncle," more accurately defined his relationship to me, and my feelings for him, than "prime minister" could ever have. His photo hung prominently in our house, its inscription testimony to Father's close ties with him. "To every respected and beloved member of the Phathanothai family," Pibul had written, "with my eternal gratitude. I pray that the highest might of the Lord Buddha may protect you all."

"Though you are children," Father said, "you must not lose face for Thailand. You will be well taken care of. Zhou Enlai will be like a father to you."

Looking now at Wai, he continued, "You are the children of a politician, and our lives and futures are only partly a matter of our own choice."

Wai shifted about uneasily, listening carefully as Father went on. An important duty was being entrusted to him, a highly unusual role for a second son. He did not seem to be envisioning the adventure I had in mind.

"You will learn to adapt yourselves to the new world you are about to enter. Hopefully, you will do so fairly quickly. Sometimes it might not be a lot of fun; you may have to do things you don't want to do."

When Father spoke in that tone, there was no challenging his words. Wai was quiet. Finally he said, "Father's desire is my command." Absolute loyalty and obedience had been part of his traditional Thai education.

"In the old days," Father was saying, "the children of the leaders of small nations were often sent as gifts to the emperor of a big nation to show their goodwill, while learning the habits and thinking of the emperor and the big nation. That is what you will do in China."

Father carefully folded up Zhou's letter. "In any case," Father added with renewed enthusiasm, "your new life will certainly be full of discovery and excitement. Premier Zhou is a wonderful and exceptional man who will give your lives in China great meaning and much adventure."

Father turned to an obviously reluctant Wai. "Look at Sirin, so willing, so brave."

Father didn't say he would miss us. He didn't say how long it would be. He gave us no specifics at all.

DURING THOSE NEXT THREE DAYS before we went, my sense of dread increased as my parents, seemingly unaware of my feelings, praised my determination. I clung more than ever to the admiration and attention directed at me. Mother quickly stepped in to make the final arrangements, and we busied ourselves with the preparations. She spoke proudly of my going with Wai, but underneath I detected a profound uneasiness. Wai and I didn't speak about it either; our worlds had been rather separate, and he was making his own preparations to go.

Mother had always been a highly efficient person, organizing both the household and my father's newspaper. From the beginning, she had evidently known what it meant to be a politician's wife, or at least what it meant to be married to my father. She was a reliable emotional presence for us, but my father's decision to send us to China showed just how much their marriage had been founded on a commitment to Father's political life. "We have five children," I overheard her say to Father. "and we want all of them to have a bright future. I trust your judgment. If you think this will be a fine opportunity for Warnwai and Sirin to make their lives meaningful, I as a mother cannot object. If their going is for the better, we cannot hold them back." I turned away, very sad. Her voice had been both strong and deeply pained.

For reasons I did not understand, practically no one was to know where we were going. Mother took me to say good-bye to my teachers. I'd be on leave for a term, she had told them. That briefly cheered me. A term was not so long. My teachers did not ask where I was going; Mother had not implied that they should. Only abroad. Father's relation to the prime minister precluded their even indirectly expressing curiosity.

I stood there in the empty hall, trying to figure out how to tell my friends I was going. Mother was waiting in the car for me to make my good-byes. I listened to the drone of the recitations from the classrooms, and for a brief moment I felt happy to be leaving. The bell rang; I hesitated; what was I to say? I turned away and walked down the corridor, stopping only when I heard one of my closest friends calling to me above the din of the morning break. I ran back. She began to question me as a growing circle of friends surrounded us. Where had I been the last week? Where was I off to now?

Even if we had been alone, I could not have told her anything of the truth. Her father was the head of the Thai Air Force, but he was not part of my father and Pibul's discussions of China. I knew it was dangerous to speak. "Loose lips kill," my father often said.

I proudly announced that I was preparing to go abroad and was leaving the next day.

"Where are you going?" they cried.

For a moment I was stumped. And then out popped "Bandung." It could have been a country, a town—all I remembered was that it was a fine place where Zhou Enlai had first met and so impressed Prince Warnwai, Thailand's most famed diplomat. It was after that meeting that China had become my father's virtual obsession.

Then the bell announced the end of the break. I waved good-bye, running off to the car, where Mother was waiting anxiously.

"Don't worry," I whispered in her ear. "I told my friends I was going to Bandung." She looked immensely relieved.

We picked up Wai and then drove to the bungalow compound where Pibul lived. I had spent many happy hours in those rooms, the scene of some of my most outrageous behavior. Each time I dashed in, I'd pause long enough to glance at the large portrait of Pibul in full field marshal's uniform in the entrance hall. He stood there so impressive and handsome, a perfect military commander. I loved that sense of strength and discipline in him, but I loved even more how he greeted me in his relaxed, playful way. In person Pibul was rather short and slight. His eyes always seemed bright, their liveliness accentuated by his easy smile. He stood very erect, and his composed manner exuded refinement and neatness. He loved to walk with Father, but he was so fast that I could never keep up with them.

After I'd passed through the entrance hall, I'd usually run upstairs to his study, where he often received Father. His golf clubs, a source of considerable pride, stood in one corner. Books neatly lined the walls of his study, and pictures of his family were prominent, as they were throughout the house. Pibul had loved French art and furniture ever since he had lived in Paris in the 1930s, and there was much of both everywhere, offset by the highly polished wood floors. The windows were almost always open, the wind blowing gently through the rooms and corridors.

I remembered coming the previous year to Pibul's annual birthday celebration, waiting along with the various government ministers, generals, and foreign diplomats for Pibul to make his entrance.

Per Thai custom, guests were expected to bring baskets of flowers as birthday gifts and to leave them outside the entrance to the house with their calling cards suitably inscribed with birthday wishes.

Father tended to shun such official occasions, but he was particularly adamant about avoiding this one. He and Pibul had had another of their ferocious arguments. They often argued over the years, and Father would then quietly sulk, withdrawing into his study. On those occasions it was Pibul who always made the first move to thaw the ice.

I knew the two of them had been in prison together before I was born; what a prison was, or why they had been there, was not entirely clear to me. But it was certainly a place that forged strong friendships. Pibul often spoke of how the past had shaped their ties.

"One can see a person better when one is in difficulty, but one can trust that person as one would oneself when in prison and facing the death penalty," he'd say about my father. "Sang knows me better than my wife." Pibul, who was reserved and often pessimistic, was cheered by my father's determined optimism. After the two of them had been sentenced to death, Father had written poems on the prison wall to boost Pibul's spirits: "Even if one is in prison now, one is sure to be on one's way soon, even if one doesn't know when. The days of freedom will come!"

Perhaps because they knew each other so well, they could allow their disputes to rage on. Whatever the current one was, Mother and I were expected at the party. I left our basket of flowers prominently at the head of the enormously long trail of bouquets and baskets, then joined Mother in the large waiting room. Wanting one last look, I dashed out again. The flowers were gone! At first I thought others might have been placed in front of them, so I looked carefully through the others lined up near where Pibul would enter. Nothing. I searched everywhere until I felt the cold eyes of someone turning away as I glanced at him, a person I knew did not wish my father well. I was frantic. Pibul might be coming at any moment.

I rushed back into the house. Mother was not to be seen. I edged my way up the stairs toward Pibul's private quarters. No one was around. I walked through several quiet rooms, then toward the bedroom. Suddenly there waas Pibul, standing in front of a mirror, finishing his shave. First startled, as was I, he bent down to me.

"Whatever is the matter?" he asked gently, seeing my tears.

"Someone has taken my flowers for you, Grandpa Pibul," I cried.

"Well," he said, "find them we will." Whereupon he loudly called for the soldiers to search all the gifts. He would not descend the stairs until mine was found! By now he had added the jacket and a colorful sash to his splendid white satin suit. As we stood there together, he asked about my father. Unbeknown to me, he was taking the opportunity to mend their most recent rupture. Soon the flowers were found, and Pibul was informed that they had been placed at the very front of the presents.

"Time for us to make our entrance," he said. Taking my hand, he led me down the steps, and we emerged together to greet the crowds. I bowed down, reached for my flowers, and proudly presented them to a much-amused prime minister. Hours later I overheard Mother's account to Father and swelled with pride as he praised my courage and cleverness.

FOR SEVERAL YEARS Father had been taking me with him when he went to see Pibul. I'd sit on Pibul's lap, enjoying my favorite perch from which to listen to their words on various weighty subjects. They were just big words to me, except that I seemed to grasp the significance attached to particular ones. What was important, what not; what words had a particular emphasis or concern associated with them: these I learned. I came to learn when I could interrupt, and when not. And I learned how to venture right up to the boundary of the acceptable, how to be blunt, and what never to repeat to even my closest school friends.

Pibul often encouraged me. One morning when Father had all but ignored me for several weeks because of his work, I made him promise to take me and my friends out for ice cream that afternoon. After school my friends and I gathered expectantly at my house, playing hide-and-seek as we waited. As my friends became impatient, I became more and more embarrassed. Clearly Father had forgotten. Furious, I called up his office. He wasn't there. He was meeting with Pibul and was not to be disturbed.

I immediately picked up the phone and dialed Pibul's personal number. "I want to speak to Grandpa Pibul," I said, telling the aide who I was. When Pibul came to the phone, I said, "Grandpa, Father broke his promise to take my friends and me out for an ice cream. Could you please send him home right away?"

Pibul burst into laughter, and I heard him speaking with my father. "I guess the government will have to wait awhile." Father rushed home, took us out for ice cream, and then disappeared back to Pibul's compound. All in all, it was a most triumphant ice cream party.

My antics quickly began to revolve around politics, and I learned to use those big words in ways that amused without being silly. I had grown up hearing about the war in Korea, evidently a place where Thai soldiers had gone. Father had long been uneasy about what had happened there, I sensed. When the words came up, he became quite serious. Toward the end of the Korean War in 1953, Father had watched films of various battles between the United Nations and the Chinese troops. He was shaken by what he saw. Thailand, he repeatedly said, had committed itself by sending troops to fight on the allied side, and the Chinese had held their own against the greatest military power on the globe. I sat on Pibul's lap one night as he, too, watched the films. It was during one of their discussions afterward that, perplexed by their evident distress. I turned to Pibul and said, "Grandpa, we lost the war, didn't we?"

Pibul did not say anything. He just softly placed his fingers over my lips.

Because our house was so filled with political words, with men enveloped in their endless meetings, my brothers, Man and Wai, assumed my father's ways as well. Father was the secretary-general of the workers' union, and truckloads of representatives, sometimes a hundred or so, would cram into the huge meeting room in our house. Wai and Man watched the proceedings secretly, later acting out their own rendition of the drama they had observed. They and their friends would sneak into the empty room and bang on the table, shouting, "This is a serious matter, we must do something about it. We demand government action!" And they would lard their speeches with the long words they had heard. They were more adept than I, who was so much younger. And they totally excluded me from their games; indeed, I was always largely separate from their world of friends.

But I had my revenge. By the time I was three, Father had brought me into his world, where I would sit on his lap listening to the raucous discussions or watch him speaking to the groups that gathered. He had a powerful voice. Beneath the eloquent language was a mesmerizing force. It made him an effective propagandist for Pibul.

Often I saw him argue with others. I learned to sit through even the most vehement and heated discussions, bewildered at times by the intensity but able to take it in. Though I knew Pibul and Father fought often, they did not do so in front of me.

Once, while playing in our courtyard, I saw an unfamiliar car turn in through the gates. From the smart salute the guards gave, I knew a "high" uncle or grandpa had arrived. I did not know that it was General Pao Sriyanon, head of the Thai police force and one of Pibul's top lieutenants. Called the "Iron Man of Asia" by friends and enemies alike, he was greatly feared. When I saw his tall, well-built, imposing figure emerge smoking a cigar, I approached his car. I wasn't sure of his name, but that cigar brought to mind vague images of things I'd heard—perhaps from Father, perhaps in the union hall where the many speakers declared what had to be changed by the government.

Not at all intimidated, I ran up to this visitor and asked who he was. "Uncle Pao," he replied.

Pao, cigars, guns: this I somehow knew in a flash. I looked at his cigar and pointed. "Uncle, can that shoot?"

"Yes, like this." He burst into laughter, blowing out huge rings of smoke and stopping only to resume laughing.

When he picked me up, I asked if he had come to see Father. When he gave the expected reply, I said, "Follow me." I led him into the house and toward Father's study, and when Father ushered him into the room, I climbed onto Pao's lap, claiming my undisputed right to remain.

Pao and Father argued vehemently for some time.

Pao was adamant. "We must exterminate those Communist bastards. He must be put to death."

What, I wondered, was a Communist? Pao and Father seemed to share a dislike of them, but Father did not wish them killed, or at least not this one. Tempers flared; in my father's world words were direct and blunt. I was not particularly afraid: I detected that Father and Pao did not dislike each other.

The words made little sense to me, but I quickly perceived from the shifting tone the course of the discussion and its likely outcome. Pao slowly gave way to my father's arguments. While he left without some of the customary amenities, he was not hostile.

Father seemed unusually relieved. That night, before he left for his nightly meeting with Pibul, he took me out for ice cream. "Is your friend a good man or a bad man?" I asked.

"He is a political man," he replied. "You are the daughter of a political man, and someday you will understand what this means."

I nodded. I had gotten an equally evasive answer, I thought, when I had tried to find out what a Communist was. This "political" world, with its special, unfathomable words, was a strange but alluring one. I became ever more determined to master it.

ANY SENSE THAT I WAS BEING LEFT OUT engendered in me an even greater passion to be included. Perhaps that is why I felt so responsible for my going to China. One day, Father took me to yet another of those meetings that were filled with discussions of China. But this time I felt something had been resolved between him and Pibul. Though in later years the words had to be recounted for me, emotionally I never forgot that moment.

"In the old days," Pibul said as I sat on his lap, "we small nations often sent our rulers' children to China to show our loyalty and devotion to the emperor. By your suggesting that I send your son on my behalf to study in China under the care of the Chinese government, we could once again show Zhou Enlai our sincere determination to improve relations and our implicit trust in China. No trust could be greater than parting with your own child. It is the beginning of a relationship that will be carried on by your children and by their children to the third generation and beyond. Furthermore, it's good to have a little living bridge between our two countries."

I knew from Pibul's voice that something extremely important was happening; I knew as well that Pibul's children were not the ones being considered. My brother Wai—why him? What about me? Why was I being left out?

"Grandpa Pibul, I want to go! Let me go, too. I'm a politician's daughter. I won't cry."

Pibul laughed, then stopped. In an unusually quiet voice he asked, "What do you want to be when you grow up?"

I knew exactly the right answer: A diplomat for Thailand."

Getting those words out proved difficult. But even as I stumbled, Pibul said, with a knowing look at my father, "This child will be something special when she grows up, I'm sure."

I left satisfied. I had seen the look of approval in my father's eyes, and I proudly thought I had come up with the idea of going to China all by myself. Little did I know that it was Father who had suggested the whole idea to Pibul after carefully studying China's old tributary system.

I REMEMBERED MY IMPULSIVE ACT WITH CHAGRIN as we pulled up to Pibul's house the morning I left my school. Why was I still acting as though I wanted to go away?

When I saw Pibul, though, my doubts gave way; I moved into my accustomed role, feeling very much my claim to a starring part in the unfolding drama. Unlike me, Wai was quiet, standing there in his white sharkskin suit, the latest fashion in Bangkok.

At lunch Pibul seemed relaxed, swapping stories with Father of their early years. Father talked about Wai's early years in the fishing village with his grandparents and how Wai had returned from school one day after coming to Bangkok with his new shoes tied around his neck, preferring that to getting any dirt on his first pair of shoes.

Pibul laughed. "Nothing to be ashamed of. We got our first pairs of shoes much later than he did, and I can assure you that what happened to us was much worse. I screamed the first time I saw shoes and caused no end of trouble at school by insisting that I did not need to wear them." He paused, then looked directly at me. "You will find many new things in China: different food, different clothes, new habits, all strange and unlike what you are used to. Try to learn about them and adapt yourselves. You are going on my behalf, so you have a heavy load. You will be a bridge between Thailand and China. I hope this bridge you are building will turn out to be a strong one."

Never had I felt so proud. It had certainly not occurred to me that our trip was to be so important. Although Pibul's advice about living in China was uncomfortably clear and direct, I was intoxicated by my role. My brother was not. He was somewhat reserved, uneasy about his new responsibility. But his reluctance seemed to have made him all the more earnest. That day he began his practice of taking notes of all our "official meetings" and recording the events in a diary.

After lunch and a Thai dance performed by the leading dancer of the Grand National Theater, Pibul presented Wai and me with gold Parker pens to encourage us in our studies. We sat on the floor to give the Thai *wai*, placing our foreheads on his knees, and said good-bye.

That night we continued our round of farewells. Father took us to see Admiral Luang Yudhasard Kosol, the supreme commander of the navy and one of his closest associates in his work on China. I had been to Luang Yudhasard's palatial house many times. Its roof, covered with wires and antennae of all sorts, made it stand out eerily against the evening sky.

He embraced us warmly, but he seemed sad. "Sang, are you sure you are right to send these two children away tomorrow?"

Father quickly dismissed Luang Yudhasard's uneasiness. For a while they talked about a secret visit of a Thai naval delegation to China, and Father assured him that premier Zhou would give it a warm welcome. Kosol seemed relieved by that and turned to encourage us.

"China is a great country. The language is hard; perhaps it is the most difficult in the world. But you are lucky. I wish I could go myself."

He gave us two handsome traveling bags as parting gifts, kissed our heads fondly, and murmured a few Buddhist prayers to protect us on our journey.

I returned home that night exhausted, but I could not sleep. I heard the breathing of my baby sister, Tukta—and imagined that I might never see her again. I heard my mother moving about, packing the bags Luang Yudhasard had given us, and occasionally I heard the faint sound of Father's voice.

I fell into a troubled sleep only to awaken with a start. "I'll never see them again, I'll never see them again," I thought. When I dozed off once more, it was into a nightmare of explosions and furiously burning fires that left me shaken. I sought out my mother, put my head into her arms, and finally fell back asleep.

At 5 A.M. I was awakened and dressed in a new blue traveling suit. I told myself I felt better, so grown up. But the tears kept threatening to come. Ba Yiad, the chief cook, and Jit, my maid, had been up for hours, preparing for my departure, but they could not understand why I was being sent away. Jit cried as she fixed my hair.

"Where are you going?" she kept asking. "Do they have somebody to do your hair? Who will prepare your clothes?" Jit had always tended to all my personal needs—my dresses, my hair, my baths. It was her passion to try out different hairdos on me, and often she made me fancy dresses, laughing as I paraded around like a little princess in her creations.

"If you are left with nobody to care for you, please tell your mother. I will come to serve you," she continued, tears streaming down her face. Then she dashed out to kneel in front of the Buddhist altar in our home and pray for my safe trip and safe stay.

It hadn't occurred to me that I might have to leave my maids behind.

I went downstairs to say good-bye to Ba Yiad. Tradition prevented her from ever coming upstairs, but often I'd watched her preparing our food. She had been with our family almost from the very beginning. She, too, fought back tears as I said goody-bye. It was getting harder and harder to maintain my composure.

The guards seemed unusually solemn and forlorn.

Father came to say good-bye. He explained that he could not be seen with us at the airport. Too much attention would be aroused, and the very well-being of the family depended on our trip's remaining a secret.

For once he said little and with no ceremony. He hugged us both tightly. "Sending you away, you two loved ones, is like cutting out a piece of my heart. But be brave. Don't be afraid, children. Look after yourselves."

The airport send-off was simple, more tense than sad. Mother's smile was a thin mask over her worry. Wai and I struggled to stay composed, he by quietly withdrawing, I by continuing to chatter. Abruptly I embraced and kissed everyone and walked to the plane without looking back. As it started down the runway, my tears began to flow.

The date was August 19, 1956.

CHAPTER 2

The World of My Father

IN THE LATE 1940s, when I was born, my father was at the pinnacle of his power. He was Field Marshal Pibul's closest adviser, and Pibul would come to serve as Thailand's prime minister longer than anyone else in the twentieth century.

Of their history together I knew little. Up to the day he died, Father himself rarely talked about it. He had been born in 1914 in a fishing village in the province of Samut Prakhan, not far from Bangkok. His own father, the fisherman with whom Wai would later live as a small child, chose my father, the youngest of four, as the child who should receive an education. He was sent to a monastery attached to a well-known temple to study with a Buddhist monk. As was the custom, he served as the monk's attendant and errand boy as well. His lifelong love of words began at that time. He read everything he could, saving all his money for books, some of which remained from those early years to line the walls of his book-filled study as I grew up.

When, at seventeen, he won a government scholarship to the nor-

mal school in Bangkok, he found it difficult, as Wai also did, to adjust to urban ways. Like Pibul, he had never worn regular shoes. But
if some urban ways were difficult to master, others were not. He
soon found himself swept up in the politics that were to shape Thailand's future for several generations.

In 1932 Pibul and Dr. Pridi Phanomyong led the revolution that
changed Thailand's absolute monarchy into a constitutional one.
For years the friendship and conflicts between these two men signif-
icantly shaped the course of Thai politics. They had lived and studied together in Paris and had been deeply influenced by the French
Revolution. In those days they had complemented each other well.
Pridi studied law and politics, Pibul military science. When they returned to Thailand, they and other Paris-trained students organized
an underground People's Party. As Thailand was suffering the effects of the collapse of the world economic market in the early thirties, they launched their revolution.

To some, this upheaval that created a constitutional monarchy was
merely a realignment of power within the Thai elite; to others, a decisive change in the structure of Thai polity and economy that
broadened the base of power and introduced an element of genuine
democracy. Father clearly felt it was the latter. It won his immediate
support and enthusiasm, and its swift success plunged him into new
areas of study. He quickly taught himself English in order to read
the classics of Western political theory and to study international
politics. Throughout his life, he would turn to books whenever he
sought to understand a new subject. In the early 1950s, when he
started collecting books about China and communism, it was merely
the continuation of this old habit. Over the years, though, his interest in Buddhism remained; he became extremely learned in its theo-
ries, once making a pilgrimage to India to trace the footsteps of the
lord Buddha. He seemed equally at ease in both that world and the
new one to which Thailand was seeking to adjust.

When Prince Boworadej sought to restore the former regime in
1933, a year after the revolution, Father joined the forces defending
Bangkok. After this failed attempt by the old order to regain its
power, Father returned to his native province, afire with the hope of
spreading modern education. He began to write regularly on political and international subjects and soon became a daily commentator

for the national radio station. His strong, deep voice and oratorical skills served him well. By twenty-one he was a radio star earning two baht per show, a princely sum at the time, enough to cover a person's food needs for a month.

Pibul heard Father's broadcasts; within a year he had gotten my father to join the State Department of Propaganda. But it was Father's radio show, *Mr. Mun and Mr. Kong*, that first made him famous. The program was broadcast every morning at seven. Father wrote most of the dialogues that constituted the show, and he took the part of Mr. Mun while a colleague spoke the views of Mr. Kong. The subjects ranged from domestic household issues to global politics, but it was obviously the witty, humorous, sharp-tongued exchanges and the intense Thai patriotism that made the show such a success.

Father became a sought-after political figure. When he traveled to a seaside resort to rest one weekend, a colleague told him to look up the governor of the district.

Father arrived late in the evening, but as the governor was eager for news and proclaimed himself an avid fan of Father's radio broadcasts, he insisted upon talking until all hours of the night. Since a well-known businessman and his family were already staying with him, the spare rooms were taken, but Father was quite happy to sleep on the floor in a corridor.

Finally, Father was able to bid his host good night. Soon sleeping deeply, he heard nothing until a young lady opened her bedroom door and, not expecting to find anything on the floor, stepped on top of him, stumbled, and fell, hurting herself. Father awoke to find a quite attractive woman sprawled beside him.

Father was infatuated. He extended his stay at the governor's residence, spending as much time as he could talking with her. The governor was not terribly obliging. He much preferred that Father talk with him.

The young woman's name was Vilai Chaiyakarn, and like Father, she was born in 1914. Her parents were Vietnamese, but they had died when she was three and she had been brought up by her maternal grandparents, who had emigrated from Saigon years earlier. When she was twelve, both grandparents had died and she had become the ward of a distant uncle, K. Thow, an overseas Chinese. He was was the head of a highly successful business that by the early 1930s had become very prominent in foreign rice markets, maintaining close contacts with the East Asia TIC Company, the Borneo Company, and such big Japanese firms as Isube Mitsui. He built his own docks in Bangkok to handle the growing exports and successfully founded a business empire. The company owned some eight ships and virtually dominated the rice export trade. Vilai was very talented at finances herself, and by seventeen she was deeply involved in overseeing the family's financial interests. She was sought after and well respected, and her uncle was eager for her to make a marriage that would strengthen the family's economic position.

My father was not what her uncle had in mind. Uncle Thow and other family members feared any immersion in Thai politics: a business family, particularly an overseas Chinese family, linked with a Thai politician risked great danger when political tides shifted. He quickly stepped in to forbid her from seeing Father, and tradition strictly enjoined a young man from calling on a young lady without permission.

For weeks after their meeting at the governor's house, Father tried to contact her. He received no answer to his notes, and he lacked an appropriate way to reach her directly. Then one afternoon he found himself walking around the high wall enclosing her house. Impulsively, he clambered up and jumped over to the other side. Her servant girl stood transfixed in horror at his unexpected appearance. But she quickly led him to Vilai's room, where Father proposed and my mother accepted.

Uncle Thow, of course, was not pleased. He was not even slightly assuaged when Lord Prachakrit Kornchak, the lord mayor of Bangkok, whose son was Thailand's foreign minister, called on him and formally asked for his niece's hand on Father's behalf in accordance with Thai custom. He could not refuse. His effort to avoid politics had now placed him in the position of offending politically powerful people if he did not sanction the marriage. Prachakrit Kornchak himself officiated at the large wedding attended by many senior government and business people.

But Uncle Thow could refuse what my mother knew he would— any future contact with her. Their relations became distant. Even when she faced the most difficult trials in the years ahead, she never turned to her family, nor did they ever seek to help her. She had chosen to live in a political world, and there she remained.

The year after they were married, Father was appointed the head of the radio and newspaper sections of the Government Publicity Department. In 1938 Pibul became prime minister. Shortly thereafter, as the Japanese threat grew, he made Father the government spokesman and put him in charge of all government propaganda.

This marked the real beginning of their intimate and tumultuous relationship. Father was the intellectual, always ready with ideas, quick to analyze situations, eager to argue and discuss. Pibul was down to earth, a man of action, a soldier. Like Father, he came from a rural family. He, too, had been a pupil in his hometown's temple school and had gone on to study in Bangkok, winning a scholarship to the Royal Military Academy at the age of twenty. After World War I he was sent to France to continue his military studies. In 1932, when he was thirty-four and a major in the army, he became the key military leader of the revolution.

Pibul loved to talk, and with my father the topics ranged from the daily world of politics to the recondite details of the history of Buddhism. Father's irrepressible sense of humor appealed to him as well. Father was moody—he could sink into depressed immobility at times—but Pibul seemed to know how to deal with his moods, and his stubbornness.

With the German occupation of France in June 1940, Pibul knew that French colonialism in Indochina would soon give way. The precarious balancing act that had so successfully allowed Thailand to maintain its independence among the great powers throughout the period of European expansion was threatened as never before. In the days immediately before Pearl Harbor, Pibul issued orders to the troops to be prepared for a Japanese invasion. Though he had little faith in the course of the negotiations in Washington between Japan and the United States, he did not expect them to collapse as quickly as they did. On December 6, 1941, he left Bangkok for an inspection tour of the eastern border. Twenty-four hours later the Japanese were deep into Thailand, having landed at various sites along the coast.

As resistance flared and casualties mounted, Pibul met with the Japanese ambassador, who came accompanied by twenty senior

Japanese military officers. The Japanese demanded Thai cooperation. Pibul and his cabinet agreed to end resistance and to allow the Japanese troops passage through Thailand on the condition that Japan at least nominally respect Thailand's independence and territorial integrity. A committee headed by Prince Warnwai and Pridi was set up to negotiate Thailand's surrender. Thailand was forced to declare war against the Allies, and on January 25 my father read the formal announcement over the radio. He was to remain Thailand's chief public spokesman throughout the war.

Had I not gone to China, my father's and Pibul's roles in "collaborating" with the Japanese would never have been a critical issue for me. In China, "collaborators" were bitterly condemned. The lives of the heroes of the Chinese revolution I came to know, the texts I read in all my classes, were imbued with the sacrifices of those who had died fighting the Japanese. Yet I was an honored guest, and my father was held in high esteem by Zhou Enlai and others. Publicly, collaboration was vehemently attacked; in private, hardly a word was ever said to me. What was I to make of my father?

I knew that he and Pibul had spent six months together in the same prison cell. My mother's visits were part of the family folklore: how she would peep through a small wooden hole day after day to talk to them; how she returned each day with various Thai dishes, bringing Man along; how again and again Man asked Father through the bars, "Why have they locked you and Grandpa Pibul up?"

"This is a special school for politicians," Father would reply. "Perhaps when you grow up you will go into politics."

Why they had been there was not clear to me as a child. Something about people opposed to what my father was seeking to accomplish, perhaps. The stories I heard were of his opposition to the Japanese, not of his collaboration with them. Once, when Father had heard that the Japanese military were about to arrest an editor of a Chinese-language paper, he had called to warn the man to flee. Father had not known his own phone was tapped, and when the tip was traced back to him, a coterie of Japanese army officers with samurai swords hanging from their waists had charged into his office. "You dared to help a Communist!" the officer shouted at him.

Father had rebuked them, accusing them of undermining his position as head of the government department in charge of radio broadcasts and newspapers by plotting to seize the editor secretly. What would my father say to the people under him? What would he say to the man's family? Was this the friendship the Japanese talked so much about?

His audacity left the officers unsettled. They withdrew. But immediately afterward, Father noticed that a tail had been placed on him, one so evident, so unconcerned about being noticed, as to be almost impossible to shake. Father called up the Japanese press attaché, related the story to him, and asked him to repeat it to the Japanese ambassador. A few days later the ambassador sent an apology. The tail disappeared.

This was the father I knew. His intense Thai nationalism was always a part of the stories of those years. He had persuaded Pibul to have the Thai national anthem played on the radio every morning at eight and every evening at six. Everyone was to stop work and quietly pay tribute to the country, thereby expressing their resistance to the Japanese.

These were the stories I heard during my earliest years. Of the way Pridi and Pibul had ended up complementing each other's efforts to protect Thailand from the ravages of World War II, I knew nothing. That it was the Americans who had demanded that Pibul and Father be tried for war crimes was unknown to me as well. Later Father told me how Pibul had refused to arrest resistance leaders and had looked the other way as Pridi developed contacts with the Allies in World War II. Pibul wanted Thailand to emerge as unscathed from the war as possible, thus the only policy was to play off the big powers against each other, Pridi with the Americans, Pibul with the Japanese. The victory of the Allies brought Pridi to power, but he, in turn, refused to turn over Pibul and his generals and important government officials like Father to the Allied tribunal in Singapore, insisting that Thailand's sovereignty required that they be tried before Thailand's Supreme Court.

Pridi certainly knew the likely result; Thai politics was that kind of game. Six months later Pibul and my father were quietly released, the Supreme Court having ruled that they could not be tried under the war crime statute imposing the death sentence that had been enacted after the end of the war. Released from prison, Pibul and my father remained close. Pibul retired to his village, gardening and attending to his flowers and chickens. Father stayed largely at home, working as a free-lance columnist.

In June 1946, shortly after Pibul and Father's release, young King Ananda was mysteriously killed. Pridi was the prince regent and thus was held accountable for what happened. In addition, the government was widely criticized for failing to deal adequately with the enormous problems left in the wake of the war, and thus the charismatic figure of Pibul was turned to once again.

On November 8, 1947, a coup brought Pibul back to power. He invited Father to join the cabinet. Father refused. He remained Pibul's confidant, but his only official post was that of secretary-general of the workers' union. With Pibul's restoration to power, Father could turn himself wholeheartedly to journalism, setting up a daily paper that he himself edited. Mother quickly put her financial and accounting talents to use as acting general manager. The paper, called *Satienraparb* ("Forever"), soon exerted considerable influence in Thai politics. Father's ties with Pibul ensured a ready audience, but his skills as a journalist and propagandist rendered it a far more important and successful venture than it might otherwise have been in the ten years Pibul was prime minister.

As secretary-general of the workers' union, Father was given an official residence in a peaceful residential area in Klong Teny. The large wooden house, shaded by immense tropical trees, bordered a canal and a spacious walled garden. Four gardeners were employed just to keep the flowers and plants in perfect condition. Father had a passion for orchids, so he added an orchid lodge to the garden area. No matter how busy or preoccupied, he could be found tending his orchids early every morning. Each one that bloomed he celebrated as a personal triumph.

The house had three floors and some twenty rooms. An enormous conference room was on the first floor, while outside the house was the kitchen and, attached to it, the maids' rooms. Although I would play with the cook and talk with my maids, I was not allowed ever to enter the houses set aside for them. They had come, as servants often did then, from the countryside, recommended by relatives, and it was expected that they stay for life. They wore colorful sarongs and always kneeled upon entering the house, moving quietly and discreetly. When serving my parents or talking with them, they sat on the floor. When passing by they always bent so that they never stood taller than, or looked down on, anyone who was their superior or a member of the older generation. Often they looked down at the floor while talking.

Near the entrance gate was a small house for our Indian guards, who were on shift twenty-four hours a day. They carried large sticks but not guns. My brothers and I often wondered what went on in the "Indian house." The guards and their wives kept largely to themselves and never talked much to us.

Man was particularly curious about them. "They don't brush their teeth," he announced with great authority after several days of spying on them. "They chew some kind of root instead."

"I think it's sugarcane," Wai suggested. "Maybe we should stop cleaning ours and chew the roots." We all knew that their teeth were much whiter and stronger looking than ours.

"So what do they do all day?" I asked. They never seemed to leave their house.

"They cook," Man said, "and they are very strict with their children."

Mother understood our fear on the latter point. Whenever one of us really misbehaved, she threatened to send us to live in the "Indian house."

Behind the house was another large tract of land, where Mother had constructed a chicken coop so that we could have fresh eggs every morning. Man and Wai, however, thought it made a wonderful meeting place for their friends, and so they drove the chickens out (and the girls away) whenever they convened. Their mischievous activities included throwing stones at passing cars and disappearing before they were caught. Of course, people would be too intimidated to complain about being hit by flying rocks coming from such a large house. I watched my brothers happily pursuing such pranks until they happened to lob one particularly large stone at what turned out to be the car of the American ambassador. The car came to a screeching halt and abruptly drove into the entrance. An angry-looking ambassador was soon knocking at Father's conference room door. After his meetings that night, Father stormed into the bedroom, where some five boys were all pretending to sleep. Only little Wai's eyes were unable to stay shut. Father spanked each in turn, and neither Man nor Wai was let out for the house for three days.

Such discipline was rarely ever part of my own life. I was adept at the rules of my father's world. I knew as I sat with him for hours in the library that amid all those books one was to show a proper reserve, as though it were a sacred place. He spent hours writing or arranging and rearranging his favorite books. Often scholars came to discuss philosophy and history. Their big words, however, I did not remember. I had chosen the political ones with which to play.

CHAPTER 3

Secret Missions

CHINA HAD FILLED MY FATHER'S world for more than a year before Wai and I left. People who had been to China came and went. Gifts were brought. Chinese movies were shown. Friends of my father's would sit and tell him about their trips. I was puzzled to see pictures of them in the papers later, arrested for having gone. The higher-ups, Father explained, were not pleased. The Americans opposed Thai contacts with China, but Father wished to establish a relationship secretly and then begin to raise the issue publicly through his newspaper. Zhou Enlai had invited Thai politicians to come and see China for themselves.

"We know so little about China," Father would say.

At first Pibul was vehement in his opposition. To my father's argument that Thailand needed to learn to live with China, that America was far while China was near, Pibul protested that Thailand needed American dollars and could not afford to alienate the United States. Nor could it afford to ignore the Chinese, Father countered: Thailand would find them on its doorstep long before the United States could send troops.

The dispute between my father and Pibul had erupted one week-end at Pibul's retreat at the Lopuri military base, where my family would often visit so the two of them could discuss matters informally. For once the door was closed to me, but I could hear their angry voices for hours.

"I cannot just let your people go to China and come back. What will I tell the Americans?" Pibul said.

"We must learn to live with China. We can no longer ignore her. . . . We lost many, many men in that war . . . it was a mistake," Father said.

Finally, late at night, Father left in a fury. When Mother urged him to approach Pibul with some gesture of conciliation, Father was as obstinate as ever. As usual, Mother drew me into her mediating efforts, taking me with her to Pibul's house to offer him some of his favorite foods and to give him an indirect opportunity to assuage Father through his gracious reception of Mother and me.

In the months that followed, he and my father reached a compromise.

"I have to send them to prison," Pibul said of those returning from China. "I must be able to tell the Americans. So I'll arrest them, you'll take lots of pictures and publish the news, and I'll let them out an hour later.

"Thus every delegation that went the year before I left was greeted by the police upon return, arrested, and then whisked away, often to our house, where Father excitedly talked of their visit and their meetings with Zhou Enlai.

"You know, my life has changed from the back of my hand to my palm," Father frequently said to the visitors that came.

In Thailand Father was still publicly seen as a virulent anti-Communist. The images of Communists with huge, cowlike teeth threatening to chew us up were his creations. No one had more ferociously denounced the Chinese Communists in the press. That, in part, was his job for Pibul. He supported Pibul in his pro-American orientation and throughout the late 1940s and early 1950s was the country's most prominent orator and propagandist against the Chinese Communists, especially after they came to power in 1949.

In school, my teachers spoke of China as a land where the leaders terrorized their own people. Their big-toothed caricatures were prominently displayed. Of the very differrent China I heard about at home I said nothing to my friends and certainly not to my teachers.

I was part of a secret inner world, dangerous but alluring. Sometimes, driving back in the car from a meeting, Father would remind me of what I was never to talk about. He rarely had to repeat himself. I was a quick study.

Father became obsessed with China. From his trips abroad he brought back numerous books on communism, Mao's speeches, and Chinese history. He began to listen to the English-language broadcasts of Radio Peking. He read Marx and Lenin in order to understand better what lay behind Chinese Communist theory and practice. And he began a long study of Chinese history.

The Korean War had made relations a matter of life and death for Thailand. At the outbreak of the war in June 1950, a unified, Communist China had only just been established. Father had been disturbed by Pibul's decision to send troops to fight the Chinese in Korea. Often I'd hear him repeat the old Thai maxim: "If you must make an enemy, do not make him the one on your own doorstep. Make him the one who is far away."

How was Thailand to maintain ties with both the United States and China? Pibul could not afford to offend the Americans, but he feared China's power. Could he balance the need for some long-term basis on which to live with China against the immediate pressing needs for American support—both for Thailand and for himself? Pibul perceived Thailand as surrounded by Communist insurgencies: might not China appeal to the overseas Chinese community in Thailand to take up arms or to otherwise subvert or undermine Thai sovereignty? Pibul's "pro-Japanese" policy in World War II had not endeared him to the Americans. Could they be counted on in such an event?

Other Southeast Asian countries with far greater insurgency problems, Father had replied, were developing friendly relations with China and having to modify their domestic policies. The Chinese community in Thailand made it all the more imperative to establish normal relations with China. The danger was clear. All of Thai history, he insisted, spoke to the need to balance two paramount powers. Thailand's survival, its integrity, its independence as a small nation among the great powers demanded drawing on its traditional ability to play one foreign devil off against another. Had not Thailand, alone among its neightbors, successfully done this, even if at great cost, during World War II. Why abandon that proud and valued tradition because of pressure from the Americans?

I heard these arguments in bits and pieces all the time. Our lives, I sensed, were shaped by them in some profound and fundamental way, inseparable from the very foundations of my family.

The link with the Americans worried my father in other ways as well, tapping into his deep pride in Thai independence. American dollars were pouring into the country—and into the pockets of well-placed individuals. People around Pibul certainly were not immune to temptation. "They disgrace politicians," Father said. We had our government house; we had innumerable privileges. But using one's position for wealth offended him deeply. He saw Thailand's independence being sapped that way, and it made him resolute about his own.

Mother handled most financial questions, both for the household and for the newspaper. To help subsidize the newspaper, she decided to set up a small export-import business. It was an area she understood well. One evening she asked Father to help her arrange several transactions. It was impossible to do so without assistance from someone in the government. Meeting the right quotas required getting through to the right people and getting around the others.

Father looked startled. I was scared. I knew an explosion was coming.

"You may never use my name for such a purpose!" he thundered. "I will not allow it. If I had realized what was involved in this export-import business, I would have forbidden it from the start. I am not going to have my name sullied by it. Never will my family get involved in commercial transactions that profit us. I will leave this house and never set foot in it again if you do!"

Mother looked stunned. She had done what everyone did, what she had been trained to do as a child. Her standards were impeccable by the current norms. She had struggled to find sufficient money in other ways to keep the newspaper going. And now this.

Father seemed surprised by his own rage. It had welled up from his deepest sense of himself, as though his integrity were being violated in some profound way by her request. But he also knew what had motivated my mother. After he calmed down he apologized for the outburst, but not for his stand.

"There are too many corrupt people around who are bringing disaster to Thailand. I must set an example. We will have to make it a different way."

His refusal to accept the corruption spreading around him reflected his profoundly imbedded notion of the role he sought to play. "To be a lotus," he'd say, "that is what I want. Its roots go deep into the muck, but it flowers so beautifully on the surface of the water." Anything of pettiness, corruption, even the mundane details of daily life seemed to imprison his spirit.

Perhaps for him establishing relations with China seemed a way out of such dilemmas, a decision based on the basic needs of Thailand and not on minor policy disputes and struggles over political influence. In 1954 his great opportunity had come, and he had seized it. In that year Thailand joined the SEATO alliance organized by the United States against China. Pibul had been unable to resist the American pressure to join, but having gone so far publicly, he began to waver privately in his commitment to the United States.

Partly in response to SEATO, India, Ceylon, Burma, Indonesia, and Pakistan at their Colombo conferernce in 1954 agreed to sponsor a large conference of Asian and African countries to be held in Bandung, Indonesia, the next year. China quickly accepted the invitation, announcing that Premier Zhou himself would attend.

Father had long awaited an opening like this. Pibul worried that sending a Thai delegation would anger the Americans. Their aid was at an all-time high, and they invariably protested if Thailand showed any sign of pursuing an independent path in foreign policy. Thailand was their anchor in the region. They were not at all pleased by the prospect of the Bandung conference.

Father quickly developed a rationale for Pibul to use with the Americans to explain Thailand's participation: Not going would isolate Thailand from the very neighbors America was counting on it to influence. Thailand would not need to take an active part; it would simply observe from the inside what was going on. Pibul found the argument effective and agreed to send Prince Warnwai as Thailand's representative.

I had been to the prince's house several times with Father. I had had to observe the strictest Thai etiquette and be careful of my political frivolity. His room, too, was filled with books, and when he and my father talked the normal political repartee was often absent. They could go on for hours about poetry and literature. The prince himself was considered a great poet, indeed one of the great learned men of his time; we had studied and memorized some of his writings in school. I was to call him Tan Lung, "Your Excellency Uncle."

Prince Warnwai had been a quiet benefactor of my father's from the time they had first met in the late 1930s. It was he who gave Father the surname Phathanothai, "rising sun," to symbolize his spreading fame as a radio personality. When my second brother was born, the prince bestowed his own name, Warnwai, on him.

He got on well diplomatically with the Americans; he had been elected president of the U.N. General Assembly, serving in 1950–51, at the height of the United Nations' involvement in the Korean War. But he, too, was worried about Thailand's deepening commitment to America, and he wished to observe this much-publicized premier Zhou in action.

The first time I distinctly remember Zhou Enlai's being discussed was when the prince came to dinner with Father after Bandung. I was particularly taken with Zhou's gift to the prince—a colorful length of silk in a beautifully decorated box. The prince had been very impressed by Premier Zhou, but he had been careful to keep a correct and distant attitude in the early part of the conference. He recounted to Father what had happened at the first meeting.

The last item on the agenda had been the election of a rapporteur to summarize the proceedings of each session. Indonesia had nominated Prince Warnwai. Zhou had strongly objected: China had no faith in Thailand, with its membership in SEATO and its staunchly pro-American record. He knew only too well of the close association between Thailand and Generalissimo Jiang Jieshi (Chiang Kai-shek) and of the harsh official persecution of overseas Chinese suspected of having friendly feelings toward the People's Republic of China. Despite all this, when Ceylon's delegate whispered to Premier Zhou that Prince Warnwai was the senior diplomat present and that he had the most experience in international conferences, Zhou not only withdrew his objections but even voted for him.

Over the next few days, Prince Warnwai had been relieved to hear Premier Zhou's comments on the controversial issue of the Chinese attitude toward the overseas Chinese community, a difficult problem in Thai politics. But when Premier Zhou had invited him to a private banquet at the end of the conference, he had felt uneasy. The rationale for Thailand's attendance did not include opening up discussions with China. It was all very well to talk with memebers of the Chinese delegation in his role as rapporteur; no implications about Thailand's attitude need be drawn from that. But a private dinner was quite a different matter and would certainly be so seen by the Americans. Secretary of State John Foster Dulles had refused even to shake Zhou Enlai's hand at the Geneva conference the year before, and the act had clearly symbolized just how America thought others should behave as well. Prince Warnwai asked Indian Prime Minister Nehru for his advice. Nehru strongly urged him to accept.

Prince Warnwai told my father that discussion at the dinner had been frank but friendly. The prince spoke openly of the Thai government's fear of Chinese armed intervention across the Laotian border. He spoke of the persistent rumors in Thailand that China was training the Dai minority in Xi Shuang Banna near the Chinese border with Laos in preparation for an invasion of Thailand to be led by Pridi, who now lived in China.

Zhou had laughed and had replied with great directness. "China," he said, "has no intention whatsoever of organizing an underground movement to topple the Thai government. No military training is taking place to prepare for intervention or infiltration into Thailand." Zhou emphatically denied that the overseas Chinese community was a Trojan horse, fomenting unrest in Thailand, ready to do the bidding of Communist China. "Thailand is welcome to send any delegation to China, where it is free to visit Xi Shuang Banna and see for itself whether China is making any preparations."

"As for Dr. Phanomyong," Zhou continued, "he has been staying in China as a political refugee with our permission, but he has engaged in no activity against Thailand. I can assure you of that."

Prince Warnwai did not think Zhou was making an empty offer. Pibul would have to decide what to do, but the prince had been impressed by Zhou, particularly by the adept way he had let Nehru take the credit for the five principles of coexistence drafted at the conference. Zhou had expressed surprise to the prince about the degree of anti-Chinese hostility that pervaded other Asian governments. He spoke of those who sought to isolate China and urged Prince Warnwai to help bridge the gap between their two countries. And he reiterated that only contact would foster genuine understanding. "To see something once is better than hearing about it a hundred times," Premier Zhou said. Zhou was an extraordinarily charming man, the prince concluded, and a natural diplomat: astute, patient, unfailingly courteous.

"Who said Zhou was a Communist bandit?" Prince Warnwai smiled. "He is fit to be a lord of our time."

In his quiet way, the prince made clear that he gave his blessing to Father's efforts to develop contacts with China. Father left to see Pibul that very night and was gone for long hours for days thereafter. From that point on the name Zhou Enlai was a common one in our hosehold.

"PIBUL USED TO ASK MEevery day if I had discovered a way to develop relations with China secretly," Father said in later years about this critical moment. "But we needed the right person, and I didn't have a clue as to whom to turn to. It had to be someone who could vouch effectively for our sincereity and who already had contacts in China. We had none, and there were no formal channels to go through."

Then one day Aree Pirom, an old acquaintance, dropped by to see Father. He had just been released from prison, where he had been held as a suspected Communist sympathizer, and he looked worn and weary from the experience. His wife had come to Father sometime earlier to ask for help in getting Aree released. Father had agreed, and Aree now came to express his thanks.

After a few minutes of casual talk, my father told him that Prime Minister Pibul wanted to establish secret government-to-government communications with China.

"Sang, you must be joking," Aree said.

"I'm absolutely serious," Father replied. "It is imperative that Thailand do this. At the same time, the Chinese must come to understand that owing to America's tremendous influence and pressure, Thailand cannot be overt in its relations with them. I've discussed these matters very carefully and at length with Prime Minister Pibul, and he is intent on developing a direct line to the Chinese government. To accomplish this, we wish to hold official talks in Burma with the Chinese ambassador there."

"But Sang, why tell me this?" Aree said, his face now quite pale. There was nothing comforting about being told such sensitive information.

"I want you to go to China. You surely have old friends there. I want you to locate them and get their help."

Aree sat quietly. He had worked in the Government Publicity Department since 1934 and for many years had worked under Father censoring Chinese newspapers and radio broadcasts in Thailand until his political problems overwhelmed him in the early 1950s. He had been born in Thailand to a Chinese father, a native of Hainan Island, and a Thai mother, but his father had sent him back to China when he was two, and he had not returned to Thailand until he was twelve. During the Japanese occupation of large areas of China during World War II, he had secretly raised money among the overseas Chinese in Thailand to send back to China, including to the Communists. In 1947 he had founded a first-rate municipal Chinese school in Bangkok that employed many of the Chinese teacher who had come to Thailand after the outbreak of the Japanese of China in the 1930s. Through his role in the publicity department and in the school, Aree came to know some of the most politically active students on both the left and the right. In 1949 many of his left-wing friends returned to China.

My father and he talked for some time. Aree's diffidence was understandable, but he began to see the suitability of his background and contacts, the rareness of the opportunity presenting itself: my father was often a very convincing man. Aree, a patriotic Thai with a genuine attachment to China, could no longer resist, despite the obvious danger.

"Who is going to go with me?" Aree asked. "And how can I possibly succeed in convincing the Chinese government of the Thai government's sincerity?"

"Three people will accompany you," Father replied. Except for the key contact person, he had had a plan worked out for some time.

"First, Karuna Kusarasai will go as the secretary. He is a friend of mine and is thoroughly reliable. The other two will be Amporn Suwarnabon and Saing Marangoon. They are both members of Parliament."

I knew Karuna well. He was the foreign editor of Father's paper and a professor of Hindi at Thamasart University. A disciple of Rabindranath Tagore, he had fallen under the influence of Mahatma Gandhi, whose work he had translated into Thai.

I had not been very close to him. He loved to engage Father in what seemed to me interminable and tedious philosophical topics. Himself invariably attired in plain, simple clothes, he never commented on my beautiful dresses. He talked rapidly, and whenever he dined with us he made ponderous comments about the millions of starving people in the world if we left any food on the plate. But to Father, his eccentricity translated into a rigorous, discreet discipline that allowed him to accept adversity stoically. He had been Father's first choice for such a dangerous mission.

When Aree agreed to go, Father continued; "You will be the head of the operation. We must move ahead as quickly as possible."

Aree became a frequent visitor to our house, the only place he and Father could meet without attracting notice. With each meeting Father grew more excited.

The obstacles were formidable. How was Aree going to get into China, let alone sneak members of the Thai Parliament in with him? Once in China, whom was he to get in touch with? He knew key members of several leading organizations in China, but he did not know exactly where they were or how to reach them.

Although Aree had a sense of who might help him, he had to gamble that his Chinese friend in Thailand was utterly trustworthy. The friend turned out to be very enthusiastic, providing the necessary letter from one of his friends to another in Hong Kong who could help Aree get the visa needed for China.

Luan Buosuwan, an overseas Chinese banker in whom Father had considerable faith, often joined these meetings, the only other person who did. He was financing the trip.

Aree came straight to Father's study when he had obtained the precious letter. By then Father had made the final preparations. Aree and Karuna were to leave for Hong Kong the following day,

December fourth; Amporn and Saing would stay behind in Thailand until Aree established contact with the Chinese. It was too dangerous for all four of them to travel together. Foreign agents of many countries were in Bangkok and Hong Kong, and the mission could readily be sabotaged if anyone got an inkling of it.

"You are acrobats on a tightrope," Father warned him. "Doing this runs counter to the policy of the American government. We must be very cautious."

Then he outlined to an amazed Aree just what was to be conveyed to the Chinese. Father had said nothing of it until the last moment to prevent any possible leak.

"In ten days, beginning on December fourteenth, Prime Minister Pibul will pay a state visit to Burma. Luan and I will accompany him as official members of his delegation. You will inform the Chinese authorities that, while in Rangoon, I wish to hold official talks directly with the Chinese ambassador to Burma and therefore the Chinese government should instruct him accordingly and empower him to negotiate as its plenipotentiary. Since Prime Minister Pibul will himself be in Ragoon and immediately available for me to consult with on all aspects of my talks, we can clear up with him any problems that might develop. It is also the necessary cover for me. I am being watched very closely by the Americans and the Nationalist Chinese in Taiwan."

Until that moment, Aree had not known that Pibul himself was to be so directly involved.

"Ten days is too tight a schedule," Aree protested. "What if I cannot get in touch with the right people in the Chinese government? What if they refuse to believe me? What if they refuse to authorize the Chinese ambassador to negotiate with you?"

Father cut him short. "You must do all that you can. I am counting on you."

I saw these comings and goings, but the bits of memory only made sense years later when I heard this story from Father and his associates and from the Chinese who were involved.

Aree and Karuna arrived in Hong Kong the next day. That afternoon, after settling in at a hotel, Aree slipped out to the address he had been given. He trembled as he knocked at the door, praying that Mr. X himself would be there.

When the door finally opened, Aree found himself gazing at a tall Chinese who welcomed him with a smile of immediate recognition. It was indeed Mr. X. Aree handed him the letter. Mr. X. sat down, reading it carefully and deliberately. Several minutes passed, and then Mr. X rose with a now considerably warmer smile on his face and greeted him in Mandarin.

"Please return this evening to my place. My car will get you."

They did not talk for long that night. Mr. X told Aree only that he and Karuna should be ready to leave from Macao by boat with two of Mr. X's friends the next day.

Early the next morning they were on their way. Immediately after landing, the companions Mr. X had provided to escort them went to report their arrival as "tourists" with the Portuguese immigration authorities. They then took Aree and Karuna to a hotel and disappeared.

Twenty-four hours passed before the escorts returned to the now almost frantic Aree. Time was short, and he pressed them. The senior man smiled, holding out their visas to China. "But I advise you, Mr. Aree, to enter China first, by yourself. Mr. Karuna can follow if all goes well for you. We shall look after him until then."

Aree had little choice. Karuna reluctantly acquiesced, and Aree left for Guangzhou by public bus. He arrived in Guangzhou late in the afternoon and asked a pedicab to take him to a hotel. But all the hotels were full, or so he was told. He rode around for several hours, looking for a place. Near despair, Aree suddenly thought of an old friend, Fu Fongcha, who had helped him establish the Chinese school in Bangkok eight years earlier. He had Fu's address with him, though until that point it had never crossed his mind to use it. When he arrived there and rang the bell, he was answered by an annoyed—and sleepy—woman's voice. But Aree recognized it as Fu's wife's, and overjoyed, he shouted back his name.

There was a long silence. Then Fu himself yelled out, trying to make sure who it was. Assured of Aree's identity, both Fu and his wife greeted him warmly before asking, perplexed, what he was doing there and why, in the middle of the night, he was standing in front of their house calling out to them. Was he in trouble? Had he fled Thailand?

They were not prepared for his response.

"Prime Minister Pibul has instructed me," Aree said, "to make secret contact with the Chinese government and to pass on an urgent message from him."

Fu looked astonished.

"I need your help," Aree continued. "You must help me."

Fu needed little convincing. Aree was an old friend, and the situation seemed surprisingly straightforward, if still astonishing. He thought that Huang Sheng, the mayor of Shantou, would be able to help Aree. As it happened, he was in Guangzhou on business.

For the first time in days Aree felt some relief. He knew Huang Sheng well from the days when Huang had edited a left-wing Chinese-language paper in Thailand.

The next morning, Fu took Aree to meet him. When Aree told an amazed Huang why he was there, Huang offered to telegraph Peking immediately for a response. Whether it would be favorable or not, he added gravely, he couldn't venture to guess.

Aree agreed to what seemed the most direct and effective course of action.

Two days passed. No response. Only five days remained until Pibul's arrival in Burma, and Aree was becoming anxious again. That night be could barely sleep, wondering what to do next.

The next morning Huang came earlier than usual. "Beijing is sending Qiu Ji by a special plane to meet you. He will be here this afternoon."

The two men smiled. Both knew that this meant the response was positive, but Huang could say nothing more.

Aree knew Qiu Ji's reputation. A founder of the Thai Communist party as well as the Malayan Communist party, he had for years been a highly talented leader of the underground Chinese Communist party. Now he was one of Zhou Enlai's chief aides. In the following years he often reminded me of this first strange contact between China and Thailand: it had led both to my coming and to his own involvement as one of those directly responsible to Zhou for my life and safety in China.

Late that afternoon, Qiu Ji arrived with Huang Sheng. Qiu Ji first exchanged the formal Thai greeting with Aree and then embraced him. They all knew time was short, and so it was quickly agreed that Aree should immediately return to Macao and bring back Karuna,

Saing, and Amporn so that the four of them could go on to Beijing together.

Aree cabled Saing and Amporn, who took the next plane to Hong Kong. Two days later all were assembled and ready in Guangzhou. Qiu Ji took them to Beijing on a special plane. Theirs was the first Thai government delegation to China since the Communists had taken power in 1949.

Aree pressesd Qiu Ji about timing. That very day, December 14, 1955, Pibul and my father were due in Rangoon. When would they know if their message was being acted on? Qiu Mi gave no specifics but reassured him. Their greeting in China was warm, although not public. They were whisked to the Beijing Hotel only long enough to prepare for a dinner hosted by the mayor of Beijing, Peng Shen. Aree immediately asked about their message. Peng Zhen told him that the Chinese ambassador in Rangoon, Yao Zhongming, had already been instructed to act on behalf of the Chinese government in the forthcoming discussions with Pibul's designated representatives.

After three days with no news, Aree feared the worst. The meetings had not taken place, something had gone wrong. Or the discussions had gone awry. There had been disagreement, and he had not been told.

He waited impatiently for Qiu Ji's expected visit. When he saw his buoyant smile, he felt relieved.

"Mr. Phathonothai and Mr. Luan have met the Chinese ambassador in Rangoon," Qiu Ji said. "For two days they have talked in a most cordial and friendly atmosphere."

Aree was delighted.

"Discussions went so smoothly," Qiu Ji continued, "that they have culminated in the signing of a peaceful coexistence agreement between the two governments." He held up a copy of the agreement that Father and Ambassador Yao had signed.

Qiu Ji laughed, "It was a very successful meeting once it took place." Then he told the full story of what had happened.

Zhou had instructed the Chinese embassy that Father and Mr. Luan would make contact with it. But when the embassy checked the names on the list of Pibul's delegation, neither Father nor Luan was on it. At the last minute Father and Pibul had decided it was safer to have Father and Luan go separately and quietly and not as members of the delegation. The Chinese had no way of contacting them, no way even of knowing where they were staying. Thus my father and Luan had also been waiting. Two days passed, and in some desperation, they had put a small notice in all Rangoon's English-language newspapers:

> Mr. Luan Buosuwan, chairman and managing dirctor of the Ayuthaya Bank, is now in town to prepare for the opening of a new branch in Rangoon and would like to interview suitable people for the position of branch general manager. Please contact Green Hotel reception if interested.

An alert reader in the Chinese embasssy had spotted the message, and Father and Luan had been reached.

The mission had floundered at several points, but it had succeeded far more than anyone, except perhaps Father, had hoped. There was more to come. The next afternoon, the mission was awarded the highest Chinese accolade, a meeting with Chairman Mao Zedong and Premier Zhou.

Almost twenty years later I read Aree's notes of this meeting and saw the pictures of him with Chairman Mao. For years the notes and pictures had remained buried in a polyethylene bag in a remote suburb of Bangkok where he had attempted to hide himslf during the military coup in 1958 that was to destroy his world. He had feared the cost to him of this effort from the beginning, and he and Karuna were to pay with years of imprisonment. In the years to come, no one who went down Father's path of seeking a friendly relationship with China was to emerge unscarred.

Mao, Zhou, Peng Zhen, and others met with Aree and his delegation for several hours. Mao urged them to tell Pibul and Father that all Thais were welcome to come to China. "Those who curse China are welcome as well," Mao said. "And I don't mind if they continue to curse us. Just let them come. China contains no mysteries. People can come and see whatever they want."

Aree mentioned Thai fears that China might invade Thailand.

"The Thai government should stop worrying about any such Chinese invasion," Mao laughed. "We have no military bases beyond our borders. We ourselves have been invaded by foreign aggressors several times, and history proves that sooner or later invaders are bound to be defeated. It is only a matter of time, as it was for Germany and Japan in World War II."

But what should Thailand do? Aree asked, implicitly referring to its ties with the United States.

Mao looked slightly embarrassed. "I am not a Thai military adviser," he responded. "It is not for me to suggest an option. It is an internal Thai affair." After a considerable pause, he added that he personally felt that the most advantageous policy for a small country like Thailand was to remain neutral. That would not be an easy road for Thailand, he said, but Thailand should try to have as few enemies as possible. The way would be long and difficult, and there would be many twists and turns in the road. They should be patient and cautious.

As the delegation prepared to leave, Mao praised the courageous and farsighted vision of Prime Minister Pibul and Father, and he asked in particular that his respects be made to His Majesty, the king of Thailand.

AFTER THE SIGNINGof the secret agreement between China and Thailand, the Chinese embassy in Burma became the point of liaison between Premier Zhou and Father. Father's letters to Zhou would be delivered by hand in Rangoon by one of Father's trusted aides. Upon arrival in Rangoon, the messenger would call up the commercial attaché at the Chinese embassy, speaking as an Indian businessman. The attaché would then meet him at an agree-upon location. Or if a letter from Zhou awaited Father, he would receive a telegram from Burma, and the messenger would be sent to pick the letter up.

In January 1956, just after their own successful trip, Father and Pibul decided to send a nongovernmental "friendship" delegation to China headed by Thep Chotinuchit, the leader of the Economy party. This was to be a fact-finding mission, and Father hoped to air its observations publicly, thus opening up the taboo subject of China for the first time in Thai politics.

Thep looked a little like Father, with thick glasses and an almost invariably serious expression. He had a booming voice, a caustic tongue, and a repertoire of anti-American jokes that seemed too sharp-edged even for Father. Indeed, I wasn't sure Father liked him. He never seemed to invite this man into his study and never once asked him to sit down. Instead they always huddled in the garden. Once, when I followed him into the garden, Father uncharacteristically sent me away.

Father had decided to try something enormously risky. Thirty minutes before the delegation was to leave, Thep held a press conference to announce that he was leading a group to China. Everything had been carefully worked out: the announcement, the plane about to take off, the police unable to arrive in time to interfere. The move caused a furor—and enormous curiosity about what the delegation would learn.

On its arrival, the delegation was greeted openly by Zhou Enlai and invited to travel widely, particularly along the sensitive southwestern border near Thailand. Zhou told the group that he wished to promote friendship with Thailand and to make it permanent. "China is ready to sign a nonaggression treaty with Thailand. But the absence of such a treaty in no way detracts from the sincerity of our friendship. We would be very honored," he added, "if Prime Minister Pibul himself could visit China." And Father's own role was publicly acknowledged: "We appreciate Mr. Sang Phathanothai's efforts in promoting Sino-Thai relations."

Chairman Mao received the delegation the next day. The Chinese were sympathetic to the efforts of the Pibul government to improve Thai-Chinese relations, Mao said. He knew it was dangerous and difficult to undertake such efforts. There would be sacrifices, he warned, many ups and downs.

The Americans were furious, as was the Nationalist government on Taiwan led by Generalissimo Jiang Jieshi. Jiang may have lost the civil war, but he still insisted that his government represented all of China. The United States strongly supported this claim, bitterly opposing any steps other governments took toward recognizing the Chinese Communists or supporting their admission to the United Nations. Accordingly, Pibul, who had planned to let the delegation return to Thailand without reprisals, had the men arrested as soon as their plane landed. The action was meant to look severe to the

Americans, but the men, although imprisoned, were allowed to spend weekends and evenings at home. The head of the police, General Pao, had been in favor of the mission; one of his key aides had gone with it. They were all well treated.

Pibul faced the dilemma he had long feared. The Americans were very angry. Would Zhou understand Thailand's difficulties? Pibul asked Father. Try to explain to Zhou how delicate the situation is, he said. The arrests are purely symbolic, an empty gesture to keep the Americans at bay. But henceforth the trips cannot be public.

Pibul was not sure that such explanations would prove satisfactory to the Chinese. He worried more and more about how to deal with the problem—especially how to show his sincerity and his commitment to improving relations. This was the context in which Father first proposed to Zhou that Wai and I be sent to grow up in China.

Zhou wrote to Father in early April 1956 to say that he well understood what was happening. He warned Father to be more careful and to beware of plots against the government and against friends of China. "While the Chinese people sincerely hope to promote Sino-Thai relations in the spirit of 'Bandung,' " Zhou wrote, "they fully understand and sympathize with the difficult situation confronting the Thai government." Zhou cautioned against becoming impatient. And he feared that if Father sent his own children to China, he would be politically at risk:

"Regarding the question of sending your son and daughter to China, we are deeply grateful for your friendship with and trust in China. Nevertheless, after due deliberation, we feel it may not yet be the right time for your children to come from the point of view both of the present political situation and of your own personal welfare." Our coming, he concluded, might provoke those opposed to good relations between the two countries, provoke them even to take ruthless steps against Father. "I firmly believe in your courage and tenacity and realize you despise these people. Yet for the sake of long-term political interests you should not expose yourself inopportunely and bring yourself this heap of troubles. Therefore, from a political point of view it would be more convenient if your children came to Beijing in more favorable political circumstances."

In the months that followed, other, lower-key trips took place. Visitors were arrested, then released, soon appearing at our house bearing gifts from Zhou. One night I went with Father to Pibul's to watch a film of the Korean War that Zhou had sent.

"I'm determined to go ahead with our policy," Pibul said after watching it. "It is fortunate that the Chinese understand our situation. You continue with your plans. I will go along."

But Pibul knew he could not himself risk a trip to China. Even sending Father was risky. How long could the Chinese be persuaded of Thailand's goodwill if the alliance with SEATO continued and the American presence remained so strong? Zhou had asked him to come. What could he do?

Often when I saw my father reading in his study during those months, I asked him what he was studying. "China," he always replied. Years later, I saw that he had marked the parts of his books that explained about the old tributary system, how the rulers of the past had sent their children to Beijing. This was to be his and Pibul's way out—the proof to China of their sincerity, the human link without which, they felt, the policy could not effectively endure. To Father, sending his own children would plant the seeds of future Thai-Chinese relations. The Chinese government would tend to our upbringing and in so doing would nurture the seeds as well.

As negotiations over my fate proceeded, Father continued to open up other avenues to China. In June he asked Aree to lead the first Thai trade mission to Communist China. Once again Aree would be secretly representing the Pibul government. In the past the Chinese government had bought Thai tobacco through third parties in Hong Kong; now Father wished to arrange a mutually beneficial govenment-to-government basis for trade. Thai farmers were suffering from a huge surplus of tobacco caused in part by British domination of the world market. In time the trade Father proposed might lead to further quiet support for his policy toward China.

Officially, the Thai government subscribed to the U.S. embargo on all trade with China. Since 1949 there had been no open trade, no discussions of commercial activity between the two governments. A small number of middlemen had become rich by buying goods from China and changing the labels of origin to "Made in Hong Kong" or selling Thai goods in China through Hong Kong middlemen. Father wanted to reduce their role or at least make it advantageous to both governments.

"Zhou has already been informed of your trip," he told Aree. "Ambassador Yao in Rangoon will give you the delegation visas." Hong Kong was now too dangerous for transit to China by Thai visitors; they were being watched very carefully, and the threat of sabotage was real. Burma, therefore, had become more and more the route through which Father sent people to China.

Aree and two businssmen—Prasert Siripipat of the Bangkok Bank and a close associate of the Thai minister of finance, and Uthai Tongkapalin, a tobacco expert—left in early 1956, traveling on three different planes and only joining up in a hotel in Rangoon. Chinese embassy officials dropped by to give them visas that did not have to be entered in their passports, so there would be no record of their visit. The next morning they quietly left for China on a regular Air China flight.

Qiu Ji greeted them in Beijing, and the next day they met Liao Chengzhi, a member of one of twentieth-century China's most illustrious revolutionary families and the man with whom my life would be inextricably tied until his death in 1983.

Aree informed Liao of the Thai government's intention to establish direct trade contacts with China and of my father's effort to move toward the normalization of Thai-Chinese relations. He also explained the crisis confronting the Thai tobacco farmers. Liao had the delegation meet members of the relevant foreign trade organization. Then he and Aree talked into the night about Thai-Chinese relations. Liao repeatedly urged him to tell Father to take great care and be patient.

Agreement was soon reached. The Chinese government committed itself to spending about $20 million with payment to be made to the London branch of the Bangkok Bank. Zhou Enlai met with Aree and his group to celebrate the successful negotiations. A month later the tobacco was on its way to China.

Pibul was pleased. China, he felt, had reached out to help Thailand with its surplus tobacco problem. The Americans had done nothing to pressure the British to ease up. "Only other Asians can understand our situation with sympathy," he told Father. The Americans were different. "They are so generous, our best friends when they need something from us. But when we are in trouble and in need of help, it's no use going to them to ask for it. They would kick us out."

Yet Pibul knew he could not govern if the Americans opposed him too strongly. Father was to go ahead, but as carefully as possible.

When Zhou wrote to Father on July 9, 1956, he reiterated his understanding of the "awkward situation" of the Thai government. He stated his belief in "active but prudent measures" to develop relations "step by step" in the hope that they would gradually improve.

"I expressed my views on the question of your children coming to China to study in my last letter," Zhou continued. "You must, of course, be the only person who can make the final decision on this issue. If, after the most careful deliberation, you think it is sufficiently safe, there is no problem from our side. We will respect your opinion and do our best to take care of your children."

#
"A Glorious Place"

THE SKY CRIES ALL THE TIME,"I said to Wai as we rode through the streets of Rangoon. It was gray and rainy, but at least we were back on the ground and being driven to our hotel. The airplane had terrified me, conjuring up the previous night's images of fiery destruction. My fortitude in front of my family had utterly given way to fears of abandonment and death, but worse still were the waves of nausea that lasted the entire two-and-a-half-hour flight. Wai had withdrawn into a deep quiet, emerging occasionally to mutter, "He's crazy to send us."

Two of Father's most trusted aides, Chareon Kanokratana and Pisit Sripen, were our chaperons. Chareon had been the messenger between Father and the Chinese embassy in Rangoon, carrying Zhou's and Father's letters back and forth. A prominent journalist in his own right, he had worked for years on Father's newspaper.

Only Rangoon's temples and pagodas made me feel that the world was not totally alien. The women wore sarongs, but why, I wondered, did the men dress like women? Thailand is much better, I thought.

We arrived at a fancy new hotel in Rangoon late that afternoon. Having recovered enough to be ravenously hungry, I said I wanted to go to the hotel restaurant.

"Not there," Chareon said. He was edgy, not his usual affable self. "We can eat in a private room."

That seemed all right, but afterward, when Wai and I said we wished to be driven around to see more of the city, he gave a firm no.

I objected.

"I can't take any chances," he replied. "We are going to stay in our suite and not leave the hotel. Sripen and I will sleep on the sofa in the sitting room tonight."

Wai joined my protest.

"No, we must be careful. Your father stressed how critical it is to keep our trip here secret. After Mr. Luan's death, we can't ever afford to be careless. I don't think anyone is following us, but I can't be sure yet. I'll try to take you out in a few days, but first let me get a sense of what is happening here."

Luan Buisuwan, the friend of Father's who had accompanied Pibul on the state visit to Burma, had been murdered just a few months earlier. Uncle Luan, in whose house I'd first seen Chinese art, scrolls of calligraphy, and intricate carving utterly different from anything I was familiar with, had always stopped to tell me stories and to admire my pretty dresses on his visits to Father. The last time I had seen him, as he and Father discussed a trip they were taking on behalf of the government to deliver food, clothing, and radio equipment to the remote province of Korat, some hundred miles from Bangkok, Luan suggested that Man might like to accompany them as well.

I had jumped right in. Why just my elder brother? Why not all of us? I had never been on a plane, and this sounded like a wonderful opportunity. I loved seeing Father off at airports and joining the large groups of trade union workers welcoming him back with huge, sweet-smelling garlands of flowers. I always insisted he write me postcards from abroad—and send them to me at school. I loved the moment when the headmistress walked into the classroom holding a beautiful postcard in her hand and announced, "Sirin, a postcard from your dad!"

To my surprise and delight, Luan and Father had agreed that our entire family could go. Only after warning that I'd get terribly airsick unless I was sufficiently rested did Mother finally get me to sleep that night.

I awoke the next morning when the alarm went off a little before five. Quickly dressed, I hurried off to find Father in his study. He seemed tired and preoccupied.

Father said he had just returned from an all-night meeting with Pibul. He still had to write his newspaper column. "I'm afraid I will have to tell Luan that we can't go this time. I'm sorry, my daughter."

I fought back my tears, but not my anger, as he turned back to his writing. "I want to go. How can you just cancel the whole trip at the last minute?"

He lookd at me quietly.

"We're all dressed up and ready. If you can't go, we will go with Mother."

"That would not be very nice," he said.

"Well, you not going is spoiling it for us. And Uncle Luan expects it so much," I pleaded.

Father had been just about to phone Luan. He reluctantly agreed to indicate to him that while he would prefer to stay at home and finish his work, he would go if Luan felt it was essential for him to do so.

I was heartened. He and Luan had seemed inseparable of late. But this time Luan did not insist. Furious, I nevertheless knew I could protest no further. I withdrew and went back to bed bitterly disappointed.

That evening, I sulked around the entrance to Father's study. He was talking to Pibul, though his voice seemed strangely distant. I crept up to hear. "Another murder plot," Father was saying as he hung up.

I asked what was happening.

"Luan's plane crashed," he replied grimly. Turning to Mother, he said, "Luan is dead. Pibul says a bomb had been planted; the plane exploded shortly after taking off from Korat." He paused, adding softly, "Pibul is sending more guards for our house."

At the funeral, Luan's wife clung to my father and then fainted in his arms. Luan's body had been burned beyond recognition; only his gold teeth had identified him. Pibul came, as did many dignitaries. Not publicly commented on but significant in its presence was a wreath from Premier Zhou Enlai.

This was not the first assassination attempt on Father. A few months earlier, on a trip with Pibul to a religious ceremony in one of the provincial capitals, he had been in an auto accident that, Pibul told my mother, had been no accident. My sense of security was shaken; with Luan's death shortly afterward, it vanished. As China became more and more a part of my father's life, so did danger. By day I easily assumed my expected role, full of the confidence and even brashness Father and his visitors enjoyed in me. But at night I was often terrified. Father would sometimes come to comfort me when he returned late from his meetings, but he did not deny the danger he faced. "Life is like the waves of the seas, sometimes up, sometimes down," he said. He would remind me that he was a politician and that if I was afraid of death I would never be able to follow in his footsteps.

Now Chareon's admonition reinforced my dread. It also temporarily sapped my curiosity and energy. This secret world was not proving so exciting, I thought, feeling suddenly tired. Far from adventure-filled, Father's world now seemed very constricting, as though all that was left was this hotel room. When I couldn't be active, everything loomed harsh and suspicious.

That night I dreamed of my baby sister, Tukta, in my house in Bangkok. She looked so lovely and seemed so comfortable there. When I woke I remembered how I had taken her to one of my school parties, proudly showing her off as my "doll." Now I was far away, and she was there. I looked around at the two large rooms and the large balcony that jutted off from them. Only the mosquito nets draped over the bed reminded me of home.

Life was already so different. Jit was not here to comb my hair or dress me. My chaperons lacked her many talents, though not for want of trying. Chareon and Sripen took turns picking up our things, and Chareon even borrowed an iron from the hotel staff since both Wai and I loved the look of crisply ironed clothes. With my hair they were a total loss. Both of them tried and tried, but finally we all gave up and decided I'd better stick with a simple ponytail.

We stayed in the room all morning. Chareon's games barely passed the time. He seemed tired and nervous.

"I stayed awake most of the night," he said.

Finally, after lunch, Chareon told us he was going out to phone "Uncle" to tell him of our arrival and find out what arrangements had been made for us.

"We'll go with you," I said.

He refused.

"You can't just keep us locked up here!" I cried. Father's people had never treated us like this before. Wai was equally adamant.

"You shouldn't be afraid," Chareon soothed me.

"I'm not afraid," I said.

"Well, you're safe here. But people tried to kill your father. They killed Luan. They might try to kill you. We must take every precaution. Perhaps the next time I go out I can arrange something. This time I must go alone."

I peered out the window when Chareon left, wondering where these people lurked who were so intent on harming us. Even this did little to divert me from my increasing boredom.

Chareon was smiling when he returned late that afternoon. "The Chinese ambassador, Yao Zhonming, is delighted to learn that the two of you have arrived safely in Rangoon. He is sending his secretary to pick us up for dinner tonight."

I was momentarily cheered. Ambassadors, I knew, were important figures.

"Why did it take you so long?" Wai asked.

"Where did you go?" I added. "Is the ambassador far away?

Chareon laughed. "I simply called the embassy and arranged to meet someone in a coffee shop nearby. The man from the embassy brought the invitation and filled me in on the details."

I listened with growing excitement. This was to be my first diplomatic performance without Father. Wai and I quickly dressed, I in the blue-ribboned dress Chareon had washed for me and Wai once again in his white sharkskin wuit. Wai was particularly nervous; he was feeling the full weight of being the prime minister's personal representative. For several hours he walked back and forth, slowly and solemnly, imitating the powerful leaders he had seen. Shaking hands posed a dilemma. Should we follow Thai custom and give the ambassador the *wai*, the traditional greeting, or shake hands, which Father said was the Western practice? Wai gravely walked up and shook my hand. Again and again, back and forth, trying to do it just as he had seen it done before. Finally, unsure, he decided we should *wai* first and then shake hands.

At seven sharp the embassy secretary came to the room to get us. He was tall, well built, in his middle thirties, and neatly dressed in a Western suit and tie. Chareon and the Chinese secretary spoke English, a language slightly familiar to me since my father spoke it as well.

As we walked out of the hotel, a brand-new Mercedes pulled up for us. I was impressed; only a few people in Thailand had such cars. The embassy secretary spoke briefly to the driver. It was the first time I had heard Mandarin. Was this what Father wanted me to learn?

The car soon stopped before a tall steel gate. A guard ran out to open it, and we drove slowly down a long tree-lined road to a large building. As I got out, I looked up and saw a slightly built, scholarly-looking man with thick spectacles. I sensed it was Ambassador Yao come out to greet us. He and his wife approached, smiling warmly. Wai forgot all the protocol he had been practicing. We all shook hands, and Ambassador Yao lightly stroked my hair as he bade us welcome.

Madame Yao embraced me, and I looked carefully at this beautiful woman dressed in an elegant traditional Chinese dress. She embraced me, the led me by the hand into the embassy.

We sat around a little table piled with sweets and nuts, and as I helped myself, Ambassador Yao told us how pleased he had been to meet our father and to sign the agreement they had worked out. "How do you like Burma?" he asked

"It hasn't stopped raining since our arrival," I said. "The sky cries all the time."

"That's well said. You may be a writer like your father when you grow up," the ambassador said. "Did you cry when you left home?" he asked gently.

"No!" I exclaimed firmly, though suddenly feeling a flicker of loss.

He laughed when I recounted how I had told my friends that I was going to Bandung. Now quite at ease, I talked freely.

"Is Chinese hard to learn?" I asked.

"Yes, it is," he said. "But you will learn it quickly, and when you do I hope you will remember me and write me a letter in Chinese."

I laughed: what an absurd idea. I was not going to be staying that long. She showed us pictures of the Children's Palace in Beijing, where dance was taught, and I allowed as how I'd like to learn Chinese dance.

"Premier Zhou Enlai," the ambassador said later as the dinner ended, "has sent a special plane to Rangoon to take you to China. He is concerned for your safety. You will leave the day after tomorrow."

I curled up with my held on Madame Yao's shoulder to watch a Chinese animated film. I awoke the next morning in the hotel to find Wai upset with me for falling asleep at my first formal diplomatic function.

Again we spent the day in the hotel, waiting for Chareon to keep his promise and take us out for a look that evening. Finally, we got our way. But no sooner had the taxi entered the main street than I wanted to return. Everywhere I looked there were Indian beggars, pitifully undernourished people who seemed to be waiting for death. "I want to go back!" I cried. Reluctantly, Wai agreed.

That night everything was packed up for our early morning departure. Well before daylight, we were up and speeding toward the airport, where we pulled into a quiet spot toward the edge of the runway. Ambassador Yao had come to see us off. He walked us over to the small plane, introduced the pilot to us, and gave me a warm embrace. Wai and I and our two chaperons boarded the plane; we were the only passengers.

The pilot introduced us to the crew members and then took us up to the cockpit. He showed us all the switches and knobs on the control panel and let us sit in his seat. When the plane took off a few minutes later, my fears rushed back until nausea pushed even them away. As I looked around the tiny plane, I felt utterly helpless and alone; Wai was preoccupied with his own thoughts; Chareon and Sripen were talking quietly.

Four miserable hours later the plane landed in Kunming. I perked up quickly when I saw a caravan of three cars drawn up to greet us. A Mrs. Wu, speaking Thai, came forward and introduced a Chinese official. As we talked for a few minutes, I looked around, curious for a glimpse of what made this country so exciting for Father. Everywhere I looked, men and women were dressed alike, in the same clothes, the same blues and grays.

Brief formalities over and still dazed by the flight, I settled back in the car to watch the houses as we were driven to our government lodging. The houses along the road were old—hardly as beautiful, I thought, as those in Bangkok. People stared at the car as I looked out at them. Bicyclists wove in and out around the car.

As long as I don't have to live in houses like that, I'll be okay, I thought.

When finally we drove through the gates of the guest house, we entered an utterly different world. Set within a magnificent garden, surrounded by fruit trees and flowers, it seemed almost magical, and for a brief moment I could envision playing hide-and-seek with my sister and father, tearing around the huge rock garden with its small streams and little bridges, a setting at once wild yet well managed. The house was old-style Chinese, Mrs. Wu said, pointing to the gilded red roof. Two enormous lions with smaller ones under their feet heralded the importance of the place. Only in the movies from Zhou Enlai that Father and I had watched had I seen such entrances.

Mrs. Wu was explaining that she had lived in Thailand for ten years, including under the Japanese occupation, returning to China in the early 1950s. She spoke Thai well but with a noticeable Chinese accent.

"Did you like Thailand? Did you teach Chinese there? Were your students Chinese?" I peppered her with questions.

"How did you guess?" she said, laughing.

"Well, then," I replied without answering, "did you know one of my father's friends, Mr. Aree, who had a Chinese school with lots of Chinese children?" It had also had, I did not add, a dwindling number of Chinese teachers in recent years.

"That is where I taught," she replied.

"We all know him, then." I smiled, pointing to Chareon as well. "This will make him very happy." I stopped. I knew I should say nothing more about Aree's role in my coming. Mrs. Wu already seemed suitably surprised and impressed by my knowledge.

"We are invited to dinner with the mayor of Kunming tonight," she told us with evident pleasure.

I was not very impressed. Where, I wanted to know, was Beijing? Was it far? Why couldn't we go now?

She had no idea when we were going, but Beijing, she said was far away. We were fortunate to be going. She had long wanted to visit but had never had the chance.

That night at dinner the mayor seemed to enjoy entertaining two youngsters. With Mrs. Wu interpreting, he told us Chinese jokes and stories, but it was less what he said than how he acted that surprised me. His subordinates sat at the table with him, as they would not have in Thailand. Mrs. Wu and the others laughed and talked together with great vivacity and seemed equals in the conversation. We heard all about Kunming, its history of fifteen hundred years, and the relics for which it was known. "Stay a few days, rest, and see them," the mayor suggested. I knew full well our stay had been carefully planned. But they were so friendly, I thought. What would my school friends think? Would my teachers ever believe me? These people did not seem wicked or cruel. I decided that one day, when I had got to know such people better, I would summon up my courage and ask whether they were actually Communists or not.

They kept referring to "liberated" China. Wai and I knew what coups d'état were; Thailand had those. So Wai asked the mayor whether the Comminists had staged a successful coup d'état.

He laughed again and said no. Wai and I both felt uncomfortable. Wai was trying hard to talk sense; it was his duty, he felt. He was sitting in the place of honor and feeling every bit of importance attached to it. I was very tired and restless, and I knew I shouldn't move about too much. I looked around longingly for a decent soft drink.

"I'd like a Coca-Cola," I said finally.

Wai gave me a dirty look.

"We don't import from abroad," the mayor said. "We make our own."

My "soft drink" tasted horrible. It sat there in front of me, barely touched. I kept myself from saying what I thought of it, but my face was evidently expressive enough. I would get used to it, the mayor assured me. And in Beijing there were many more choices.

Over the next few days we saw the sights—temples, pagodas, and the lovely park along the lake. Mrs. Wu told us fairy tales about the stone forest. Where, I asked, were all the beggars? I realized I had been looking for them, still haunted by those I had seen in Burma. Starving people and beggars were everywhere in China—Wai and I had both been taught this in school. I saw Wai blanch when I started to suggest as much.

"They may be offended by what you are saying," he warned me. "Try to control your comments."

Chareon heard him, however, and told Wai not to worry. "During my first trip to China with the delegation of members of Parliament, they asked lots of embarrassing questions. They wanted to know where the 'low women' were. 'Bad women,' our Chinese guides insisted, 'are no longer to be found in China. The new society has trained them to become factory workers or to take other jobs.'

"They were quite proud to talk about it," Chareon continued. 'You can talk with former "bad women" if you like,' the Chinese hosts said. Our Parliament members felt they could not be expected to believe such propaganda; they would be made fools of if they returned from China saying that. So during some of their spare time in the days that followed they wandered around the streets to see if they could find any."

Did they find any "bad women"? I wanted to know, not quite sure what bad women would look like.

"No," he laughed, "and some of them certainly knew how to spot them. They had to admit failure and settled for interviewing several former prostitutes."

I nodded uncertainly.

That evening we were told to get ready for bed early. The next day we were to make the long and tiring trip to Beijing. No sooner had we gone to sleep than a loud knock on the door announced the mayor coming to say good-bye. We greeted him in our pajamas and told him all that we had done the last few days.

"Please come back to visit us," he said and wished us a good trip.

The next morning, August 25, we left for Beijing. Once again the trip was a nightmare. The plane landed every two hours for refueling, and the ascent and descent made me ill each time. By the time we arrived in the early evening, I only vaguely recognized my name being announced. Evidently we were expected to disembark first.

As I stumbled down the steps, holding Chareon's hand tightly, I saw a serious-looking man of about fifty with thick black eyebrows and an engaging smile standing at the bottom. It was Qiu Ji, the man who had welcomed Aree on his first trip. And next to him was a younger man in his mid-thirties, short, sturdy, with a square face and impressive dark glasses. Lin Shanan, or Uncle Shanan, as we soon came to call him. Was to oversee every detail of our lives in the next few years.

Qiu Ji greeted us in his accented Thai and ushered us into a special waiting room, ordering tea and insisting when he saw my state that I lie down and rest. When our baggage was ready, we set out for the old Beijing Hotel. I collapsed into bed for the night.

BEIJING IS A DUMP,"Wai said. "What did Father have in mind, sending us to a place like this?"

I had tried to block out the dismal mud brick houses I had seen as we drove in from the airport. Ugly, I thought. No paint, no blue and green Thai colors. Where were the tall buildings and the wide streets bustling with traffic? A few antiquated buses could be seen, a trickle of trucks and cars, but they were lost among the horse- and donkey-drawn carts. There were even camels wandering amid these squalid surroundings.

Father had called China a "treasure island to explore." We would have "a fascinating adventure," he had said. Beijing was "the capital of a great and powerful country." It would be a "glorious place" to travel to. Father should have known better, I thought. He had traveled widely—and for me going abroad meant Austria or Switzerland. It meant exotic presents, like my first talking doll, which he had brought from Switzerland. Or it meant the beautiful gifts sent to Father and Mother by Premier Zhou: the colorful silks, the beautifully crafted boxes. With each glimpse of the city, with each outing, my spirits sank further. Beijing was dusty and dirty; it seemed like a small provincial capital, hardly up to the standards of even a backwater in Thailand.

For the first few weeks Shanan wanted to introduce us to both the old and the new China. He took us to the Temple of Heaven. I was willing to concede a certain aura about it, but it was not as grand as Thai temples, I pointed out to Wai. A little drab, with its monotonous blue color. Only the so-called telephone wall appealed to Wai and me. Again and again we called out in order to hear our voices return, ten seconds later, from around an edge of the long wall. We could have stayed and played for hours, waiting to hear ourselves, somehow reconnected to something outside this alien environment.

Next Shanan took us to the Summer Palace. He described the luxurious lives of the people who had once lived here. Then he pointed to the big stones and told us how many people had been required to move them. Those were the ones with the miserable lives, he added.

I was not impressed. I couldn't even see why they bothered to move such wretched stones.

Shanan remained undaunted. He spoke harshly of the dowager empress, of how her long fingernails reflected her refusal, and that of her class, to do any work.

I was getting annoyed. I liked my nails long. "Did hers look like mine, Uncle Shanan?" I asked.

"Hers were longer, he said tartly.

Perhaps hoping to educate us more graphically about the horrors of the old society, Shanan took us to a film that portrayed the inequities of the feudal past. The elite ate all the good food; the peasants starved. The privileged loved their long nails; the hands of the workers were rough and callused. The rich had nice clothing and silks; the workers wore rags. The officials had servants and were well taken care of; the rest existed to serve them. The life of the privileged didn't seem so evil to me. I disliked the blatant brutality and heartlessness of the old ways, but I saw nothing wrong with the privileges. I argued that the despised elite seemed to like most of the same things I was coming to miss.

China seemed a world of absences. No Coca-Cola, no sweets, no special desserts. I couldn't find a decent chocolate anywhere in Beijing. No English underwear, either. Where were the handbags, the ribbons for my hair? And such ugly Chinese shoes, shapeless, made of flimsy, unwearable cloth.

Even worse, if possible, Chinese girls seemed to plait their hair into two short braids. I had naturally wavy hair tied back in a fancy ponytail, and my maid at home knew just how to change my hairdo from time to time so I wouldn't get bored. Clearly there were going to be no maids here to help entertain me with new hairstyles.

I expected people to dress up occasionally, but all I ever saw were the same blue and gray clothes and hats. The only colors were on children's clothes, but they seemed almost grotesque, a shocking contrast of brilliant pinks and greens, and everywhere there were the same rabbit hats and shoes with cat designs.

Our Thai clothes were anything but drab. Wherever we went people stared at my bright dresses. Embarrassed, I would fall to muttering angrily under my breath when I saw those looks, unabashed stares that seemed to examine me like an object from another world.

As the days passed, Shanan began to speak more of my father and of Father's friend Premier Zhou Enlai. We were Zhou's guests, he said. Zhou had assigned him to look after us. That I liked; it sounded a little like my Thai world. But my confidence faded quickly when Shanan continued, speaking of how we were there to study and how our role had great significance. Being a guest was pleasant enough; a visit, even a long one, bearable. But no one seemed to envision the time when we would ever leave.

Wai and I grew more and more agitated. "Father must have sent me because I'm not his favorite son," Wai said. I decided that it was time to take matters in hand and write to Father, appealing and demanding, as was my way with him, to let us come home.

Wai helped me draft the letter. When it was ready to mail, I insisted that Shanan escort me to the post office.

"You may not mail the letter at the post office," he told me quietly but very firmly.

"How dare you refuse?" I said. "You take me to mail the letter."

"Letters can be sent, but only through me and through the Chinese ambassador in Rangoon, whom you met. It is not possible for anyone to mail letters from China to Thailand. We can send letters to your father, but I don't think it would be wise to send such a letter. Your father would not understand, and it is our responsibility to carry out his wishes."

"His wishes? Do you think he expected us to stay here?" I demanded, though now a little unsure of myself.

"He sent you to study here. You will be here for some time," Shanan said. "Now you have to start learning Chinese, and I have arranged for a teacher to come work with you."

"Why do we have to learn Chinese? Nobody told us we would

have to do that."

"You will start immediately," he said. "We have instructions from your father."

I stormed into the next room and slammed the door. Fury welled up in me, as though to fill the sudden emptiness. We had been dumped here. With Wai, however, I rallied myself to plot our way home.

"Something funny is going on," Wai said that night. "I don't think things are quite right here. Father never told me I had to learn Chinese."

Perhaps, I conceded, Father might have said, "You must learn the language." But he had never suggested that we would actually have to go every day and learn the characters and study. Nor had he said how long we would really be here.

The next morning Wai asked Shanan how long our stay would be. "I thought it was going to be a few months," Wai said.

"Ask your father someday," was all Shanan said. Then he changed the subject. "Cold weather is coming, and you will need to get some warm clothes. We will do that today."

"I don't want clothes." It was my turn now. "I hate what they look like here anyway." Warmer clothes sounded like a long stay, and I had no intention of cooperating.

"You must," he said, his voice rising.

Shanan, I sensed, had become quite frustrated with our behavior. For me to answer back so directly was shockingly unacceptable behavior in his eyes.

"You can complain to your father if you want, but I am going to take you to buy clothes. I am responsible to Premier Zhou for you. It is not just you that is at issue here."

I relented somewhat. It was September; for me it already felt chilly. The one department store, the Bai Huo Da Lou, or "Hundred Goods Big Building," on Wangfujing Street was crowded even at the entrance, more so inside. I looked around. One bland-looking thing after another. Where were the foreign goods? I asked.

"There are none," Shanan answered. "Everything here is from China."

"But you promised me we would see beautiful things here," I blurted out. I was in no mood to hear about how China was working to be able to clothe its own people. Or how so many people could go shopping in the store every day because of the staggered workweek.

"Those are on the third floor," he said.

We climbed the stairs, people pushing in both directions, seemingly oblivious of one another. Except, that is, for the stares directed at us.

"Pick out whatever you like," Shanan said as we arrived. "There are colors to choose from, different patterns."

I looked around silently. Nothing. I thought maybe I should try to find something passable. The assorted clothes were heaped in piles. Hopeless. In a corner, though, I spotted some turquiose silk. This was more promising. I asked the clerk to show it to me.

"It's too long, way too long," I said as nicely as I could.

"Well, you will grow into it in a year or so," she replied.

"A year from now?" I said, shocked. "I want it to fit now! I don't wear things that are too big. And I'll want several of them."

The clerk looked at Shanan, speechless.

She looked even more startled when Shanan picked up the silk, looked at it for a minute, then took out a special card, showed it to her, and said firmly, "Please see that it is altered."

"And I don't want the pants that go with it," I added. An altered silk top I could live with, but those pants, three times my size, never. We left with the promise of delivery in a few days.

Shanan tried to explain why the Chinese did not have the choices we did. "China was a very, very poor country, and for a long time people never had enough even to cover themselves. A lot of them died in the cold in the old days before Liberation. Now at least everyone can dress decently and warmly. That's why a single padded jacket to last for several winters is sufficient. We have to think of everyone's having warm clothes, not just of what we would like to dress up in."

Shannan knew I was not particularly persuaded. But he would prove tenacious in the days to come. He seemed proud of this poor country, and he spoke with a firm confidence that was both infuriating and compelling.

Perhaps because he realized how hard it was for us to enjoy ourselves in our alien environment, Shanan took us one night to see an acrobatic performance. Wai was especially taken with the juggler, who kept three, then four, then fives balls going at the same time. On our return Wai resolved that he too should master the trick. We had never seen a juggler in Thailand, and learning this skill would certainly prove much easier than learning Chinese and would greatly impress his friends as well. So we made large balls out of plastic and started to practice. Soon we had broken all the lightbulbs in the room.

The ever-courteous room attendant came, looked at the broken bulbs and at us, then quietly cleaned up the mess and replaced them. Soon we had them all broken again. For several days we happily set about breaking the bulbs. "Surely," Wai said, "they will send us home when they see how spoiled and bad we are."

It was such a pleasant thought that we gave ourselves over entirely to the challenge. When Shanan, having certainly been informed, walked in one day and saw the shattered bulbs for himself, he sat us down on the bed. He talked about how children in China collected wastepaper and turned it in to be reprocessed into newspaper. Everyone in the new China was being taught a sense of public property, he said firmly. It was a governmental slogan that one should be proud of being frugal and ashamed of being wasteful. China was still a very poor country and needed to become careful before it could become strong. "If every Chinese wasted a grain of rice at a meal, that would mean several hundred million grains of rice lost, he concluded. He had not mentioned the lightbulbs.

I was not appeased. "Father told us what a wonderful place China is. You have taken us all around, and all I can remember are those stinky toilets and that miserable Tiananmen Square."

Shanan turned crimson. I couldn't understand his anger, in part because I couldn't quite figure out why he was with us every day. He was certainly not our servant. No servant had ever criticized us before. Nor did he quite seem like a bodyguard. At times he was gentle and caring, at others firm or exasperated.

Shanan asked us to remember why we were there. But he knew we were homesick, he said. He reminded us that Father had sent Chareon to Beijink with us to work on a conference organized by the Chinese Buddhists to celebrate the 2,500th anniversary of Buddha's birth. Our father had arranged for four Thai Buddhist monks who had been studying in India to attend. They were coming with

Pibul's blessings.

"I will be their interpreter," Shanan said. While he was with them, we were to live on one of the dowager empress's private estates near where the conference would be taking place. "You will like the orchards," he added, by this time well aware of my fondness for fresh fruit.

Trying to gain some semblance of control over our antics, he told us that Uncle Qiu had agreed to this special arrangement.

"Uncle Qiu is a very influential man," he added. "He is as important in China as General Pao is in Thailand."

Wai and I were both impressed, but only a little. General Pao was merely one of many powers in my father's world.

Qiu Ji had a commanding appearance, I noticed the next day when he came to pick us up, but unlike General Pao, he radiated good-humored vitality, not power. Yet I sensed in him and in the way people responded to him a tacit assurance of the power he held. Thai power, I knew, did not necessarily lie with those who seemed to flaunt it. It could be very quiet, more like my father's indirect influence. I had been with him once when he was stopped for speeding. Father had apologized to the policeman who had pulled him over, and then he had showed his card. Immediately, the officer saluted. Father did not say, "Don't you know who I am?" "How dare you?" He said it was right to stop him. His power seemed all the more impressive for the way he bore it. Angry and lonely as I was in China, I never stopped watching for the various indicators of a person's power and what it revealed about his character.

F OR SEVERAL DAYS WE PLAYEDamong the antiques and ornaments in dowager empress's quarters. But Shanan was right: I loved the orchard most. Fall had already begun in Beijink, and the crystal blue sky was the perfect backdrop for the manicured orchard, its trees bending with apples and peaches. Neither was grown in Thailand, but Father would bring apples back from abroad as a special treat for me. With great ceremony. he would unveil them upon his return. The peaches, though, were my first—big sweet, ambrosial peaches, the best I would ever have in China. I wondered why he hadn't brought those! The old gardener, whose family had been court gardeners for generations, had clearly been told to give us the run of the place. We obliged. He called me *Shui guo Gong zhu*, "Fruit Princess," and each day when we returned to the orchard, he greeted us like old friends.

Chareon came one evening to tell us that Zhou Enlai had received the delegations of Buddhist monks. Zhou, he reported, had gone out of his way to pay special attention to the Thai monks and had expressed to Chareon how much he appreciated our father's proposal that the Buddhist monks of Thailand be represented by those studying in India, thus circumventing U.S. opposition to Thai participation in the conference. Chareon had met the monks as Pibul's representative. Uncle Shanan had been the interpreter.

Chareon talked about the conference at some length. For him it had been a great success, a moment to savor. Your father will be pleased, he said. Father would find his account of Zhou's remarks very helpful in Thailand. Zhou had spoken of the difference between Buddhism and Marxism. "I don't know much about Buddhism." he quoted Zhou as saying. But there was still important "common ground" between them, and China respected the right of Buddhists to practice their beliefs.

"Even with my scanty knowledge of Buddhism," Zhou said, "I know that Prince Sittata abandoned his throne and became a monk in order to contribute to the people's peace and happiness. Therefore we should uphold this principle of Buddhism in the interest of the people."

I listened to all these big words. It certainly seemed like my father's world. I had heard Zhou's name so many times by now it had become an expected part of certain political conversations. Always it was somehow linked with Father. But it hardly seemed relevant to the problems Wai and I were facing. Zhou was still no more than a name to us, a sign, in fact, that I had been cast out from the political world in which I had once moved so easily.

I was slightly mollified when Shanan told us that Premier Zhou had asked him to convey his personal welcome and that Qiu Ji was acting as our host on Zhou's behalf. Then Chareon gently told us that he was leaving, returning to Thailand now that his work for the conference was over. I felt more alone than ever. He, at least, was able to go home.

A few days later, however, Shanan reported that a delegation of senior Thai naval officials was coming to see us. Admiral Luang Yudhasard had asked them to bring us greetings from him and Father.
We received them in our room at the Beijing Hotel, and Admiral
Luang Jian, whom I had never met, spoke warmly of Father and his
work. He said he had asked Premier Zhou for permission to visit us,
and he told us of the delegation's trip to the Jiangnan naval base in
Shanghai, where they had witnessed a mock naval battle. He came
with presents, giving us money as well, something I knew Shanan
disapproved of.

Wai and I found the visit difficult. Although desperate to find a
way home, we did not feel free to tell the Thai delegation. We could
say as much to the Chinese but not to Father's representatives. For
them we put up a front. More than ever, I felt excluded from my old
world, set adrift. My father's world seemed everywhere yet nowhere,
continually spoken of by others but no longer part of my daily life.

Sequestered in the Beijing Hotel, Wai and I were pleased one
morning when Shanan told us we were invited that evening to a big
show at the Beijing Theater in honor of the opening of a conference.
A Thai writer was giving the first speech, and Shanan was to translate; Premier Zhou had assigned him to accompany the delegation.
We, however, would sit with the Chinese dignitaries, as their guests.

"Qiu Ji will also be there," Shanan said. "When you see us,
though, you are in no way to give any indication that you know us.
You must keep your ties with us a secret. Your security and that of
your father depend on it."

This was at least a familiar request. For a moment I had a sense
that our worlds might have something in common and that there was
something special about the world I was moving in. That night for
the first time I saw Shanan as something besides a bodyguard. He
stood there in his jet black Zhongshan suit looking very distinguished, and he translated into fine Thai the speech of one of the
Chinese ministers. He seemed very poised.

Our routine was broken on Sundays, when Qui Ji joined Shanan
to take us out. Usually he brought his three children, two of whom,
though older than Wai and me, at least spoke Thai, having been
born in Thailand. Qui Ji had more than once called, however, to say
that he and Shanan could not come as planned, and, anxious that

they might cancel at the last moment, I could not tolerate even their arriving late. One Sunday morning, I was put out, too, when Qiu Ji came without his children. It was going to be a dreary day.

Qui Ji clasped my hands in greeting, feeling for my pulse as well. He had mastered the old Chinese art of analyzing the pulse and used it on us each time he saw us to see if we were all right.

"How cold they are," he said. "Even our fall weather is fold for you," he said. "Here we have four seasons, and we have to change our clothes according to the weather."

The message about clothes was clear enough.

"Uncle Shanan has taken us to buy clothes," I replied. "But I hate wearing them; they're too thick and uncomfortable." Ugly, too, I said under my breath.

"Look at my cardigan." He smiled and opened his Zhongshan jacket.

He was smartly dressed in a dark blue suit. I had never seen him that way before.

"Where are we going?" I asked.

Qui Ji cleared his throat. Warming my small hands between his big palms, he said, "Premier Zhou Enlai has asked me to make regular reports to him about how you are and what you are doing. He is very concerned about you."

His words were familiar. The intensity behind them was not.

"Ever since your arrival Premier Zhou has been eager to see you, but he has been very busy, particularly with the preparations for National Day on October first."

He paused. "Premier Zhou has at last managed to find some time and he has asked me to bring you to his home today for a family lunch. Indeed, our premier so much wanted to see you that he has gotten up especially early to receive you. Normally he works at night and sleeps in the morning."

My first thoughts were not happy ones. I had long since dismissed the idea that we would see Zhou Enlai. Now that we were going, what would he say about all the terrible things we had done and our atrocious manners? Surely he would mention the lightbulbs and all our schemes to be sent home.

I shuddered at what he must have heard about the way we had treated our Chinese-language teacher. Each time she had come, we had reduced her to tears, deliberately drawing the characters with the wrong number of strokes and mispronouncing every word.

What explanation could I give? How could I deal with his anger? I'd say my brother made me do it.

Wai was also afraid. He knew we had not lived up to our responsibilities to Prime Minister Pibul. "If worse comes to worse, we can promise him we won't do those things again," he whispered.

The car had gone only a few blocks from the hotel when it stopped at one of the large gates of Zhongnanhai, the great walled compound where, we had been told on earlier outings, all the top leaders of China lived. I waited expectantly as the two security guards walked to the car. Qui Ji showed them his pass and exchanged a few words with them The guards made way and signaled us through.

For several minutes we drove slowly past a beautiful lake lined with willows so bent you could hardly see the sun as we passed under them. The place was immense, and as we drove further in the sounds of the city receded. There was an enormous serenity there; even the birds seemed to sing softly and with reverence. In the lake fish swam leisurely, at times sending big bubbles up to the smooth surface. Along one bank we passed imperial buildings with roofs of glazed tile set among thick, tall, ancient trees. The buildings seemed more like temples than houses. We came to a stop in front of one of them, a half-hidden, attractive old building close to the wall. Qui Ji told us it had been a Qing palace.

"This is the residence of the premier," Shanan said. "And Chairman Mao lives back over there," he added, pointing at a large clump of trees more toward the interior.

The minute the car stopped, two men ran down the steps to open the car doors, I sensed that this would be like visiting Pibul. We would be well received, not punished.

I bounded up the steps, holding Qiu Ji's hand. The protocol man led us first into a large unpainted corridor, then into Zhou's private sitting room. Although it was simple, I appreciated the imperial beauty of it. We had been seated for barely a moment when in he walked. He was just like the photos I had seen all over—thick eyebrows, straight shoulders, straight back. He was very handsome.

"Welcome, welcome," he said, smiling.

Wai and I made our Thai *wai* greeting. He returned it, the first person in China to do so. Smiling even more broadly, he said *"Sawadi,"* "Greetings," in Thai. Then, with Shanan interpreting, he added, "I love these customs you have in Thailand. In Burma, too, but in Thailand it is even more elegant the way the lady bends."

"How old are you, my little friend?" Zhou asked, leaning down to put his arm around my shoulder. I was already inching toward my accustomed spot.

"Eight," I replied.

"How old is your father?" Zhou asked.

I turned to Wai. "In his forties, maybe. I'm not sure," he said.

Wai was quiet, but already he was picking up what he had begun at our farewell meeting with Pibul, taking notes, a sign to all that, even if he was only a boy of twelve, he had an official role to fulfill.

Zhou talked on. "The forties are good years. You've started to understand the world. You've made a fool of yourself lots of times by then and become wiser, and you still have the energy to work. So perhaps it is the best time of a person's life."

"Is that your age?" I asked.

"I'm over fifty," Zhou replied. "At fifty we still have a few more years. it depends on how we use our lives."

Turning to Wai as well, Zhou asked us how we liked China.

"I'm bored stiff," I blurted out. Then I made a very sad face to show how I felt. Wai looked as though he would have kicked me under the table if we had been sitting at one.

Zhou laughed at such bluntness, and thus began the very direct relationship between us that was to last until he died. He made an equally sad face in response. "I think I understand how you might feel. I was older than you when I was in Japan, but I was bored stiff too. Nothing to do and I didn't understand the language."

Zhou turned to Shanan. "Have they taken Chinese lessons?"

I looked uneasily at Shanan, but he only smiled and said we had started.

I gave Shanan my dirtiest look. "Don't tell all the bad stuff!" I said.

Zhou laughed when Shanan translated. By now I was quite relaxed. I told Zhou about telling my friends I was going to Bandung, about Wai's being named after Prince Warnwai, whom he had met at

Bandung. "Father told me that his name might remind you pleasantly of the prince."

Zhou looked at Wai. "I hope you'll grow up to be someone like him. I'm told he is a great writer and poet."

"Yes," said Wai. "We have to study his poems from primary school on."

"And he likes me," I added.

Zhou laughed and pulled my ponytail gently.

"Prince Warnwai," Wai continued in his most serious tone of voice,. "wished us the best in coming here to China and asked us to convey his best regards to you. He told us that his meeting with you was the most memorable." Wai went on to express both Grandpa Pibul's good wishes and Father's and then presented Zhou with a pair of small elephant tusks from Pibul and an engraved silver cigarette box from father.

Zhou thanked Wai. "Your father is a courageous man," Zhou said. "China was once a backward country bullied by Western powers. Now your father too is trying to assert Thailand's independence and integrity. Someday I hope to visit your country, but maybe I should wait until it is less awkward for the Thai government to receive me."

I nodded.

"But for now," Zhou continued, "I am going to try to make you as comfortable as possible. Prime Minister Pibul and your father have entrusted the two of you to my care, and we'll certainly do our best."

Wai was writing all this down. For the first time in China I felt fully back in my natural element.

"You are a very political little girl," Zhou said to me. "We understand how difficult it is for your father and how bravely he is acting."

For some time we batted comments back and forth.

"Qiu Ji," Zhou asked, "why haven't you taken them out more? I know what it's like to be cooped up in a hotel room. Let them see the changes in the city."

I hoped Qiu Ji would not bring up what we had been doing while cooped up. But he only mentioned the difficulties of getting us around and promised that he would follow Zhou's suggestion and take us to the Beijing duck restaurant.

"Have you tasted Beijing duck yet?" Zhou asked.

"No, but I don't like Beijing food. It's too oily for me."

Zhou patted my head and said, "Ah, but you are sure to like this special duck. It is so special that the Russians have just invited some of our cooks to open a restaurant in Moscow." Evidently the Russians had tried to prepare it themselves but hadn't known the secret.

What was so special about the duck? I wanted to know. Zhou made gestures to show how the ducks were force-fed to make the fat and the meat so tender. That and the sauce were the secret.

Food made me think of his teeth. "You don't look at all like some of your pictures in Thailand, an ogre with big jutting teeth," I said.

"Can't you see them?" Zhou said, opening his mouth wide. "My enemies always try to make me look like a monster to scare off people."

"But how do the Thai enemies know you?" I asked.

"They don't know me personally. But they don't like what we are doing. They don't like the new China. Who knows, perhaps the decision your father made to send you will help set a new path for Thai and Chinese relations. You could build a beautiful bridge between us."

Though Wai had warned me to sit still like a good Thai lady, I forgot, and as we talked I got up and began taking the lace doilies off the couches and the chairs. Shanan watched with some shock when I asked Zhou why these doilies were to be seen everywhere in China. Then I folded them into lotuses, something my mother had taught me.

Zhou was very amused. "Thailand has many fine cultural works. Look at this!"

I glanced at Shanan in triumph.

"My dolls in Thailand would look very nice dressed up in these," I said.

"But did you bring them with you?" he asked, apparently quite concerned.

"No," I said. "I never thought I would stay away from them for so long."

"Well," Zhou said, hugging me closely, "we will try to find you new dolls here."

"But I've looked in the big department store, and I can't find any to dress up that I really like." China had few dolls, and none like the ones I was used to.

"We shall see," Zhou said. "Shanan can take you to the Dongsi market next Sunday. Perhaps you can find one there."

By the time Little Chao, as Zhou called his wife, announced lunch, I had fully accomplished my task of ridding the room of its doilies.

Deng Mama, as we were to call her, seemed a total contrast to Zhou. His purposeful aristocratic bearing, his simple, neat, courtly style and enormous charm, were nowhere mirrored in her down-to-earth plainness and quiet demeanor. She was solicitous, however, and full of advice for us. But it was Zhou who set me to talking as of old.

When I told her how bored we were and how I hated the hotel, she took my hand and told us her "good news." A special place was being prepared for us: an old house that had once belonged to a high Qing official would soon be ready. It was a typical Beijing-style one-story building, she said, quite spacious and with a courtyard. And once modernization was completed, it would be one of the few buildings in Beijing with central heating. She smiled at me.

"How many servants will we have?" I asked.

Zhou just laughed and patted my head again.

"When can we go see it?" I asked.

Zhou asked Qiu Ji how the work was progressing. "The workers are on the job from early morning until late at night, including Sundays," he said. "It is nearly finished. In a week it should be ready for a visit."

Lunch was ready. I noticed a small dish of fried peanuts beside Zhou. Was it his favorite? I wondered. Yes, he said. Then I asked about another dish. Zhou said it was *mantou*, steamed bread. My question elicited a Chinese folktale about its origins.

"*Mantou* means 'the heads of Man tribesmen,' " he said. "*Man* is the name of a minority group, *tou* means 'head.' The Man tribesmen lived over seventeen hundred years ago, during the period of the Three Kingdoms. They were considered backward by the Han people, and they lived in a region extending from southern Sichuan and Yunnan into present-day Burma and Thailand."

I tasted a piece of one as he spoke.

"The Man king launched several attacks on the southern Chinese kingdom of Chu, all of which were defeated by the brilliant General

Kongming. Each time the Man king was captured, Kongming released him without any conditions. On the occasion of his surrender to Kongming after the failure of his final invasion, the Man king wanted to offer the heads of forty-nine of his subjects to scare away ghosts and demons, but Kongming persuaded him to substitute lumps of dough shaped like heads. There were to be no more sacrifices of human beings. So now we make these heads and call them 'Man' heads—and eat them."

With the fish dish came another folktale.

"See the flesh on the cheeks of the fish?" Zhou asked. "We consider it the choicest part of the fish. It's the way the robber picks out his victim."

Zhou gave me a piece of the cheek.

"A bandit came to a village with the intention of robbing the richest man. But the people were unfamiliar to him. He couldn't tell from appearance who that was; apparently many lived quite modestly. So he invited the whole village to a big fish dinner. Then he watched. One very nicely dressed man plunged his chopsticks right into the tail." And Zhou put his chopsticks there, removing a piece of it for me.

"So the robber said, 'That's not the person for me.' Another person put his chopsticks right into the belly of the fish, and the robber said to himself, 'That one's not for me either.' " This time Zhou took a piece from the belly and gave it to Wai.

"Then there was a quiet old man, dressed in rags. He quietly put his chopsticks into the cheek of the fish and tried to get the piece for himself. And the robber said, 'I will visit him tonight.' "

The folktales and stories came effortlessly to Zhou. Father had never suggested that he would have such a sense of humor and be so entertaining. Every dish seemed to have its special story.

Deng Mama pointed out that the dishes contained young sweet corn and green peppers from the Zhongnanhai vegetable plot. Gardening, she explained, had been a hobby of many of the leaders ever since the Yan'an days during the war against the Japanese in the 1930s.

When she tried to show me how to hold chopsticks, I knocked over my glass of orangeade. Until that moment feeling confident, I was mortified now. Only when the mess was cleared and the lesson temporarily ended for the day did I feel better.

After lunch Deng Mama took us out to the back garden and loaded us down with corn. We were preparing to leave when Zhou said, "Let's talk about your studies now. Chinese is a very important language. You will never regret learning it. Don't let me hear you are not making progress and working hard."

Zhou didn't talk the way Father did. Not "Life is hard, life is struggle." He was very precise and clear. "Do your lessons well. Next time I see you I expect to hear Chinese. Your father is an extremely farsighted man," he continued. "He entrusted you to me to learn about China and its civilization. That way you, too, can do great works in the future."

As he walked us to the car, he stroked my head lightly and said to Wai and me, "Make my house your own. The door is always open to you."

I was happy as we drove off. Wai was less so. "How could you talk like that in front of the premier?" he said. "This could be very bad. He might think from what you said that the staff had failed to take care of us. How could you go on and on like that?" I was unfazed. I felt I had at last been thrown a lifeline to a world in which I might survive.

"You have a very lively sister," Shanan later said to Wai. But he did not say it disapprovingly. He had seen a different side of me, some-one who showed off, perhaps, but was at ease, as my Father was at ease, with power and powerful people. After that I began to under-stand Shanan's role in a different way as well. He was our closest guardian and caretaker, Zhou's immediate representative. He re-ported to Qiu Ji and through him to Zhou. Zhou, I soon realized, knew all about our antics. But he had said that I would be seeing him again, that I was always welcome. I now had my own contact. Not since our plane had left Bangkok almost two months earlier had I seen as certain a glimmer of a world in which I could once again be safe.

CHAPTER 5

"Ni Hao, Zhou Bobo"

WAI AND I WAITED impatiently to see our house. Every day we asked Shanan about it. Each time he told us we had to wait a few more days. Construction of the central heating system was not finished. There were still repairs to be done. I consoled myself with the exciting prospect of an old palace made completely new for us.

"What color are we going to paint the house?" I asked Shanan. "Let's paint it pale green," I decided, thinking of a color then fashionable in Bangkok.

"When in Rome, do as the Romans do," Shanan replied.

"What's a Roman?" I asked.

"Well, in Thailand the houses are wooden. You can paint the wood green, blue, gold, almost any color you want. But in China I can't build you a wooden house. In winter you would freeze to death."

"You mean no pretty colors?" I asked in disbelief.

"It's a beautiful house with a cresent moon–shaped entrance," Shanan said. "Very modern. Like all the houses in Beijing, though, it's made of earth and bricks."

"Still, I would like it to be painted pale green," I said.

"Not possible," Shanan replied. "A pale color would quickly be covered with dust in Beijing, and nothing would be seen of it."

His reminder of Beijing's dust left me feeling doubly thwarted. I was going to have to live in a drab house in this dirty city.

He continued in great detail, drawing us diagrams and pictures, explaining how one walked through the entrance into the courtyard. As he went on, I stopped listening. I was sure we had gotten an ugly house, certainly nothing as large or colorful as mine in Thailand.

Still, we insisted on seeing it, construction or not, and Shanan finally agreed to take us. He explained that it was in the eastern part of the city, near Chao Yang gate. During the Ming and Qing periods from the fourteenth to the early twentieth century, princes and court officials had lived both in this area and slightly south of it. It was also a commercial center, once the site of granaries, an antiques bazaar, and markets for meat, rice, lanterns. The streets still retained their old market names. Ours was Brewery Lane in the Shao Jiu Hutung.

As our car turned into the lane, I saw two large lions out front. My spirits rose. Then I saw the dark red door. "That's the house?" I asked incredulously. In Thailand we associated a red roof and red doors with madness and mad people.

Dust swirled from the debris as we passed through the cresent-shaped entrance and into the courtyard. I stared aghast at the painters busily at work. They were painting the corridors and the ceiling shockingly bright colors—red, green, and gold.

"Why are they splashing the colors all over?" I asked Shanan.

"These are artists we brought in to decorate the house," he said. "You said you liked colors," he added.

Soft colors, I thought; I like soft colors. The artists were diligently working over the fine details, delicate motifs of birds and forests along the corridor between the glassed-in areas and the house walls. I tried to show an interest in what they were doing.

As we continued down the corridor, Shanan proudly pointed out the central heating system that was being completed. "Only Premier Zhou can approve such a costly system," he said.

We walked into the glassed-in porch. "I have rarely ever seen one in Beijing," Shanan said. "It will keep the cold out in the winter and the heat out in the summer."

I suddenly felt I couldn't breathe. Thai houses were open so breezes could flow through them continually; here all the windows were sealed shut. Even the exits and the entrances were glassed in. It wasn't even cold, and already the house felt completely self-enclosed. I couldn't help but gasp. Shanan didn't seem to notice. He led us from one room to another.

The south side, he explained, was for our cook, his family, and the guards. We would live on the east side. My room would be next to Wai's. A large door connected our two rooms. In each room there was a big iron Russian-style bed, the type, Shanan told us, that all the top leaders preferred. Momentarily, I was pleased. I sat down hard on mine. It was quite springy. In front of a window that faced the corridor were a large table with a glass top and a wooden chair.

"Is there a dressing table?" I asked.

"You can use the big mirror on the wardrobe," Shanan replied. "But if you wish, we can get you a dressing table as well."

It was one of the first times Shanan had not tried to make me simply accept what was given. Since our meeting with Zhou, he had become more flexible.

"We can finish decorating the rooms soon," Shanan added, perhaps noting my unusual quietness. We walked into the big sitting room. There was a large, thick maroon carpet with Chinese motifs on the floor. The same official khaki-covered settee and armchairs as we had seen at Zhou's were carefully placed, as were the requisite lace antimacassars for the arm- and headrests. A large glass table sat in the middle of the arrangements, with smaller glass tables by the sides of the chairs. Everything seemed big and heavy; brown was the predominant color. When Shanan said we would get pillows for the room, I pleaded for something with nice colors—"a soft pink, please."

"We will get plants too," he said. "When visitors come, this is where you will receive them."

Shanan pointed out the two bathrooms, each with a bath big enough to hold an entire family. There were old-fashioned toilets, with strings to pull the flushing mechanism but otherwise new and clean, and a big sink with separate hot and cold water taps.

We continued through the two guest rooms, the large kitchen, the equally spacious dining room, and a playroom on the west side that briefly aroused my interest. A Ping-Pong table was already in place. A smaller game room was next, then the driver's room and a spare room where Shanan said he would sometimes stay. Behind the house and separate from it was a building for the boiler.

I knew Shanan was very proud of this house, an accomplishment of the new China he so ardently wished us to know about. He wore a satisfied look on his face when we'd finished. I looked down at the dirty tiles. I couldn't walk here with my shoes off as I did on the smooth wood floors in our house in Thailand. Several times I had scuffed my shoes on the rough edges.

"I told you," Wai whispered to me. "All we would get would be a big house—nothing else."

The days that followed were tedious and excruciatingly uncomfortable. I had broken out all over in a skin rash. Still, I consoled myself with the thought that the house would surely be better than being cooped up in the Beijing Hotel. I tried a little harder to study Chinese. Each morning we had lessons for two or three hours. Unlike Wai, I also spent much of my time memorizing the characters and practicing Chinese with the hotel staff. Wai hated memorizing characters and was shy about speaking Chinese. I had not forgotten what Zhou had said, although he seemed far away and our daily life unchanged. Even so, we often did not cooperate with our teacher. She was not free to criticize us because of our privileged status, of which she was perhaps more aware than we. One day she could stand it no longer and abruptly left in tears.

When Qiu Ji came that night, Wai and I knew we were in trouble. Since our meeting with Zhou, I had held Qiu Ji in higher esteem. People who appeared at ease with such a powerful person were usually of great prominence in their own right, I knew.

"What do you want to do with yourselves?" Qiu Ji asked. He was firm and direct. No pulse taking that night. "No one else can learn Chinese for you."

We remained quiet, our heads down.

"In two months you will be attending a Chinese school. You will be lost there and unhappy if you can't speak at all."

I continued to look down. Going to a Chinese school had not occurred to me.

"Your father made it very clear that he wanted you both to learn Chinese and to attend a Chinese school. Premier Zhou has entrusted me with the task of making sure that you get a proper education. You have a responsibility to your father. You will find that when you try it will not be so difficult."

He took my hand. "The next time I see you I expect things to be different. I know it is hard for you, but you must make up your minds about how you are going to act."

For the next few days we worked more earnestly. Shanan came every day to take us out and sometimes succeeded in entertaining us with his stories. He took us to the Beijing duck restaurant Zhou had mentioned. Wai and I were indifferent to the duck but liked being able to associate the place with Zhou.

The next morning Shanan announced that he was going to take us to a very special place, that we were sure to like. I was curious, but Wai was appalled when Shanan led us down a small side street into a dingy little eating place.

"Why are you taking us to this kind of a place, Uncle Shanan?" he demanded.

"You'll like it," Shanan replied. "It is one of our most famous restaurants, and it serves food fit for an emperor."

Afterward we thought that for once Shanan had been right about something.

TWENTY-FIVE YEARS LATER I was able to read Zhou Enlai's and Qiu Ji's letters to my father reporting on us. "You have put your two lovely children in our care," Qiu Ji wrote. "This kind of confidence makes us feel the greatest honor and happiness." As we tortured our teacher, Qiu Ji wrote of how "their Chinese has greatly improved. Every day they find it easier to express themselves."

He also wrote of the house I initially so disliked. "To assist us in caring for your children, a house is in the process of renovation, and soon they will be able to live there. We are planning to ask for a special teacher to consolidate the children's Chinese studies. We will wait until they have a basic level and then have them go to school. This is the way we are arranging their lives. Do you or your wife have any suggestions for us?

"We will do our best to give them all our love. We will take them and love them as our own children. Rest assured of this."

His hope, Zhou wrote to Father that fall, was "to try and create a warm home atmosphere. You and your wife should not worry about this."

ON THE EVE OF NATIONAL DAY, October 1, 1956, Qiu Ji came to tell us that we had been invited by Premier Zhou to the greatest ceremony of the year. Day after day we had seen and heard the preparations under way near the hotel.

When Qiu Ji and Shanan arrived for us the next morning, we were ready, Wai in his sharkskin Western suit, I in a multi-colored, long-sleeved Thai dress. We walked the short distance from the hotel down the brightly colored avenue to the reviewing stands. There were twelve of them, Qiu Ji pointed out, and everyone would be given a red, pink, or green satin ribbon to show what stand he or she were meant to sit in.

As we passed through the crowds and approached the stands, we were given red ribbons with "West No. 1" inscribed on them. Once up in the reviewing stand, we saw that we were the closest to the Tiananmen rostrum, where the top Chinese leaders would stand. The square was a sea of red flags flanked by giant portraits of Stalin, Lenin, Marx, and, directly beneath our section of stands, Mao. I felt a pang of regret that Zhou's was not there. In China it had been confusing at first not to see Zhou's picture everywhere. He seemed not even to be number two—or three. Perhaps number four, I thought—after Mao, Zhu De, and Liu Shaoqi. In Thailand, Pibul, the prime minister, was clearly the top person, much as I had expected the premier here to be.

Thousands of children now filled the square, each holding a branch of colored paper flowers in either hand. Only Chang An Boulevard was left open for the parade to pass through. Wai and I looked around our reviewing stand. We were the only children there, and many of the well-dressed foreign guests seemed as curious about who we were as about the parade itself.

At ten o'clock sharp, Chairman Mao, Premier Zhou, and the

other leaders of the Chinese revolution appeared. It was my first glimpse of Mao, who towered over his comrades. Just as I spotted Zhou, a twenty-four-gun salute began. Next came the national anthem, and when it ended, a military jeep drove up to the stand with Minister of Defense Marshal Peng Dehuai in full uniform standing inside. He gave a snappy military salute, got out, and walked quickly to the rostrum to salute Chairman Mao again. When he was in place, Peng Zhen, the mayor of Beijing, delivered the official speech.

Then began the parade. First came the military part, with each of the three branches of the armed forces displaying themselves. They were followed by workers from most of Beijing's factories and by peasants from outlying areas. Then came athletes and sports officials and, after them, dancers in brightly colored costumes, twirling and swirling through the square. Folk music, popular Chinese dance music, and military marches echoed through the square as the troupes of dancers, soldiers, and ethnic groups passed by.

The parade ended at noon, when all the children with paper flowers in their hands rushed forward chanting, "Long Live Chairman Mao! Long live the Communist party of China!" Mao, Zhou, and the others walked back and forth, waving to the paraders and the children, finally bidding good-bye to all the guests.

We had been told we could watch the fireworks that night. But we were surprised to find ourselves on the Tiananmen rostrum with the leaders. The children of the leaders were running around, so I too ran to the end to look at the people far below, many of whom were singing and dancing to the music as it blared over the loudspeakers. At eight the fireworks began. I watched, dazzled, as they exploded, then looked toward the center to see Mao walking in with a short, fat, bald man. "Khrushchev is here," I heard someone say. Mao stood erect and tall, an imposing figure compared to the Russian.

I saw Zhou approaching. I had practiced for this moment. *"Ni hao, Zhou Bobo,"* I said. "Hello, Uncle Zhou. I can speak Chinese to you, Uncle."

Zhou greeted me and smiled, patting my head gently.

"I love the fireworks," I stumbled on determinedly.

When he answered, though, I became confused. Shanan interpreted.

"I enjoy hearing your Chinese as much as watching the fireworks," Zhou said.

A few minutes later we headed back to the hotel. It was the first day in China that I had enjoyed from beginning to end.

That night, as Wai and I discussed all we had seen, the telephone rang and I ran to answer it. The connection was bad, but I immediately recognized Mother's voice.

"Where are you?" I asked.

"In China," she replied. "In Guangzhou. Tukta is with me." It was hard to make out the rest, but I understood that she would be in Beijing in a week or two.

Qiu Ji arrived early the next morning and confirmed that Mother would arrive in about ten days and that we should go to our house now and see if it was ready.

"If it is, you will move in in the next few days. It will be more enjoyable if you can all stay there with your mother during her visit," he said. We moved into the house two days later.

I had a terrible first week there. At night, shut up in my room, I became depressed and frightened. I felt closed in, totally alone, and I spent the first night gasping for breath. Shanan quickly understood part of my problem. I had never been alone in a room at night in my life. A maid had always slept next to me on the floor in Thailand. In the hotel, Wai and I had slept in the same room. The next day Shanan cut a special door in the wall so that I could see Wai in his room at night.

With this I could at least sleep. But now, whenever I did, I rolled over and fell out of bed, awakening everyone with my screams of pain. The beds were high off the floor, and landing on the hard tile floors hurt. Shanan resorted to tying me down at night so I would not fall out. Somehow I still managed to do so. Finally Shanan put a thick carpet under my bed to break the fall.

Shanan's next task was to persuade us that the house staff were workers, not servants. We had our responsibilities to look after, they had theirs. In the Beijing Hotel everything had been taken care of; the staff had patiently seen to our every whim.

The day we moved in, Shanan introduced us to everyone. They were all Chinese born and raised in Thailand. Zhou insisted we were to retain our Thai culture and language; our house was to be Thai-speaking.

There was a driver, Lai Liesheng; a cook, Feng Liangming, and his family; a cleaning person; and two guards. A car was in the garage, always ready for our use. Only Old Lai, as we called the driver, and Shanan knew or were authorized to know who our father was. I saw the bafflement on the faces of the others: what could it mean that two kids lived in a house all by themselves under Premier Zhou's auspices? One look at Wai and me told them we were not from a revolutionary background. Perhaps there was a revolutionary hero in the distant past, surely dead. Or more likely we were the son and daughter of some high Communist party leaders. Not even the children of princes or kings were so well treated. But none of this was said to us, nor, I learned in later years, was it discussed much among the staff. In those days secrets were kept; it was part of Communist discipline. Zhou had made it clear from our first meeting that we were special guests, for whom security considerations were paramount. "You are not to go out alone, even when you learn the language. You are to go by car, and always accompanied."

I was familiar with secrecy. Father had taught me to know almost instinctively what was secret and what not. Assassination attempts made such knowledge a matter of life and death. Zhou, too, I learned, had narrowly escaped death when a bomb had exploded on one of the two Chinese planes that had gone to Bandung. Whenever Wai or I complained about always having to be escorted, Zhou or Shanan would sternly bring up the plane incident. On this Zhou brooked no disagreement.

In China I was to live with secrecy far more pervasive than anything I'd known in Thailand. Our past was a secret; practically no one knew who we were, why we were there, and why we lived in the midst of such privilege. For my first fourteen years in China I was never asked about my background except by those who, for official reasons, had the right to know who we were. Neither my school friends nor my teachers asked. They knew not to.

In the house Zhou set up for us, my Thai background became an abstraction. I spoke of missing Thailand to those who took care of us, but I wasn't to speak of my family. The little stories I might have about them, my memories—there was no one to tell them to. Although Wai and I could have spoken to Shanan of our past, we soon learned not to. He had no reason to like Pibul and his government: they had driven him underground and had forced him to flee Thailand in the anti-Communist campaigns. He knew far better than I did how prominently my father had once figured in those. To Shanan, Father was a "bourgeois intellectual." He was clear, in his idealistic bluntness, that our ways represented much that was wrong with the world, and so naturally he sometimes lost his patience with the unruly behavior of his spoiled wards. With Wai, however, he tried to be tactful, for while Wai might say Father was crazy to send us, he would not tolerate critical comments from anyone about Father or Pibul. He was Pibul's representative, he insisted. It was a matter of honor for him.

Our driver, Old Lai, was about thirty. A short, rather quiet man, he was everything to us—driver, playmate, carpenter, guardian, bodyguard. He lived with us, usually staying in his small room at the far end of the house. His wife and children never came to the house, and we rarely saw them. His wife belonged to a different organization, we were told, one not in the premier's office. Sometimes we talked of Bangkok and Thai food with Old Lai, but more often than not, he was simply there, a comforting presence, playing with us, acting as an intermediary with the rest of the house staff. In Shanan's absence, he was in charge. If there was a problem, he would phone Shanan.

Shanan made sure we knew of Old Lai's heroic past. He wanted us to realize that we should respect him as well as the cook for their past deeds.

He is not an ordinary driver," Shanan said before we moved into the house. "He fought against the Japanese in the war. He led strikes in Japanese-owned factories. Once he was caught by the Japanese, but he never gave in, never said anything."

Wai stiffened at these moment. He knew a little of Father's role in Pibul's government under the Japanese occupation.

Old Lai, however, never talked about his past. When Wai needed companionship, he gave it. "Now you come and box with me," he'd say, and Wai would, though Old Lai was so bad that he ended up serving as a punching bag. At night he would sit up with us and play cards and games. He was never rigid with us; he never simply "applied the principle" to us. He seemed to understand that our lives had been quite different.

From Old Lai we learned of Shanan's past in the Thai underground and we learned, as well, that Shanan sometimes translated for Chairman Mao when he needed a Thai interpreter. This was impressive, although Mao, despite my glimpse, seemed a remote figure.

From the first, our cook, Old Feng, and his family resented our privilege and thought us very spoiled. We liked the food well enough—it was Thai—but as children we had eaten what we wanted when we wanted. When he served chicken, we ate only the parts we liked and left the skin. When he served fish, we ate only a part of it.

Unless Shanan joined us, we ate alone. Old Lai was not allowed to eat with us, and even Shanan required permission to join us. The cook and his family ate nearby, and I could see what they had. It was not the same. They gave us the pork chop, while they had the bone cooked with vegetables. Compared to us, they ate quite poorly.

"Why don't you have meat?" I asked Old Feng.

"Where would I get that?" he replied. "I am not in your position. You are the special guest of the premier. Of course, I will try to cook whatever dishes you like. But as for my family and me, we have our own ration card and it is sufficient."

"Still, can't you have any meat?" I asked. No one had ever told us that food was in such short supply.

"I am not you," he repeated. "If I were you I could get any meat I like. For everyone to have some meat, we must ration what we have. We are big but poor, and the ration system is the only fair way."

Perhaps we should be very careful, Wai said later. Perhaps we shouldn't throw away any of the food. I was not about to agree. I couldn't possibly eat it all, yet it gave me pause when I learned that while we had rice, only a few people in northern China ate it regularly. Every day our cook went to a special supply shop for the high cadres to get the goods that could not be gotten in the marketplace. Eating well with others looking on began to make me uncomfortable.

During the war, Feng had been a top chef for a Japanese army general in Bangkok while working for the Communist party. Zhou had specifically picked him for our house because of his Thai background. Feng himself knew that his role was somehow important, but it was unclear why. Not only was he stuck with two little kids, but we seemed impossible to please. He produced dishes with great care, yet I'd often only pick at them. He thought us wasteful but made a great effort to learn what we liked. I sensed this and tried hard in return not to think of him simply as a servant.

"We are all equals in terms of our contributions," Shanan said. "We are all comrades."

"What's a comrade?" I asked.

"It means one cause. That we are all fighting for the one cause. That we are all serving the people. You must respect all the tasks people do. In the new China, we don't treat people as servants."

We are all equal, I said over and over to myself. Nobody is to serve anyone else. Zhou Enlai, the cook, the driver, me—we are all equal in this society. It didn't seem true, but it was fun to say it to myself.

Certainly our house staff did not act like Thai servants. Initially, despite Shanan's admonitions, we behaved as though we were in the hotel. They might not be servants, but still, someone had to clean up and make the beds. When it was intimated that we were to make our own beds, we responded by making an even bigger mess to signal our refusal.

In the hotel Wai and I had continued our custom of changing our clothes several times a day. In the blistering Thai heat, we would drop our things into the wash, and the servants would wash and dry them, returning them within the day—the intense sun could dry them in just a few hours. Nobody told us not to do the same thing here, but gradually we noticed that our clothes were disappearing. Within a few days we were practically out of clothes. So one day we decided not to dress but to stay in our pajamas.

That afternoon Qiu Ji came unexpectedly. He walked in and found us in the playroom. Coming up to me, he felt my pulse. What was the matter? he asked. Were we sick? Why weren't we dressed?

"No clothes," I said.

"What do you mean, 'no clothes'?" he asked with a startled look on his face. "You have lots of clothes. We just got you new ones."

"No, we don't have clothes. They're all dirty," I replied.

"That's not possible. Why weren't they washed?" he asked.

Qiu Ji called in the girl who was temporarily washing our clothes for Feng's wife, who was giving birth.

"Why are there no clothes? Why didn't you wash?" he asked.

She stood there with an attitude of respect but spoke firmly. "They change their clothes three times a day. She changes her dresses repeatedly. I can't be expected to wash and dry them all."

"Very well," Qiu Ji said. "Wash the clothes that are dirty, and we shall try to reduce their number."

"You see," Qiu Ji continued after she left, "in China we don't change our clothes like you did in Thailand. It is not so hot here, especially now. But we are also a poor country. We lack the facilities. She has to do it all by hand. We have only limited soap. It is very hard for her. I want you to understand this so it will make sense for you to dress differently."

"No one said anything to us, Uncle. She just stopped doing it," I said. Evidently, it was not her place to say anything. Learning the new rules of how people acted was not proving easy.

"You are going to be learning many of our ways as you live here," Qiu Ji said. "Shanan and I are here to help you understand them and explain to you what is happening."

There was much to learn. Ziao Ma was a young man of about eighteen who served our food, cleaned up afterward, washed the windows, and set things in order in the morning. He was probably the son of a military man. Try as he might, Shanan could not convince him that his work for two spoiled kids had anything to do with serving the new China. He almost certainly had no idea why we were treated the way we were. Nor had I any idea what category to put him in and therefore how to treat him. He obviously hated wearing his white coat and laying a white tablecloth for us. Within a few days, whenever Shanan was not with us, he practically threw the food on the table.

"You tell your people," I said to Old Lai one day, quite outraged, "that they are not to behave like that, or I will tell Premier Zhou En-lai."

Old Lai would sometimes speak to the staff when Wai or I complained, but he was very uncomfortable. Although he sympathized with us, he was not going to get too drawn into the struggle. He particularly wanted to keep the cook happy; he saw the problems. Shanan didn't like our manners either, but he tried in various ways to make us feel that he was someone we could count on.

Several days after Qiu Ji had dropped by and discovered us in our pajamas, Wai and I were in the game room loudly singing the Chinese national anthem. We could practice our Chinese with it, and the tune was lively enough to get enthusiastic about. We were well into the spirit of it when I saw Ma out of the corner of my eye. He was at the door watching us, his body rigid, his eyes filled with rage. He charged into the room, screaming.

"Stop singing! How dare you? You are insulting our country!"

I stormed out in fury. No servant had ever treated me that way. No one in China had ever spoken to me like that.

I immediately phoned Shanan at his office. "Ziao Ma has stopped us from singing!" I complained.

"Impossible," Shanan said. "Calm down. Now tell me what is happening."

"No," I replied. "You just come quickly. Then I'll tell you."

He was there in ten minutes. I suspected he had already gotten a report from Ma about how bad we were. "He throws the food at us, and now he screams at us. What next?" I said.

"Ma did not act correctly in shouting at you," Shanan said. "His criticism was correct, but his manner was bad. In China, the national anthem is something we are proud of. It is never sung merely as a tune—it is sung only on official occasions. For us it represents the revolution and what we are seeking to build in this country. That is why we treat it with such respect. He was angered by what he saw as your disrespectful treatment of it."

"But why is it so lacking in respect for the nation if we sing its anthem?" Wai asked.

"You don't pay the proper respect if you simply sing it. It must be sung standing the proper way and with the proper attitude."

"We will not be treated like that, Uncle," we both said. But then in a softer voice I added, "But we understand about the singing."

A day or two later Ma was gone.

QIU JI AND SHANAN BOTH WENT with us to greet Mother at the airport. Wai and I had been in China just eight weeks.

From almost the moment I saw her, as she and Tukta disembarked, a great divide opened up between the way I acted and the

way I felt. Outwardly, I proclaimed my enormous pride that I could
live away from home for two months. Inwardly, though, I did not
like being in China or our having been sent here. What I liked were
Zhou and our special treatment. So, I quickly saw, did she.

Mother loved the house: she knew what its size meant, and she
knew as well the luxurious standard it set in China. "I can see that
you are secure and well taken care of here," she said with evident relief. She was amazed to confirm what our letters said, that the entire
house staff spoke Thai. She got to know them immediately, and by
the first evening she was already cooking in the kitchen and laying
out our clothes on the bed. She showed Old Feng how to make some
of the dishes we liked. They seemed to enjoy working together, and
Feng appeared pleased at our improved response.

Qiu Ji made no plans for the first few days. "Please relax and get
reacquainted," he said. Madame Zhou sent her limousine to be at
Mother's disposal for the length of her stay in Beijing. We went to
the markets, showed her a few sights, but mostly just enjoyed our
time in the house. I played with my baby sister and heard, with
mixed feelings, about life at home.

Wai was clearly unhappy and wanted to go back. He had a sense of
mission, of why he had been sent, but personally he remained aloof,
detached. I, by contrast, had no sense of mission, but I was beginning to feel the kind of involvement that had so attracted me at
home. To Mother I made a point of how I liked the house and all the
little things that were done for us. I was eager to portray myself as
fulfilling my role well. I pronounced the Chinese words I had
learned, showed her my character practice book, and chatted endlessly about my experiences.

Mother knew Wai wanted to go; she undoubtedly knew I did as
well. She didn't wait for Wai to bring it up. Instead, she told us we
could go home. "If you are really unhappy, you can come back with
me," she said. "This can be done." Then she gently pointed out the
difficulties. "All these efforts of the Chinese government on behalf
of our family imply a deep sense of responsibility for us," she said,
looking around the house. "Father expects this of you; he expects
you to meet your responsibilities." She did not say what she herself
felt or thought; she didn't say what it was like seeing two of her children alone among people she did not know. I knew she had never

trusted or liked "Communists." She was scared of them. Of this she said nothing.

Wai was depressed, sensing the inevitable outcome. Mother had left no doubt as to what Father wanted us to do—he would have been stunned if she had brought us home with her. She could have done so only if she had felt we were not well taken care of, and clearly great efforts were being made on our behalf.

Qiu Ji called early one morning to tell us we were invited to have lunch with Premier Zhou and his wife at their home. As we entered Zhongnanhai, I identified the landmarks for my mother. I told her which leader lived where, mumbling some of their names uncertainly, not quite sure who they were. Mao's house, I added, was buried deep inside the heart of Zhongnanhai, quite a distance from Zhou's.

When we arrived, the two protocol men quickly escorted us to Zhou's waiting room. Zhou and his wife entered together. He greeted my mother, then reached down, picked up Tukta, and kissed her on the cheeks. For a moment I felt very awkward. Then he bent down to kiss my hair and hugged me. I was once again in my element, and when he sat down, I snuggled up next to him on his left while Tukta was relegated to his wife's lap.

As tea was discreetly served, Zhou and my mother talked. Shanan interpreted. I had not seen Mother in this kind of role before. She began with messages of greeting from Pibul and his wife, my father, and Prince Warnwai. Then she warmly thanked Zhou for the care we were receiving. She paused at one point and, looking slightly embarrassed, told Zhou, "Please be strict with the children. They have been terribly spoiled. I give you authority to spank them when they are naughty."

"Children like this don't need spankings," Zhou said with a laugh. "They need to adapt themselves to our environment, but they are doing well. Sudden changes in their way of life can be very hard. It was for me in Japan. Time is really the only solution." He stopped and looked at Wai, who was taking notes.

"Your son is very mature. He will certainly follow in his father's footsteps. Tell Prime Minister Pibul that he has chosen the right representative!"

Wai gave a small, self-conscious smile.

Zhou asked about Pibul and his wife, then about Father.

Mother sighed. "My husband works late into the evening with the prime minister and then is in meetings all day. I rarely see him alone."

He nodded. "My wife ways much the same about me. The night is marvelous for working and thinking. I got into the habit of working late long ago, in the Red Army. During the day one had always to be on the move. Only at night, when we camped, could one really start to work."

"He walks so fast that I have to warn his secretaries to catch up with him and not lose him," Deng Mama said with an affectionate look at her husband.

Zhou's tone turned serious. "I consider your husband a close friend with whom I share certain common views. I assure you that I will do my best to look after your children myself. Please tell your husband," he continued, "to be careful. I know from my own experience that a man like him is a prime target for the CIA and Jiang Jieshi's Guomindang agents in Thailand."

These names were only vaguely familiar to me, but I knew Zhou was alluding to the assassination attempts against Father. As I looked at the expression on Zhou's face, I thought again of Luan's death.

"I understand," Zhou said, "the awkwardness of Prime Minister Pibul's and your husband's position. I admire what Thai friends like your husband and the late Mr. Luan and others have done—and at what cost to themselves. Such friends are the mainstay of our relationship."

Zhou paused for only a moment when Shanan finished translating.

"I have many American friends, and between the American and Chinese people, there are no basic contradictions. But ever since the founding of the People's Republic of China, U.S. imperialism has pursued a hostile policy toward us. They launched the Korean war of aggression. They have built up military bases encircling us and tried to isolate us economically through embargoes. They have used their followers in other countries to adopt and maintain an anti-China policy. What is the purpose of this? Solely to destroy China. The Chinese people are peaceful. We don't want war, but neither are we afraid of it."

Zhou spoke of the Bandung spirit, of wanting Pibul to understand that there was no reason Thailand and China could not be friends. "We welcome more visits from Thai friends. They build a bridge of good relations and good understanding between us. Your children are bridges, too."

Deng Mama then suggested lunch. I was relieved to find that the serious discussions largely came to an end as we went into the dining room. I had already described the room to Mother—the wood floor, the large round table in the center, the porcelain vases on tall stands in the corners. There was a painting of shrimp and cabbage by someone called Qi Bashi, I remembered, and one of horses by Xu Beihong.

Zhou surprised us by serving Thai as well as Chinese dishes. Feng had been brought over to prepare several of our favorite dishes, and Zhou had had his own cook prepare the homegrown corn and peppers I liked. He nodded when I asked in Chinese if I could show Mother the garden after lunch.

"I am pleased to see how well you are learning Chinese," Zhou said to me. "Soon you will be going to school." Turning to Mother, he said, "You should certainly make a visit to their future school."

"Zhou Bobo, you're hard to understand. You don't say the words the way I am being taught," I protested.

"I accept your criticism," he said, laughing. "There are many Chinese dialects and many local differences in accent. If you copy mine, your teacher won't be happy. When you start school, I think your Chinese will come easily. But I want you to speak only Thai in your house. Otherwise it will get rusty, and that would be terrible. You must not forget Thai," he said in his no-nonsense tone. "It is your mother tongue."

After lunch we went to the garden, where Mother was loaded down with peppers and corn. Then Zhou took us for a walk around Zhongnanhai. "I love these willows," he said. "Our great poets often speak of them. They have such gentleness and romance, like the elegant Chinese ladies in the old days swaying as they walked, soft and gentle." He pointed to the various residential pavilions with their pots of bright fresh flowers in front. The larger the pots of flowers, I soon gathered, the more important the inhabitants. Zhou helped us make out the partially hidden pavilions where the other leaders lived. Just as we could discern one, he would show us where yet another could be spotted.

As we returned to the steps of Zhou's house, he said his good-byes. "Stay in China as our guest as long as you like," he told Mother, "and rest before you return to your busy life in Thailand." Zhou waved as our car drove off. I felt sad. I hated going back to our house.

In the days that followed, Wai and I talked little to each other about going home. If Mother had said "Let's go back," I would have agreed with relief, but I could not simply ask. To ask would be to go against Father's wishes, and that would be to protest against the political world that so directly shaped my life. Clearly no one in China was acting as though we might go home—not Qiu Ji, certainly not Zhou. Perhaps even at eight I felt that asking would offend my pride. I should not have to ask to go home. I should be asked!

In the second week of Mother's stay, Qiu Ji called to tell us that Zhou and his wife would be stopping by for a visit that evening. I dashed about excitedly, conveying the news to the staff. To judge by the spotless, freshly pressed white jackets on Old Lai and Old Feng, they already knew. Mother joined Feng in the kitchen, while the cleaning person went around brushing, polishing, setting things to rights. When I had neatened my room, I took out my character book, envisioning telling Zhou exactly how many characters I had learned—ninety-three. I practiced writing several of the harder ones and prepared a piece from my Chinese textbook to read to him. I stopped only when I heard the approach of footsteps in the courtyard.

I ran out to see Zhou and his wife stepping inside. I bounded up to embrace Zhou, pulling him by the arm.

"Be gentle with my arm, my little friend," Zhou said.

I had forgotten when I had grabbed it that he could not straighten his right arm. Although curious, I had never asked why. He offered me his other one, and I led him into the sitting room. There he greeted Mother and Wai before going off with me to meet each member of the staff. He seemed to know who everyone was. "Look after the children for me. Help them to feel at home in China and to be happy," he told them.

They looked pleased to take his hand, shaking it firmly and holding it for several seconds each. Zhou looked each of them directly in the eye.

"You've been working hard," Zhou said to Old Lai. Turning to all of them, he said, "What you're doing is a part of the construction of our socialist motherland."

Old Lai stood there with no suggestion of servility in his demeanor. I had never seen Pibul act toward any of his help as Zhou now did toward his. From that time on, I never treated the people in the house in the same way.

Old Feng's wife had been nervous about being introduced to Zhou and had held back, but Zhou commented on how much he appreciated the way her family was contributing to the life of the house. And Old Feng looked immensely pleased when Zhou told him his Thai cooking had helped make the household successful and thanked him again for the meal he had cooked in Zhongnanhai.

I led Zhou on a tour of the house. In each room he first checked to see if there were enough radiators and if the room was insulated against the cold. He pointed out various things like the encased corridors to me as we walked about, and he asked what else we needed. In my room he paused while I showed him the aquarium we had just bought. Then I pulled out my reading and did some—which he applauded, although not without correcting me in several places. He glanced at the characters approvingly. Wai was too shy to utter a word in Chinese, and Zhou did not press him.

As we returned to the sitting room to drink tea and eat some of Mother's treats, I couldn't calm down. When Zhou asked Mother about her time in Beijing, I volunteered the details. He asked about seeing the school, and I filled in there as well. Then, noticing a certain tautness in Zhou's face, I abruptly responded to Mother's efforts to quiet me.

Zhou looked very sad. Softly and with hesitation he said that he had received bad news about Father. Mother immediately understood what was coming. "Premier, Your Excellency, I only want to know the truth. Is he alive?"

"Yes," said Zhou, "although he is now in the hospital with serious injuries." According to reports Zhou had received from Burma, a taxi traveling at high speed had run into his car in a head-on collision. It had been another deliberate attempt on his life.

Zhou and Deng Mama expressed their deep sympathy to Mother.

They understood that she would wish to be with Father as soon as possible. When Mother nodded, Zhou told Shanan to make the necessary arrangements for her immediate departure.

"You will need some time to yourselves now, so Deng Mama and I will leave. Please tell Sang of our profound concern for him."

He said good-bye to Mother and Wai, and then I walked with him to the gate, holding his left arm tightly. He squeezed my hand hard when he got to his car. As he left he said, "You are all very brave, keep in touch with me. You are like our own children to us."

With that I fell sobbing into his arms.

Back in the house, Mother was already packing. Perhaps, she was telling Wai, Premier Zhou had not told us everything. Perhaps he did not know it himself. For all we knew, Father might already be dead. Maybe Zhou had sought to soften the blow by letting the news come gradually. She packed quickly, crying. Tukta slept through it all.

Mother told us how much it would cheer Father to know we were doing well in China, how proud he would be. It was our duty to remain, she said. Father had long spoken to us of what it meant to be the children of a politician. She was going to tell Father of the good care we were receiving from Premier Zhou and of our close relationship with him.

"Nothing could make your father happier than that," she said.

I thought of Father carrying me around, taking me for ice cream, gesticulating in argument as I watched from my perch on Pibul's lap. Then I pictured him immobilized, unable to move, to act, to shape our world. To picture him dead was all but impossible. But now, with Mother leaving, there was no one to explain myself to. Even in those final hours before she left, I said little. It seemed I had only one world left, my new world, here in China. Here there was no place for mourning; it was either up—or down into despairing darkness.

Early the next morning we took Mother to the airport, and, armed with a letter from the premier's office, she was assigned a seat on the first flight. We hugged her, and she was off. I did not cry.

Qiu Ji and Shanan stayed with us all day, telling us stories, playing with us in the game room, joining us for lunch and dinner. When they left, I felt unbearably lonely.

A week later Shanan came with news from Mother. Father was

making a quick recovery and would soon leave the hospital. Shanan gave us Mother's account of all that had happened.

Father had been working with Pibul late at night. As he left Pibul's compound and turned onto the main road, a taxi that had been waiting in the shadows for two hours rammed his car head on. Father had hit his head on the steering wheel and been knocked unconscious. As the "accident" had occurred so close to Pibul's residence, soldiers had quickly seized the taxi driver.

The driver had not known whom he was meant to crash into. He had been told only to wait for a Mercedes coming down the road late at night and then make sure the driver was killed. When he learned from the police that the intended victim was Sang Phathanothai, he confessed. He knew Father as the president of the Trade Union Federation and had been to our house a few times. He had agreed to the job because an illness in his family had left him desperate for money.

Pibul was so angry that he wanted the man severly punished. Father asked to see the man in the hospital first. Afterward Father phoned Pibul. The man was the victim of their enemies' intrigues, he said, and had been able to identify some of those behind the plot. Father asked Pibul to spare him: "If he is punished, my soul will never be at peace." Pibul consented.

Evidently Father was sufficiently recovered to push forward plans for a visit by Zhou to Thailand. Zhou intended to visit Cambodia, and he had broached with Mother the idea of stopping off in Bangkok for a few hours. Pibul had agreed to the brief stopover; it was to remain a secret, however, until the very last moment.

"Your father is very pleased to hear of your progress here," Shanan concluded.

He left shortly afterward. Wai and I quietly returned to our rooms. We were to start school in a few weeks and to work on our Chinese even more intensively until then.

CHAPTER 6

School and Papa Liao

SOMETIMES ZHOU DROPPED BY to see us without much warning, though the house staff always seemed to know when he was coming. Ever since his first visit, they had acted differently. If it was not actually clearer to some of them who we were, they knew without a doubt that we were Zhou's direct responsibility. They evidently felt this made their task a very special one. Tensions eased a little. Shanan, too, seemed different, as though Zhou's intentions and personal sense of responsibility seemed plainer to him as well. He became more flexible and tolerant with us. And at least in small ways, we too had become more yielding.

When I heard Zhou's steps, I ran to the courtyard entrance, gave him a hug, and as usual, guided him into the sitting room. The day was cold, but we sat snugly in the warmly heated room, the big radiators steaming away.

"Are you prepared for our winter?" Zhou asked.

He inspected the new padded jackets and coats Shanan had just gotten for us. After days of looking everywhere for my size, since I would not wear anything that was too big, Shanan had at last succeeded.

"Are you leaving for Thailand soon?" I asked. "You're going there, aren't you?"

Zhou answered slowly, "I have received a formal invitation from the Thai government through your father to stop over in Bangkok."

"Then I have something for you to take to them, Uncle," I said and dashed off toward my room.

"Wait," Zhou said.

I stopped. By now I recognized the serious look on his face.

"I will not be going to your country," he said. "I wish I could visit your beautiful land and enjoy the hospitality of the Pibul government, the Thai people, and your father."

I was dumbfounded. For days I had counted on Zhou's going and seeing my parents. Wai and I had both written special letters to Father for Zhou to take. I had written about my initial triumphs with Chinese, and I'd collected various small handicraft objects to send as well, tiny little hand-painted eggs, something that always fascinated me, and beautiful Jing Tai Lan porcelain pens. I didn't hide my disappointment.

"The situation is a difficult one," Zhou said. "Your father is safe, but the situation remains dangerous. I've given the matter much thought, and I've decided that even a short visit to your country in the present delicate political situation could only cause more trouble to the Thai government. The United States and the Taiwan crowd would bitterly oppose such a move. I have no choice. I cannot stop in Bangkok."

As Wai sat nearby taking notes, Zhou continued, "I'm sure the day will come when our two countries will have normalized relations. Then I can visit. Do you understand what I'm saying?"

I certainly understood that he was not going to Thailand as I wished. He would be visiting some eleven countries but not mine.

"I will be gone for many weeks," Zhou added. "So I have asked Liao Chengzhi to take care of you. I want you to celebrate the Chinese New Year and the Spring Festival with a Chinese family. Liao will be your Chinese father. In my absence you can go to him as you would to me."

"Who is Liao?" I asked Shanan when Zhou left.

"Do you remember the picture of the little boy sitting on Sun Yat-sen's lap I pointed out to you when we visited the Museum of the History of the Revolution? That's Liao."

Shanan was clearly pleased to know Liao. He told us about Liao's renowned American-born father, Liao Zh;akongkai, and his famous mother, He Ziangning. Liao Zh;akongkai had been the closest political associate and personal friend of Sun Yatsen, the founder of the first Chinese Republic, Shanan explained. He had shared Sun's long exile in Japan, where Liao Chengzhi was born in Tokyo in 1908, and after Sun's death in March 1925 had become the leader of its progressive wing, the Left Guomindang. A few months later, with He Xiangning next to him, he was assassinated by a leader of the right wing.

"In the museum there is also a picture of Liao with his mother and sister beside Liao Zhongkai's body. He comes from one of the great revolutionary families of our country," he concluded.

Liao arranged to receive Wai and me at the Fang Shan restaurant in Beihai Park, a restaurant that served only the dishes of the dowager empress. From almost my first glimpse, I sensed there was something very lovable and a little crazy about Liao. He seemed entirely different from other Chinese I had met. He had an infectious grin and a supple, expressive face. He was stout—"Little Fatty," some of his foreign friends called him, I later learned. "The little lord," Mao evidently said. "And keep as Little Lord in the Party."

Liao was already at the table waiting for us with Qiu Ji. As often as not, one sat and waited for such high-placed leaders to make a solemn entrance. Not so with Liao. He greeted us with great liveliness and warmth, a camera around his neck.

"He's always taking pictures," Shanan had said. "He'll almost surely bring his camera."

As I went up to him, he placed his two soft hands against my cheeks and shook them gently, laughing. He was always to greet me like that.

I liked him immediately. A few questions about our going to school and how we were finding China, and he was off to lighter subjects. A superb mimic and natural storyteller, he kept us laughing the whole evening. Wai, as usual, had his pad of paper ready. But for once he would go home without any notes.

Liao told us about having been in Burma once for the New Year. His mobile face registered the shock he had felt at finding himself splashed with water everywhere he went. " 'Don't worry,' our ambassador said. 'You'll be dry by the time you get back in the car.' So hot! And it was true—my shirt was already almost dry. And you know, it felt good. I've always hated the heat. So go to Burma during the Water Festival. I tell you, it's the only time you can keep cool there!"

He could tell when he asked that I wasn't yet in love with Beijing. "I can't stand Beijing in the summer, either. Horrible. In the summer, even Premier Zhou works in the bathtub; the Russian bath, big, cold, a board over the top so he can read his papers."

By the time the first dishes arrived, Liao was onto talking about food. "When I was in Bandung, I was so hungry one night that I slipped out to get a real meal, but all that was open was an Indonesian restaurant. No one spoke Chinese. Or any of the other seven languages I speak. But no problem, I wanted chicken."

Liao got up and transformed himself into a strutting, clucking chicken. "All I had to do was to walk like one and talk like one," he laughed.

"You can be very expressive even if you don't know the language." He gave a few more lively struts before sitting down. "It's good that you're here to study and learn the language. China is a hard country to understand. Don't tell anyone"—he leaned toward me with a look of utmost earnestness—"but I think in Japanese." Then he grinned.

"How do you think in Japanese?" I asked.

"Oh, you'll soon know what I mean. One language to think in, one to count in. I read my favorite detective stories in German. Learned it when I worked with the German dockworkers in the twenties. But it's such dirty German, it's not fit to speak in decent company."

Zhou had told us that Liao had always played the villain in plays the Communists had put on at their headquarters in Yan'an during the war against the Japanese. "He was so good that the peasants cursed him and wanted to beat him up when he passed among them during the day," Zhou said.

Liao made a frightening face when I mentioned this, then pulled my ponytail. "I have seven children," he said, "and two are about your age. I want you to meet them soon."

Then he was back to a favorite topic: food. "I love your Thai durian fruit," he said. This was unusual; most foreigners hated it because of its smell. I asked where he had eaten it.

"In Burma," he answered, "when we were on the way to Bandung. The Burmese government gave us a grand banquet. Of course, it was first offered to Premier Zhou, but Zhou insisted that the honor really should rest with me. 'Little Liao,' he turned and said to me, 'you have such strange tastes in foods. You'll like this,' Well, I couldn't refuse the challenge."

Liao covered his nose with his hand and demonstrated elaborately how he had maneuvered the fruit so he could take a bite without a smell. For a bulky man he managed to slip easily into a mime, one arm bent high over his head, its hand reaching down to grab his nose, while the other arm crept slowly upward to slip the fruit quickly between his pursed lips.

"It was delicious. I was not, alas, successful in getting the others to try."

As we left that night, Liao said, "I'll see you again soon." Just as Zhou Enlai had, he told us, "My house is always open to you." He gave my ponytail one last gentle tug and was gone.

O UR SCHOOL PLANS WERE NOT GOING WELL. From the first day Qiu Ji came to our house to discuss the subject, I was unenthusiastic. Thai schools had been boring; this promised to be even worse—and much harder.

"I've arranged for you to attend Middle School Number One, which is attached to the principal teacher's college in Beijing. It's a fine school."

He explained that though I was not up to middle school level, whose youngest students were typically several years older than I, he felt it best for Wai and me to be together so we would not be lonely.

"The main thing is for you to learn Chinese," he said.

"Couldn't we just continue our study here, Uncle?" Wai asked.

"You must go to school," Qiu Ji replied. "It is the only way you will learn well, and you need to understand more about how our people live."

The next morning I dressed up in my new wool pants and silk padded jacket while Wai put on his suit. No one had told us what to wear. In Thailand, I had a beautiful uniform, but Qiu Ji had said that in China no one bothered about such things and so we nervously decided to dress as well as we could to at least show our respect. Our private Chinese tutor had arrived to take us, and she too was nicely dressed that morning in a Thai black skirt, a pullover, and a simple jacket. She tied a big ribbon around my ponytail, and we climbed into the car. Old Lai drove us the twenty minutes to the school.

The three of us were very quiet: Wai and I were anxious, and our teacher was still timid with us. She did not know much about us, only that we were somehow tied to a very important organization. Having seen the house and now the car, she was not about to ask questions.

At the entrance to the school, the doorman stopped us. He looked at us with utter disbelief, making not the slightest effort to take the shocked expression off his face. At first he refused to believe our teacher when she explained that we were the expected students. Staring at Wai and me, he told her he would not direct her to the headmaster's office, and only when she pulled out her card and a sheet of paper would he finally tell her where to go.

"I don't like it here," Wai said. I myself thought one shouldn't take any notice of doormen.

Our tutor led us into the office. The headmaster greeted us politely, but he took an unusually long look up and down us. Whatever misgivings he had, he kept them to himself. He said he wanted us to study well. If there were any problem, he was there to help.

He knew only that the premier's office had placed in his school two foreign children who were to be allowed to enter without the customary examination. That was all, and he had probably given the teachers the instructions he thought appropriate, including what to say to their students.

As we left to go to our separate classes, the headmaster's aide was staring, mouth open. "I'm never coming back here," Wai said before our tutor led me to my classroom and the headmaster's aide took Wai to his.

Everyone turned to look as we walked in, and then they began to laugh. They laughed at me as though I were a clown. They laughed so hard that they momentarily lost their expressions of amazement. They had been told a foreigner was coming, but clearly I was not what they expected. They were all in their simple clothes, and there I was in my silk Chinese embroidery.

The teacher pointed to my seat and told the class to stop laughing. They did, but the stares continued—even the teacher seemed to find it hard to stop gawking.

"I have to leave you now," my tutor said.

"Oh, please don't go," I cried, holding onto her skirt.

"I must. If you need anything, I will be in the headmaster's office all day. Come to me there."

"Please!" I wailed in Thai.

She left, almost in tears herself.

The class went on. During the head girl's speech of welcome, I heard the others continuing to giggle. I understood only a few words. As all around me heads turned for quick, furtive glances, I stiffened, confused and frightened.

Each time a period changed, a new teacher came in. They had heard, but they still could believe, and they couldn't keep from staring. During one of the breaks, some of the girls came up to look at my ponytail; they all had two pigtails—my single strand with a bright ribbon interested them. Then one girl came and sat by me, looking at me intently through her thick glasses. She seemed friendly.

"You have beautiful eyes," she said. "Beautiful, not Chinese eyes."

At lunch, my first teacher of the day came to take me to the teachers' and headmaster's canteen, where it had been arranged we would eat. It was an unappetizing place, with long, unpolished wooden tables and hard benches. Some people were sitting on the benches, while others were squatting; they or the people before them had left bones and unwanted bits of food on the tables. Wai and I were to line up at different windows to get the food we wanted, which was dished out from enormous basins. Coupons enabled one to buy grains like mantous or noodles, and most of the teachers, we were to learn, carefully regulated their coupons so as to make them last the month.

I got one of the mantous, but it was nothing like the ones we had at home or with Zhou. They were almost black, tasteless and greasy. I was still accustomed to the tasty Thai mixture of sour, sweet, peppery, and salty sauces, but here there were only two big bowls of soy sauce and vinegar. People seemed to swallow their food quickly, with no particular attention to manners; burping was evidently appropriate behavior. Wai was furious.

"Father wanted to punish us! He never would have sent us here otherwise. We must have done something terribly wrong to be sent to a place like this. I'm calling Qiu Ji and telling him we're getting out of here."

We huddled together as more teachers came in. One of them brought us each another mantou, thinking we would like them: no one else had them, they were specially for us. But we couldn't touch them. The rest of the food looked inedible, and we didn't even bother to take it.

Some of the teachers sat with their legs up on the chairs scattered throughout the room. We were horrified. We had never seen anything like that—or anything like this whole primitive canteen—except sometimes in Chinatown in Thailand. Even worse, the place reeked of toilets and disinfectant. I felt like vomiting.

Both Wai and I fell asleep in our afternoon classes, and our teachers let us alone.

At three o'clock the first day was finally over. Our Chinese tutor was waiting to take us to the car through the crowd of students who followed us as we went out. When they saw the limousine, they started pointing and talking. Some were curious; some were hostile, cursing us.

Several times I heard my teacher ask them to stop, but they stared at her as well, probably because she too looked rather un-Chinese and was well dressed. Old Lai shooed them away from the car, and at last we drove off, the students still talking excitedly and staring.

Wai and I immediately broke into a chorus of complaint. Since even our tutor was close to tears, Old Lai undoubtedly guessed what had happened: he himself had three children of school age. But it was not his place to say anything. Instead, he quickly went to get Shanan and Qiu Ji. When Qiu Ji asked us to tell him exactly what had happened, Wai gave an angry account. He was very clear. "I never want to go back there again. They were as mean to us as they could be. If we can't study here at home, then at least we can be sent to a better school."

"This is the best school in China," Qiu Ji said.

"How can that be, Uncle? Even the toilets stink," I said.

"You must try to understand China," Qiu Ji replied. "This is also part of your task and why you are here. This is how we live now. Seven years ago, when we started off, we had nothing at all. If you had come ten years ago, you would have seen dead people on the street, with people going around each morning to pick them up. Nothing to eat. So many people and so many poor. Now our government is trying to let all the children go to school. But we can only provide the rudiments. People cannot dress well yet. They have to learn to be careful with money."

Wai was not convinced.

"But why didn't you tell us, Uncle Shanan? Why did you let us go to school dressed that way?" I complained.

"I couldn't bring myself to tell you," Shanan said. "I didn't think you would understand the circumstances."

I protested that I would have, but I knew I had hated those plain cotton suits. If he had taken us to the school ahead of time, Wai and I might have refused to step foot in it.

"I appreciate that you did things differently in Thailand," Shanan said. "It's a ceremonial way of living that is not observed here, but I didn't want to tell you to take your fancy clothes off and wear others. And I didn't want to scare you out of going to school."

Wai was still fuming.

"Give them some time," Shanan said. "The Chinese people are very poor. They cannot dress like you. Some may be jealous, others don't understand. Perhaps you can wear your pants and pullover next time."

I certainly didn't want to go dressed as I had again. I was more ready to adapt than Wai.

"You have to try to understand why the children reacted as they did," Qiu Ji added. "It is not that they were hostile to you. But when Chinese people are embarrassed, they laugh. They were not trying to tease you, but they felt awkward. And having laughed, they don't say, 'I'm sorry.' Often they just laugh a little longer."

"After the first few days," Shanan added, "they will not laugh. There will be nothing to laugh at. Then perhaps you can have a few laughs on them."

Their anger, I thought, had really been about the car. Did we have to go to school that way? I asked. In Thailand, I had loved going in our car, comparing it to the others—whose was bigger, whose newer. Now I would rather not stand out that way. "All the other students come by bus or bicycle or on foot," I said.

"It is not just the distance,"Qiu Ji said. "The premier is responsible for your security. He has insisted upon it."

That night Wai and I spoke little. We dreaded the next day. In my room I wished only that I could stay home. Why did I have to go through this again? Why couldn't I just have some fun? Why had Father done this to me?

The next morning the others still stared, but when I went to my class, the teacher greeted me warmly, and in the place next to mine sat the girl who had admired my eyes. The teacher had assigned her to be in charge of me. Lu Ruier was her name, and she communicated chiefly through her radiant smile. She was able to explain to me that she liked having foreign friends, and my private tutor—who, it had been decided the night before, would accompany me this time—explained that this girl had several Russian pen pals. When the period was over, some of the students crowded around my desk, talking, using sign language, and acting out the things they wanted to say.

I had started writing Chinese characters, and they were eager to help, showing me the correct order of the strokes. When I wrote something wrong they all laughed. But it was now a friendly laugh, and they all joined in to show me what to do. When I got it right, they were enthusiastic. That encouraged me. I could barely talk, but this was something we could do together.

Wai and I still went to the teachers' canteen for lunch and the teachers were solicitous, stopping to give us what were clearly meant to be special treats. But Wai and I found nothing we could stomach. We stopped trying.

That brought Qiu Ji to our house a few days later. The school administration had informed our tutor that we were not eating. When we told him we simply couldn't eat such food, he suggested that our cook prepare box lunches for us. That was better, but the next day we had to tell him when he asked how it went that we didn't like our food cold. So the school had to be told to heat it for us. The result was that we were now able to start eating with the students, who also brought their lunches to school, and I slowly started to make some friends.

I felt awkward, though and ashamed. Every day Wai and I had meat and fried rice, while the others came with pickled vegetables and a few very simple things. They drank out of what looked like chipped jam bottles, and it reminded me of the beautiful mugs that Father had given us.

At first I couldn't tell Qiu Ji that I was far more bothered by the lavatory than by the food. I couldn't stand the smell, and there was no toilet seat: one had to squat over a hole dug in the ground. Once or twice a week city workers came to empty them. But the smell never lessened, announcing itself long before one reached the entrance and seeming somehow to remain on one's body and clothes throughout the day. I started coming up with excuses to stay home.

Qiu Ji came again. Why, he wanted to know, did I wish to miss so many days of school? I had, then, to admit that though I liked some of the students and some of the teachers were nice, I hated the lavatory. I wanted him to find me a school with toilets.

Qiu Ji said again that ours was the best school in China. "Unfortunately, this is the way conditions are in China generally. We are trying to improve them, but we are still a very poor country. I know this is hard for you," he said, "but going to a Chinese school and mixing with Chinese children really is the best way for you to realize your father's wish. If you and Wai stay at home, you will never learn anything about our life, and I just can't approve that. You can't let going to the toilet put a stop to all this."

I agreed to make an effort, but in all the years to come I never got over my discomfort and distaste.

Although school began to go better, each day we had to run the gauntlet to get to our car. Old Lai was plainly angered by the students, often ordering them aside. Elsewhere outside my immediate class, I also felt tension. I found it hard even to walk down the hallways, unsure how I was meant to greet the teachers. They were mostly quite young, and they dressed like everyone else in the school, so I seldom knew the difference between the cleaning people and the teachers. Here I was supposed to say, "Good morning, Teacher" as I walked down the hall, regardless of whether I was passing one of my own teachers or one of the others. Some threw me ugly glances when I walked by and said nothing.

One day as Wai came to join me at lunch, a boy walked past him and said, "Down with American imperialism!" There was always at least one slogan against the Americans up on the walls, but this boy had clearly directed his at Wai. Wai was furious. He phoned Qiu Ji's office and told them he was leaving the school; Old Lai promptly came and got him. When I arrived home that afternoon, Qiu Ji and Shanan were already there. This time no explanations about people being puzzled by us or unaccustomed to our privileges would wash with Wai. Wai had never asked for those privileges, and now he was being attacked for them.

"In all my time there, I've never had a single sign of real friendship from the Chinese students," he said. "We have to ride in this car. You make us do this and then let us be attacked. I won't stand for it any longer."

Shanan suggested he not tell Father. Wai was writing to him frequently, I rarely. Premier Zhou would be informed, Qiu Ji said.

We soon learned Zhou's response. He told Qiu Ji that the Chinese children had to learn to be at ease with foreigners and with other people's customs and ways of life. Clearly this was not happening. Of course Zhou well knew what the school authorities did not, that Wai was the personal representative of Prime Minister Pibul. It was not just a question of how he himself was being treated.

Qiu Ji told us what was to be done. Our private tutor was instructed to inform the school administration of Premier Zhou's personal concern about the situation and that Zhou Enlai himself would be kept apprised of future developments. The headmaster in turn called a teachers' meeting, and soon the entire school knew that Premier Zhou himself expected the students to "learn to respect others, just as they expected others to respect them." The two little "foreign friends" were "our friends," the premier had said, "and they are to be treated with greater consideration."

The next day, Lu Ruier came up and gave me a big kiss. "Our teacher has told us of Premier Zhou's concern for you," she said. My other classmates seemed pleased and not a little relieved. With all the nasty remarks going around about us, they had not wanted to be criticized as "lackeys of U.S. imperialism." Only Lu Ruier had stood out so actively on my behalf. She had argued with her friends when they had condemned our coming to school by car, telling them to mind their own business. Now there were others ready to defend me.

Wai asked once again to please be allowed to go to school without the car. Zhou wouldn't hear of it. "I am not acting hastily or on impulse," Zhou told him firmly. "What am I to tell Prime Minister Pibul and your father if anything happens to you? I have promised your father to take good care of you. You are both in a foreign land with no one else to turn to but us."

So we continued to go by car. But no longer were comments made about it. Wai was invited to join various sporting activities, at which he excelled. I found my Chinese quickly improving. After the first month I was settling in more and more. Wai was still shy with the language, and he never felt quite relaxed at school. By contrast, I increasingly began to be a part of it.

School was now my public daily world, and I felt protected there, but my private status remained unknown. My schoolmates knew only that Wai and I were under Premier Zhou's protection. "We attacked the boy tied to Zhou Enlai," one student said years later of the stir caused in the school by Zhou's intervention. Few ever learned more than this or why Zhou had done what he had.

S‌CHOOL WOULD SERVE TO BRING ME into Chinese life and culture in one way. Lia and his family would usher me into it in another way, introducing me to the innermost world of the Chinese elite. Liao was not one of the most senior leaders; indeed, his mother's status was higher. She was chairman of the Overseas Chinese Commission. But the history of his family was known to all. Zhou trusted him; their closeness was evident in the relaxed, joking exchanges that marked so many of their encounters. Placing me in Liao's family required making an exception to the standing prohibition against leaders of the Communist party mixing informally with foreigners. It also brought me into a home that the family's revolutionary fame and eminence had made a meeting place for high-ranking members of the party, the government, and the military alike.

In later years I learned just how close some of the links between Liao and Zhou were. Zhou had known Liao's father in the early

1920s, when Sun Yatsen had founded the Whampoa Military Academy and Liao's father was the Guomindang party's representative and Zhou the Communist party's. The two had become friends, and Zhou had come to know Liao's mother, He Xiangning, as well. In the 1940s her eldest daughter, Liao Mengxing, who served as Soong Qingling's secretary, had married a revolutionary, Li Shaoshi, who would serve on Zhou's staff when he was stationed in Chongqing. He and Zhou were driving down a street, Zhou later told me, when Mengxing's husband noticed a man drawing a gun. Without hesitation, he had thrown himself on top of Zhou and received the bullets intended for Zhou. He had died in Zhou's arms.

Liao soon invited us to meet his family, as he had promised that night at the restaurant. In this world I didn't have to come plainly attired, and I happily chose a colorful silk jacket. Liao's house was not in Zhongnanhai, where so many of the other leaders lived, but in the eastern part of Beijing. When the outside guards swung open the gate, there was a long drive along a road bordered on both sides by fruit trees—persimmons, apples, pears, peaches, even dates.

Liao was waiting for us at the door of a beautiful old Qing house. "Welcome, welcome," he said ebulliently, putting his two soft hands on my face.

He led Wai and me into the left-hand side of the house, his "mother's side," and explained that as chairman of the Overseas Chinese Committee she had to have the larger space. We walked through a good-sized living room used for official occasions and on through to the entrance of the old lady's study, where we stood for a moment and watched. She was bent over an enormous unfinished painting. She worked as though preparing to go to war, carefully readying her tiny body, utterly frail, to burst forth with rapid, confident brushstrokes. Then a pause, and another quick stroke.

"She paints every day," Liao said.

When she heard him, she stopped and greeted us warmly. She and Liao exchanged animated banter, much of it in her native Cantonese, which I could not understand.

She sent me over to her "special" cabinet. There she kept her "treasures": tins of candies and other treats brought by visitors from Hong Kong, Japan, and Macao. The best delicacies she put here for her little Liao. Her favorite was the British rock candy, and when I handed the colorful tin to her, she pulled out bright red-and-green pieces for Wai and me.

Then she looked at each of us.

"Feizi," she said, "tells me you don't have Chinese names yet."

For a moment, I wasn't sure whom she was referring to. Liao laughed when he saw my bewilderment. "It's my Cantonese name. Amah calls me 'Little Fatty,' " he said, rubbing his big stomach.

"I'm called Number Fifty-two in my class because I was the last one to come," I said.

"Well, let's see what names we could give you."

She looked intently at Wai, carefully pronouncing his name and Father's.

"Chang Huai," she said thoughtfully after a long pause.

She took up her pen and drew the characters. Chang, she explained, was a common family name in the south. It sounded like our father's name, Sang. And "Huai," or Wai, conveyed closeness to the heart. It would stand for his always keeping his country in his heart.

She turned toward me and patted my cheeks. "The right name for you is Chang Yuan."

Again she took the pen and wrote the characters. "You will have the same family name as your brother. And Yuan means 'beautiful girl.' "

"Now be sure to submit these names to Premier Zhou for final approval," she said to Liao with utmost seriousness.

Then she painted a tiger for Wai and a cherry blossom for me, writing our names on them and then her signature. She painted with amazing swiftness and directness of line.

"She often leaves several drawings she is working on out on the table," Liao said. "So I help by adding a few figures."

Satisfied with her work, she talked about Thailand and how she loved its mangoes. "I shall teach you calligraphy," she promised, and she gave me several examples of calligraphy to imitate.

"It's the best way to relax and to enjoy oneself," she said. "You can sense people's strengths and weaknesses in their calligraphy; you catch a sense of them as in no other way. And it's very much a part of our tradition to know how to write this way." She gave me a brush and ink and some pieces of scrap paper. "But don't learn from my characters," she said.

We all went to the lunch table. Liao explained that his mother ordinarily ate alone in her room. It was a special occasion for her to come sit with us.

Liao's mother clearly dominated the house. Liao's wife, Jing Puchun, was quiet in her mother-in-law's presence, but their six children—their seventh was away at military school—were friendly and talkative. Afterward, Liao showed us the other half of the house. His study was set off by a beautiful Japanese partition, and a statue of a nude—from Italy, he told me—stood on one side of the room. His bedroom was strewn with papers, his bed covered with books. "Those are the German detective stories I told you about," he said. But what caught my eye were the pictures. They were everywhere: pictures of the other leaders, of Mao and Zhou, of countless informal occasions among the leaders.

"I will tell you all about them later," he said.

It was a promise he and his mother kept in the years to come. I was drawn to them, to their house, and to the two young daughters close to my age. Wai, too, liked the family, but he was not looking as eagerly as I for a place to belong. He was convinced that entering too wholeheartedly into the Chinese world did not entirely befit our official role. Nor were any of the boys his age. The next time I went to Liao's, I went alone. I was adopted into the family at once—"big-eyed graddaughter," Liao's mother called me. "Amah" I called her. Soon thereafter, I began to spend most of my weekends with them. Liao's daughters could come to see me at my house as well. They were among the very few allowed to visit me there.

By THE END OF MY FIRST FIVE MONTHS in China, my life had finally settled into a routine. Every afternoon Old Lai would drive us home from school. There our private teacher would go over my schoolwork with me. After two months I could talk in textbook phrases about set topics, and by four months I was increasingly able to make myself understood. As I progressed, my classmates took me more in hand, and I was eager to reciprocate and to seek them out.

Lu Ruier invited me for dinner one night. When I asked, Papa Liao said it would be fine to go. Her father, I now learned, was Lu Dingyi, the minister of propaganda; he knew I was somehow connected with Zhou's organization, Liao told me. I had not doubted that her father was prominent. Had he not been, permission would have to have been sought merely to invite me.

Lu Ruier's family lived in a well-guarded, spartan house in the old quarter of Beijing, where Western imperial power and its embassies had settled in. Huge trees shaded the mansions, many of them built in grand eighteenth-century colonial style. Just past the gate to Lu Ruier's house a beautiful garden area opened out, shaded by bushy grape leaves that formed an elegant canopy all the way to the door. Her family, however, clearly didn't bother with objects and decorations. Unlike Liao, leaders like Lu were embarrassed to live with displays of wealth while the majority of the people lived so poorly. Regulations might require them to live in houses according to their status in the Party, but nothing regulated how they decorated the house within. There was the standard vintage Communist furniture with its khaki covers, and even the bowls and the plates were utterly utilitarian and of a simple design ordained by the Party. Although there were cartons of books and papers scattered everywhere, this was a household where there was pride in not owning a lot of things.

Liao had spoken of Lu with respect. Lu's austere style was not Liao's style, but it represented much of what Liao admired and what, he felt, had given strength to the revolution. "They were true proletarians," he had said. "They came from nowhere, and they want to stay close to their roots and what they fought for all those years."

When Lu Ruier took me into her father's study, I saw only a single bed with a padded quilt, an aluminum bowl in which to wash his hands and a cloth with which to dry them, and a big desk piled with papers. Cartons were stacked on the floor here as well, and there were books all about.

At dinner Lu Dingyi asked me about Thailand. Like his daughter, he wore thick glasses, only his served to make him seem formidable. Something about him seemed pained and sad. It wasn't until later, when Liao told me that Lu's only son, born on the Long March, had been left with a peasant family and never found, could I fully make sense of it.

I didn't think he knew quite why I was in China. Nor would it have occurred to him to ask. But already I knew that the world I came from would not be approved of in such a household. My luxuries would be condemned, my servants viewed with horror. So I began to speak of myself as coming from a fishing village as my father had. My grandfather had earned his living as a fisherman. The stories I had grown up hearing about that world I now put to good use.

In reality, Thais consider girls on a boat bad luck. No matter—I placed myself on those boats and deep in the struggles and glories of that arduous life in the fishing village. The results were gratifying. More important, they marked a transition in my efforts to accommodate myself to a world where the old ways of boasting were anathema.

Other visits to classmates' homes were quite different. Once day my class leader asked me to visit her home at lunchtime. Shanan encouraged me to go. "Make friends and see how they live," he said.

So I went to her home one noon. She had been very nice to me, helping me with my work and with the language the first few months. She was very talented and hardworking, which was why she had become head of our class. Her father was a worker, but as we entered her house I knew nothing else about her.

She lived in a mud house set in a small courtyard swept immaculately clean. I assumed the courtyard was her family's, but when we entered a crooked door off of it, I realized that, tiny as it was, it was shared by others. We walked into a small, dark room, where she introduced me to her grandmother. Then she showed me another room and stopped. I slowly understood that I had seen the whole house.

Yet she was so pleased with it, showing it to me with genuine pride. Of course there was no toilet; they used a public one. There was not even a table to write on. I asked her where she did her homework.

"We roll up the five blankets," she said.

"Five? Why five?" I asked.

"My mother, my father, my grandparents, me." I saw the blankets now, neatly folded on the corner of the bed.

"So where do you write?" I asked uneasily.

"I have a small table I put on the bed, and I sit there and do my homework. Often three of us work on it at the same time. It gives us enough room."

"Where do you eat?" I asked.

"In my grandparents' room—on their bed. We put the table on the bed and sit around it for lunch or dinner."

She spoke happily. She was grateful to have these two rooms, to have kitchen utensils, a place that was warm in the winter, and food to eat.

There were no toys, but she had her games. A skip rope, a home-made doll, a sandbag she and the others kicked and threw in their invented sports. She told me proudly about the chores she did and the speed with which she took care of her own needs. I still had someone fix my hair and add the ribbon, while she—whir, and her hair was neatly done, simple, clean.

I told Qiu Ji how shocked I was by how they lived but also about her pride in what they had.

"Mao said we are as blank as white paper, and we can draw beautiful pictures on it," he said. "We are poor, but we have spirit." I was beginning to believe it. I wrote to my mother to send me only the simplest clothes from now on. My father was very pleased by the letter.

It was rare for me to write to either of my parents. Wai did, though, and I would occasionally add messages to Mother. But reminders of that world made me unhappy; for Wai they were his world. I had already made new friends and was quickly forgetting my old ones. To remember was to sink into longing and lethargy. And adapting to my Chinese world came to consume all my energy. Only in particularly bleak moments would I wonder how my father could have done this to us, how my parents could have let us go, set us adrift. But most of the time I couldn't have cared less where I was born—Burma, Thailand, it made no difference, I said to myself. I studied the Thai language because of Zhou, but I hated every minute of it.

Wai had stronger roots, and he wanted to affirm not only them but his place in our family as well. As the younger son who had lived for seven years with his grandparents, he had always been somewhat neglected by my father, whose friends sometimes thought he had only one. But once in China Wai had a position, and in writing regularly to Father, he implicitly affirmed it. He would tell Father about our life and what he didn't like, but he was prepared to go ahead. It was his task, his duty.

Father never wrote as if to a child; he wrote in the big words I had grown up with. For Wai, in this setting, they came to mean something new. Father tried to console Wai, assuring him of what he was accomplishing and what it meant, how special it was for his country. "You are representing Grandpa Pibul," he reminded him. "You are doing a commendable job. The prime minister is so pleased with you and appreciative of your work. History will note your function." And so on.

Meanwhile, I was cast further, deeper into a Chinese world. Wai and I remained close, but as the months passed we increasingly followed independent paths.

IN THE SPRING OF 1957 Liao told us that Madame Pibul might be coming on a private visit. Pibul himself could still not come; the political risk for him was too great. But she had wanted to make the trip, and she strongly supported Father's policy toward China. In the meantime, Thai-Chinese relations continued to develop.

That April Zhou took us to watch the first Thai sports group, a basketball team, to come to China. After the match, a famous Thai singing and dance troupe performed under the direction of the well-known writer Suwat Waradeluk. Then came a worker's delegation, followed by a student delegation led by Suwit Pradermichit, a progressive youth leader from Thamasart University in Bangkok. Zhou greeted them all, often with us discreetly in the background. They had all come through Father.

Relations between Thailand and China were increasingly less of a secret, but Zhou knew that the Americans were uneasy, even angry, about what was developing, and he often spoke of the dangers of the policy. Pibul would not be coming, he said, until diplomatic relations could be established. "Your respected Prime Minister Pibul will then be able to visit our country," he told one of the visiting delegations. "He will receive a rousing welcome from our people and our government like the one we gave President Sukarno of Indonesia." And he told them what he repeatedly said in private: "Before I die, I want to visit Thailand, the land whose beauty I have heard so much of. I want to taste its sweet coconut milk myself."

When school let out for the summer, Zhou decided Wai and I

should travel in China. It would be part of our social studies, Liao said, a way to learn about the different areas of the country. And we would get out of Beijing in the hot summer.

The first trip was to be the beginning of a yearly ritual. Accompanied by chaperons from Zhou's office, we followed an itinerary of his devising, traveling to Hangzhou, Shanghai, Wu Xi, and Suzhou by train, in comfortable first-class sleeping cars. For several days we headed south, stopping at major stations along the way for local snacks sold in the little carts that lined the stations. Although we were by now accustomed to having a fuss made over us, the trip reinforced what it meant to be connected with Zhou's organization. The captain of the train always came to welcome us, asking what we wished to eat and disappearing to ensure that it would later appear.

Shanghai reminded us a little of Bangkok. It was more colorful, though, and its street life more prosperous and energetic. In the old imperial setting of the Peace Hotel, with its sweeiping staircase and a grand piano in the big hall, we could look out over a real city and big buildings, not the little huts of Beijing. For the first time since coming to China we were told to leave our shoes outside the door, and the next morning they were freshly polished. "It's like Bangkok," Wai said with pleasure when he saw them. He liked walking the streets in the evening: here in this highly commercial city, unlike in Beijing, shops stayed open after six o'clock. Our host took us to the old racing court, pointing out the sign "Dogs and Chinese forbidden!" that had been put up in the semicolonial days. We loved the amusement center most, and for five nights straight we went there, trying practically every game in the park.

From Shanghai we boarded a train to Hangzhou. Zhou and Liao had often spoken of its beauty and of the Xi Hu lake. We were met at the station and driven along the small streets until we found ourselves entering a long, winding drive shaded by big trees. At a well-guarded entrance, our hosts showed their identity cards, the guards saluted us, and we entered what seemed an enchanted garden, with splendid formations of rock, small wooden bridges over countless streams, and the glimmering light of the lake. We stopped before Pavilion Number One, where we were to stay.

"Chairman Mao has a pavilion right behind this one," our host said. "He was just here. He loves to come and think before the silken calm of the Xi Hu lake. This is where he drafted the constitution for the People's Republic in 1951."

I looked at the willows and peach trees that alternately lined the lake. "It's particularly beautiful with the blossoms in the spring," our host said, and then he led us into a huge room with a big wooden bed. "Chairman Mao's bed is twice this size." I looked with amazement. Twice this size, I thought; this was gigantic enough.

"Yes, Chairman Mao loves enormous beds and big rooms with high ceilings. His house in Beijing is like this."

We were being treated like guests from the emperor's city. Everything was meant to honor, and respond to, the organization that had sent us. But it was neither the repeated splendor of our receptions nor the allusions to the leaders who had stayed where we now were that most impressed me. It was the legend of Yue Fei. "Visit his temple in Hangzhou," Zhou had told me. "It is most important for a person to love and fight for his country. Yue Fei's example is a source of great value."

Yue Fei was a Chinese general who had successfully fought the Jin invasion in the thirteenth century. Against great odds, his campaigns had triumphed again and again. In defeat the Jin had turned to other methods, bribing the emperor's prime minister, Qin Kuai, to report falsely that Yue Fei's army was not successful. His behavior is reprehensible, the bribed prime minister reported, and so the emperor issued an order for Yue Fei to pull back and stop fighting. He ignored the emperor's order and went on with the drive for victory over the Jin. On the eve of the final battle, Qin Kuai manipulated the emperor's imperial edict so as to have Yue Fei arrested. He was tortured in the water cell and ultimately poisoned before he could present his story to the emperor.

Thus Yue Fei died in disgrace. But the people in Hangzhou who revered him devised a symbolic protest. They took two strips of dough and knotted them together to represent the traitorous Qin Kuai and his wife, who had aided the enemy and killed their hero. They they fried them. "Fried Kuais," the resulting pastry was called, and they have been a popular breakfast food ever since.

When Wai and I visited the temple, our host pointed to the kneeling statues of the two Kuais. The Chinese spat and cursed at them as they passed. "It has been like this for generations," our guide said.

• • •

WHEN WE RETURNED TO BEIJING in late July it was stiflingly hot. During the week our teacher still came to give us lessons, and my Chinese was rapidly improving. The weekends, my favorite times, were now usually spent with Liao and his family. With him I could go anywhere. If there were a sports event, he would invite me to come along with his children. We would be ushered through a special door to a front section where I could sit with all the other children. People would come up to Liao all the time and point to me, his new daughter. In China, to appear within a certain privileged group was to be accepted immediately. It didn't matter that they didn't really know who I was. If I was there with Liao, that was sufficient.

Zhou remained very concerned about security. Wai and I could not go to the swimming pools in Beijing, Shanan said. They were too crowded. By three in the afternoon, when people got off from the afternoon work shift, it was almost impossible to squeeze in among all the bodies that filled the pools. So Zhou invited Wai and me to come to Zhongnanhai and use the pool there.

Usually, I'd go with Liao. In 1958 the Chinese elite began to leave Beijing in the summers and vacation in Beidahe, on the seashore. But in 1957 they still clustered around the pool during the day and watched movies or danced in the evening, as they had since the early 1950s.

The pool was of white cement, very plain and nothing like the ornately tiled ones I had known in Thailand. The leaders clustered around it drinking soft drinks and beer; they seemed far more at ease with one another than Thai leaders were if Pibul was present at their informal gatherings. Liao had told me that the Chinese leaders did not talk seriously on these occasions. This was the one time they could unwind, he said. The air was filled with banter and jokes, at which Liao, of course, was particularly adept.

The men's swimming trunks, broad cotton underpants, struck me as very funny. In Thailand, colorful swimsuits had been the fashion, but in China it seemed that anything went. Some of the girls didn't even have bathing suits; they jumped into the pool in their light dresses.

It took only an instant to see Chairman Mao. He looked enor-

mous sitting by the pool, but in the sunshine, it was his huge forehead that was most impressive. The sun glinting off it seemed to ac-
centuate its size. A nice Chinese old man's smile, I thought as he sat
talking with one of the other leaders. I watched as he—and his bodyguard—got up to swim. He maneuvered his large body into the water slowly but once in he seemed completely relaxed. When he swam
his arms scarcely rose above the water, and as he floated, his big
stomach riding high above the surface, he looked like nothing so
much as lord of the place. He loved to swim, Liao had told me. Back
and forth he went without interruption, his bodyguards hovering at
either end. When he paused to float again, he seemed like a con-
tented sea creature. I watched Liao as he walked up to the edge, taking pictures of Mao floating so blissfully along. Mao never came to
the pool with any members of his family; he was always alone with
his bodyguards.

Many of the faces I recognized. Liu Shaoqi was often there. Various marshals were as well—Chen Yi, Li Xiannian. I was learning to
keep track of them, spotting them on various occasions, sitting with
their children at sporting events. Some I had seen at National Day
on Tiananmen Square; others in the newspaper. But mostly I had
learned about them—or was to learn about them—at school and at
Liao's. My favorite class was already history—the history of the revolution. Uncle Zhou was prominent, of course, but Liao's family was
so much a part of that history that I often wondered what their
heroic past must have been like. I thought of all sorts of questions to
ask should the opportunity arise. It usually did.

One hot afternoon I recognized Marshal He Lung by his brilliant
eyes and this thick black mustache. Zhou had spoken fondly of his
great military heroism and character, and in school I had read of his
numerous exploits. From the side of the pool where I clung, I
watched him mount the board and dive. As he surfaced, he suddenly
swooped under me, lifted me up, and lobbed me into the deepest
part of the pool. Terrified and unable to swim, I thrashed about,
choking, until he pulled me out of the water.

"I'm sorry," he apologized. "I mistook you for my daughter."

He tried to comfort me as he carried me out of the pool to his
family circle. His son was an exact miniature of his father, and his
two girls, who were about my age, strongly resembled him as well.

They huddled around me, his wife whispering something to him. I belonged to Liao's family, she must have said, for He Lung glanced at Liao, who was now walking over, laughing. He asked my name.

"Chang Yuan," I said.

Learning that I was Thai, he told me about coming across members of a Thai minority in southern China during his fighting days. He had fallen in love with their graceful dancing. Had I, he asked, seen the Peacock Dance on the last National Day in Beijing?

"Yes, I did," I replied. "But it really looked Burmese, not very Thai."

"You are a little expert. I can't tell the difference," he said, smiling. "Can you dance?"

"Oh, yes," I said, although by now I was very rusty. "My teacher was the best classical dancer in Thailand."

"Then you must come to my house and dance so I can see the genuine thing."

He seemed puzzled about where my parents might be. There were no other foreigners in Zhongnanhai.

"My parents are not with me in China," I stated simply.

"See how brave she is to travel by herself," he said to his daughters.

"My brother is with me," I assured him.

Liao's son called Wai over, but they quickly left together with He Lung's son to swim. He was making friends easily now, but among the leaders he remained shy.

"I've read a lot about you in school," I said. I knew I should not mention anything Zhou had told me. I could never assume that someone knew of my close connection.

"How could you be so brave?" I asked, mentioning a few battles during the war of liberation, when he had headed an army group in the Shanxi-Suiyuan liberated area. "Weren't you ever scared?"

"It's different when you're facing a known foe," he said. "You won't be afraid when you grow up either."

I knew that he and Zhu De had been the two chief commanders of the rebel forces in the Nanchang uprising of 1927. I asked him to tell me about some of those battles.

"The battles you seem to know," he replied. "I'd rather tell you the stories I told my men on the Long March when we camped."

Liao had explained to me that He Lung came from a large, very poor family from Sang Zhi, in Hunan province. His father had been a tailor but was also an amateur practitioner of traditional Chinese martial arts and the head of the local branch of the Ge Lao Hui, one of the most powerful of the former Chinese secret societies. Most of its members were peasants and impoverished townspeople who tried to organize against the bullying of the old officials. From his father, He Lung had learned the martial arts; it was the only education he had received. He himself became a "doubled-headed dragon," and he was known by the nickname "Black Mustache."

He Lung, Liao told me, spoke of the peasant world with great affection and understanding. His favorite stories tapped the peasant tradition of mocking officialdom. The Qing mayor of Swatow, famed for his stupidity, was a favorite target.

"One day the mayor received orders from Beijing: 'Tell the people and the horses to keep the to right.' But if everyone walks on the right, he complained to his subordinates, what shall we do with the left lane?"

His was a very different humor and temperament from Zhou's or Liao's.

" 'I can't understand these crazy foreigners,' the mayor said one day after watching a soccer match. 'They're all fighting and pushing one another over one ball. I could easily have bought them each a ball.' "

He Lung told his stories with gusto. "Come by my house. Come by and I will tell you more, and you can dance. You promised," he reminded me. Then he plucked me up and deposited me once again with Liao.

One Sunday afternoon, Liao took me first to Zhou's instead of to the pool. He disappeared into the house as I played out front with one of Zhou's secretaries until I heard Deng Mama calling me to come with her. I scampered on ahead, only to realize that she was walking in a different direction entirely. She didn't tell me where we were going, just smiled and said to come along. We walked a considerable distance, protected from the fierce summer sun by the ancient trees that lined our way. Finally, we reached a beautiful building I had never seen, its glazed tile roof shimmering in the heat. Guards were posted outside, and they saluted as Deng Mama walked past into the house. She clearly knew this house well, for she immediately took me through several of the rooms, straight into a splendid garden in which an old, white-haired man was hoeing. He had on a simple vest, shorts, and a pair of slippers. As he turned to greet us, I knew immediately that it was Zhu De, the "Father of the Red Army," although he looked much more like a man who had spent his life gardening than the great general I had read so much about. The garden was one of the lushest and greenest I'd seen in Zhongnanhai.

He walked over and greeted Deng Mama warmly. "Good harvest, good harvest," he said.

He motioned for us to sit in his wicker armchairs. He had callused hands, I noticed, but fine, long fingers. When he learned I was Thai, he told me how much he loved orchids.

"My father grows orchids as a hobby," I said.

Delighted, he took me by the hand to show his off. "They are very difficult to grow in Beijing, more wayward and harder to cope with than the Guomindang generals."

And Thai orchids, I thought, were larger and more colorful.

I was to see Zhu De informally at other times in the years to come. Occasionally he visited Liao's mother or came to the dances the leaders held in Zhongnanhai to relax.

Zhou and Liao were pleased to have us meet the leaders of the Chinese revolution and would encourage us to get to know them in the years to come. They seemed to me to be immensely proud of what they had done, to share a palpable spirit of accomplishment. Wai was not as enamored of Chinese revolutionary history as I was. "Thailand is different," he would say. He respected many of these figures, but entering into their world, or into their pasts, was not what he was there for. By contrast, it became my consuming and sustaining preoccupation.

By the time school reopened in the fall I had begun to master the history of the revolution. On our tests we had to be able to match the right commander with the right army in the right battle. This I had down pat. My teacher was astonished when I got the only perfect score in the class. She was evidently not entirely pleased when she told the class, "You should all be ashamed of yourselves that a foreign girl knows more Chinese history than you do."

CHAPTER 7

"Grief into Strength"

WHEN I RETURNED FROM VACATION in the fall of 1957, the halls of the school were festively decorated, the walls awash in red. The drab grayness and darkness had given way to large banners and posters proclaiming great victories in something called the "antirightist campaign." I had asked Liao what a campaign was when this one had begun several months earlier. But I had not paid much attention to his answer, and, in any case, he had said little except that it did not concern me.

I walked down the familiar hallway looking for my old history teacher. I was particularly looking forward to her class again now that I was so much more knowledgeable about the leaders of the Chinese revolution. Everywhere I stopped to ask where she was, though, people became quiet or answered cryptically. They weren't unfriendly, but I felt a chill, a hesitation. "Don't ask" seemed to be the clear message.

Puzzled, I stood looking vacantly at the writing on a particularly large poster that covered one whole wall of the hall. Out of the corner of my eye, I saw a woman moving slowly back and forth in the nearby lavatory, cleaning the latrines. I turned back to the poster, but then I looked again. I shuddered: it was my teacher. She didn't look up even as I approached. I tried to speak to her, but she seemed mortified, avoiding my eyes and keeping her head down. Then she glanced up, but her eyes were blank. She looked right past me and said nothing.

I ran down the corridor until I saw my math teacher coming in my direction, her head bowed. Several students approached her in a disrespectful way, saying things I couldn't quite hear. As she came near, I tried to speak to her, only no words came out this time.

Bewildered, I found my friend Ru Dingyi. What was going on? I wanted to know.

"What do you mean?" she asked, surprised by how distraught I was.

"My teachers, in the latrine, what—" I stuttered.

Calmly, she reassured me, "They are rightists. They are being rectified. My father says it must be done."

I vaguely knew that her father and Deng Ziaoping were important in running this campaign. I had seen Deng on National Day with the other leaders, but I had never come across him at the gatherings in Zhongnanhai.

Certainly my friend didn't seem concerned by what she saw. No one did—except Wai. He was outraged. "It's inhuman!" he cried. He proceeded to go out of his way to speak to the humiliated teachers. And since he was protected by the premier's office, no one dared criticize him.

The next morning I was further surprised when our mathematics teacher entered the room. I started to stand, as we always did as a sign of respect. Everyone else remained seated. No one said "Good morning, teacher," and when the class ended, no one rose to say "Good-bye, teacher." As I walked from class, I saw a group of students taunting and cursing one of the teachers in the hall. She stood silent and dejected as one of the students spat in her face.

"What will Father think of the place he has sent us to now?" Wai asked me that night.

Shanan tried to explain to us that some people in China were against the building of a new China. They wanted to topple the government. They were bad elements; this was a way of dealing with them.

Security, plots, antigovernment "elements," even assassins—all these I had grown up with. But this was baffling and deeply disturbing, and the parents of my friends were running the movement. No explanations made me feel any better. None of them added up to the humiliated person in front of me. I felt sick.

Finally, I saw Zhou. I told him about our "bad teachers" at school and how upset I was that the students seemed to have come so quickly to despise them. I told him about the student who had spit on a teacher.

He didn't explain why the teachers were being forced to clean the latrines. But he responded bluntly to my account of the scenes of humiliation I had witnessed. "That was a very uncivilized thing to do," Zhou said to me. "No matter what mistakes these people have made, no one should hurt their self-respect like that." His cheek muscles were taut, as they always were when he became tense or spoke of something he disliked.

He told me that I was not yet familiar with China's problems. Understanding them was part of why Father had sent me here. But he reiterated that under no circumstances did they justify humiliating people. I should feel free to tell him what I saw.

Zhou had not told me I was wrong. He had not justified the humiliation. And I found, after our talk, that I was able to go on in the school. I tried to turn my eyes away, though I cringed inwardly at what I knew was still there. At least I had a sense that my feelings were somehow shared. I told neither Shanan nor Qiu Ji what Zhou had said.

In MID-SEPTEMBER, Liao came by our house unexpectedly, looking unusually grave. He asked to see both Wai and me.

"Prime Minister Pibul's government has been overthrown in a military coup," Liao said. "He has fled the country and gone to Cambodia. We don't know much more than this. General Sarit Thanarat seems to be the key power behind the new prime minister."

Wai and I were stunned.

"Premier Zhou will try to get in touch with your father. We are worried about him and other friends of China and fear that steps may be taken against them."

I was frightened. What was my mother doing? What about my little sister? Our house? My brother? I sank into a chair.

I heard Wai saying something about leaving. We were here as Pibul's representatives, he said.

Was this the end of our stay? Where would we go? What was to become of us? Was I to be sent away?

"You will stay here. We have a great responsibility to your father and honor his great role in improving relations between our two countries," Liao said. "We must wait to understand the situation. You will remain here, and we will look after you as best we can. We will try to get in touch with your father. We don't quite know how, but we will try."

We were to continue in the house and go on with our studies. Qiu Ji came later to talk more, particularly with Wai. It was Wai who was asking about going home, not I.

"Pibul is no longer there," Qiu Ji said. "But your father is. There will never be an end to Pibul's function in Thailand, and that is now what you represent. Pibul has gone. Perhaps he will come back one day, perhaps someone like him will emerge. It may take several years—or many years. But it will come."

That was not the only reason we should stay. "It is a dangerous moment in Thailand," Qiu Ji continued. "Premier Zhou is concerned that Pibul was overthrown because the Americans were leaning of the scope and character of his ties with China and wanted a government more compliant with its own ambitions. Your returning could complicate the situation for him. We will have to be very careful here as well. Your existence here is not to become known."

Wai asked to have all available news materials on developments in Thailand. He had read some of them before; now he pored over them and discussed them with Qiu Ji. The details were hard for me to follow. The government was first headed by Pote Sarasin, a wealthy businessman who had been ambassador to the United States and secretary-general of SEATO. He also happened to own the sole rights to distribute Coca-Cola in Thailand. He was soon replaced by Lieutenant General Thanom Kittikachorn, while General Sarit, still the main power, was in the United States receiving medical treatment. Wai told me the problems facing Thanom: factionalism in the military, an economy weakened by a bad rice harvest, demands for a more neutralist foreign policy and Pibul's return from exile.

In the months that followed, some delegations from Thailand were able to visit China. Zhou and Father continued to communicate, and Father returned full-time to his role as columnist for his paper. "I have warned your father that the dangers against him are growing," Zhou told us. He expected an effort by Sarit to return and launch a program of savage repression. The conflict in Indochina was growing. The Americans needed Thailand to be more subservient, more tightly under its control. Sarit was America's choice, he felt sure.

"Your father is welcome to come live in China," he assured us. "I have asked him to come for safety's sake. I have told him how much I fear he will be persecuted because of his advocacy of ties with China." But Father did not want to leave Thailand. He did not wish to give up his role in the Thai political scene or go into exile. He preferred to stay in Thailand and fight for what he believed.

My NEW HEAD TEACHER was a great contrast to my now-discredited first-year teacher, who had praised me to the class when I made progress with my characters. My new teacher was harshly critical of me, pointing out all my mistakes; each dot in the wrong place, each missing stroke seemed to irritate her. I became more and more disheartened, reminding myself that Chinese was not my native tongue anyway. Out of spite I begain missing strokes even in the characters I knew so as to anger her. I was quite successful.

Her annoyance built up day by day. Finally she exploded, berating me bitterly in front of the entire class. I was mortified—and furious. Tears streamed down my face as I marched out of the classroom and straight to the headmaster's office, where I called Qiu Ji and told him that I wished the car so that I could go home immediately. I added only that I had no intention of returning to that teacher. I wanted to change to another class.

For some time I stood out front of the school waiting for the car. Was my teacher reporting me to the headmaster even now? I wondered. Would he come out and punish me? What would Qiu Ji and

Zhou think of me? Well, I wouldn't take it anymore.

When I saw the car, I felt great relief. I'd soon be out of there. I was even more relieved to see that my teacher, Lin Hong, had come along. She greeted me warmly and gently asked me to get in and come home. For a brief moment I felt I should tell her I was wrong. She, at least, was being kind, and I was very worried what my guardians would say. Lin Hong listened quietly to my sobbing and my stories of how horrible my teacher was. "I'll go back to Thailand if I am not transferred," I threatened, as I often did at such moments. She urged me to calm down.

"I'll work with you at home for a few days and then see what can be done to make it better," she said.

Two days passed. No Qiu Ji. Where was he? I thought surely he would come soon to scold me. I felt as though somehow my forehead was starting to grow a horn with which to fight him. Finally, on the third morning, he arrived. I was well prepared, steeled for a showdown.

"I've brought you a little something from my labors," he said with a laugh. He handed me a bagful of peaches, my favorite fruit.

"I've been down to the countryside helping the farmers," he explained, regaling me for some time with tales of his ineptness in helping with the harvest. Finally, though, as he prepared to leave, he told me he wanted me to go back to school the next day. He asked nothing at all about what had happened. "You know all your classmates well and they are as fond of you as you are of them. So why change?"

He patted me on the head. "Your teacher is just a recent graduate, and she's new to her job. You should be kind to her," he said. "Now, will you go?"

I promised I would, though with some trepidation. When the teacher came into the classroom the next day and we had all sat down, she began with a criticism of herself for being so inconsiderate of me. "I am very inexperienced," she concluded, "and I will need a lot of help from you to teach a good class."

She seemed very earnest and sincere. After class I went up to her and said I was sorry as well. She seemed pleased and relieved. I had not made my little criticism in class, as would have been expected of my classmates, and she seemed to know that it was an unusual step on my part.

Years later, I learned that Zhou had once again told Qiu Ji to intervene with my teacher to prevent the situation from getting out of hand. Zhou had reminded him, "Remember, Chang Yuan is alone, she needs to feel secure and supported. She has no parents here. Someone has to be absolutely on her side, someone she can fall back on. She must have that trust in us."

Qiu Ji had been instructed to discuss things with my teacher. He was to tell her how Zhou had summed up my character and let that help guide her as she dealt with me. "If you develop this girl's strong character well," Zhou had instructed Qiu Ji to tell her, "she could become a heroine. But if it is developed incorrectly, she could become a villain."

At the time I knew only that my relations with my teacher changed immediately. She became quite supportive, and I once again made great progress in Chinese language and history. I particularly loved reading about the Long March. In 1934 the Communist forces had escaped Jiang's military attacks on them only by making a year-long trek of six thousand miles to establish a new Communist base at Yan'an. Only eight or nine thousand of the original eighty thousand survived, but those who did included most of the great leaders of the revolution.

The more I learned about the revolution, the more I could talk to the people Zhou and Liao introduced me to, the leaders and officials who made up our secret world outside school. The stories they told me and the network of connections among them made more and more sense.

One winter night I sat up late preparing for a history test, driving myself long past my bedtime. Zhou had been so impressed with my performance the last time. Feeling I was heroically fighting off the sleepiness that threatened to envelop me, I tore the blanket off my bed and turned the radiator off. The cold started to clear my mind, and I plunged back into the names and battles of the Chinese revolution.

The next thing I knew, Wai was trying to shake me awake, but I could barely open my eyes. My head throbbed, and I shook all over. I was sick for a week with a high fever.

Zhou phoned me when he heard the news. "I never knew you

could be that stupid!" he said furiously. "Why did you do such a silly thing, sleeping with nothing on but your pajamas?"

"I wanted to do well on my history test," I replied weakly.

"You can learn much from the heroes of the revolution," Zhou said, "but learning to be stupid and trivial is not one of them. One must learn to combine one's heroism with intelligence, not with stupidity! Don't you remember the story I told you of Liu Hulan?"

Some months before, Zhou had told me her story. "Like you," he had said, "Liu Hulan had a stormy character but she used her strong will and intelligence to fight the Japanese invaders and protected the local villages in Shanxi, aiding us with invaluable information. She was seized by the Japanese army when she was only seventeen. They tortured her for days to get more information about the Red Army, which had been severely attacking Japanese supply lines in the area. But she defied them. She never betrayed the things she knew. So the Japanese sentenced her to death by decapitation. In front of all the villagers who had been assembled, she defied them a last time before she was executed. She was a true heroine. She gave her life for something meaningful. It was the countless acts of people like Liu Hulan that finally brought about the victory of the Chinese people."

Zhou's admiration for this girl and his reference to her now made me more determined than ever to learn what heroes were. I studied their stories, searching for clues. Perhaps I might find the clue to understanding who I was and what I was to do in the world into which I had been cast.

Wai continued to read the Thai papers carefully, keeping track of daily events and analyzing the risks for Father. He read widely in Thai literature and history. I often balked; I remembered little of my own education in Thailand. I told Zhou I was too busy to study Thai—my other classes required too much of my time. Zhou remained adamant.

"If you want to be useful in your later life, you must know your own language. No, no nonsense, no funny stuff," he said.

By Thai, Zhou also meant the customs and nuances not just of the language but of the etiquette required if one was to move in Thai society. He told my Thai teacher that he expected me to know such manners well. I was deeply confused. I was trying very hard to enter a world that Zhou made quite clear I would never permanently stay in. Yet I had no desire to go back home, to return to where I had been sent from.

At school I joined in the activities as much as I could. Most of my friends were members of the "Red Scarves," a group for those who had distinguished themselves by various good deeds and by their social consciousness. Children in good health who studied hard and helped others were awarded red scarves as tokens of membership.

"Chang Yuan, we want you to join," several of them urged me. "Then you can go with us and participate in the things we do in the community."

I proudly told Liao of my latest accomplishment.

"I'm glad you're doing well," Liao said, "but Premier Zhou and I don't think you need to join. While it is true that you have to be a good child in order to get a red scarf, all the same there are many good children without red scarves."

Neither Zhou nor Liao said that it was a Communist organization or that they felt it was inappropriate for me to join as a guest of the Chinese government. But I was somehow to try to enter into my Chinese world without being a member. "A good and accurate understanding of what the Chinese people are doing is part of your job," Liao told Wai and me. "But you don't need to participate fully to do so. Being a good observer is quite sufficient."

This was fine with Wai, who had no intention of joining. But I chafed against such constraints. They held me aloof from everything I determined to join. I felt that only the acceptance and approval of Zhou and Liao offered solace and purpose in my isolation.

Liao, of course, had given some thought to the problem. I was soon invited to participate in my classmates' extracurricular activities. I became a committed campaigner in the 1957 movement to wipe out illiteracy. Every day after school and on Sundays, groups of four or five children went from house to house in the neighborhood of the school and tried to teach old people to read and write. Few knew any characters, and our task was to urge them to learn some. Our student leader was twelve and remarkably adept at organizing us. At our first stop, a clean mud hovel, the occupants laughed at us. But the student leader calmly told them that they were now living in the new China, not the old one.

"Chairman Mao says that you are the masters of the new China," she said. "So you must know how to read and write."

Several people we visited got into the spirit. We wrote characters on all the furniture and cooking utensils so they could learn them in the course of their daily chores. Then we returned to see how they were doing. We gave them reading tests every week for months, dividing the neighbors into groups of three so that they could study with one another during the week. At school we prepared colorful awards and a special prize in the form of a red paper flower to be fixed to the winner's door. Then we grandly went with drums and gongs to announce the winner.

They, in turn, told us what their lives were like in the new China, as well as their hardships in the old. They proudly showed us their homes, much as my class leader had shown me hers my first year at school. Four or five families lived around a courtyard, and there they all used one public water tap. Their few rooms were neat but lacked toilets; they had no baths, washing only with wet towels and bathing once a week at a public facility.

Sometimes when we had days off from school, I joined a group of fellow students who reported to a nearby neighborhood committee on how the old men and women were managing. When we visited them in their homes, we found that some had been left alone and did not seem to be coping well. These we talked with carefully, taking copious notes for our presentation to the neighborhood committee. We helped them get hot lunches and did some household chores and simple shopping; we read newspapers to those who were illiterate. During the week I sometimes joined those dashing off during their two-hour lunch break to spend some time with the old people they were helping.

Such activities were not required of me. I participated because I sought to be included and because I found the stories, plays, and dances designed to discourage "selfish" behavior compelling. My favorite of these was a dance called "The Blossoming of the Malan Flowers."

Malan Hua was a kindly fairy girl who loved to help all who were in need—goats, rabbits, birds, deer. One day there came into their midst an ugly black bear who wanted to show that he was the savior and protector of them all. Fiercely jealous of Malan's popularity, he decided to get rid of her. Then he would be the only "hero." He threw her into a swift-running river and drowned her. But when the animals in the forest learned what had happened, they rejected him and his selfishness. In their fury they rose up in unison and killed him. When they threw his body into the very same river, Malan, through magic, came back to life. I had wept when she had died, and I wept each of the ten or so times I saw the play. When she came back reborn, I felt as though I, too, had been restored.

As the school year went on, I no longer made a serious effort to deal with anything except language and history. I went to elementary physics, math, and chemistry, but I could make little sense of them and was not expected to take the tests. Moreover, there was little hope of catching up with the other students, most of whom were two years older then I. Wai did not show much interest either. He requested that he be allowed to read his Thai materials and work on his Thai writing during those periods. Zhou agreed, and Wai was provided with whatever material he requested. A certain stability had entered our school life at last.

WHEN WE HAD HAD DINNER WITH LIAO THE FIRST TIME, he had suggested having a Thai New Year's celebration. In Thailand, New Year's Day, April 13, was a school holiday and Father had never liked to celebrate it. Our first year in China, though, we had had a small gathering at our house. Liao, his wife, and his children had come, along with some people from Zhou's office. Old Lai had begged us not to throw water, the custom that Liao had observed in Burma and that Thais also observed. But we had impishly defied him despite the cold, lightly splashing our arriving guests with the traditional perfume-scented water and allowing ourselves to get thoroughly soaked. I performed the "Dance of Good Wishes," which I had once learned for Pibul's birthday. As host of the party, Wai seemed far more relaxed and happy than he did at any of the official functions required of him in China.

Thereafter, Liao took it upon himself to celebrate the Thai New Year. In the spring of 1958 he marked it by hosting a party at the Beijing Hotel. "No water over our heads this year!" he warned us halfheartedly. Premier Zhou would be there, and so, Qiu Ji told us, would Marshal Chen Yi.

Chen Yi, I was aware, had just become foreign minister, but I knew him as one of the great generals of the Chinese revolution. Together with his fellow Sichuanese Deng Xiaoping and Liu Bocheng, the "one-eyed general," he had led the Red Army to one of its finest victories in the Huai-Hai battle, which had annihilated a Guomindang army of 550,000. The victory had been all but the death warrant of Jiang Jieshi. Zhou was clearly very fond of Chen Yi.

I had seen him and his beautiful wife, Zhang Qian, at Saturday evening dances in Zhongnanhai. He had married late; she was still in her thirties and dressed with a stylishness unusual among the leaders' wives. His own bold, somewhat unorthodox style was matched by a mischievous playfulness. He was short and stout and always wore the heavy dark glasses that Zhou had gotten him in Germany a few years before to protect his eyes.

"Chen Yi spent years fighting the Guomindang forces at night," Liao told me. "He slept in the day and fought at night, so he became known as 'the owl,' able to see clearly only in the dark. In time he couldn't stand bright lights anymore."

As the guests entered that night, we sprayed them with perfumed water and did our Thai greeting. Liao brought his children, who were as festively and colorfully dressed as we.

When Zhou introduced us to Uncle Chen, Wai offered words in greeting and together we performed a traditional Thai dance. Liao, as usual, was taking pictures. Then Zhou began to speak. Formalities were quickly dispensed with, and he began to tell stories about Chen Yi and Liao. They often joked with one another on such informal occasions; theirs was a camaraderie not typical among the leaders. Zhou said he knew much of the heroic character of Chen Yi and his great courage. Smiling, he said he had yet another example to report of this great man's courage. His story confirmed what Liao had told us about Zhou's tending, at foreign state banquets, to pass on the occasional unpalatable local dish to an esteemed subordinate.

"On our visit to one of the African countries in 1956, the president of the country held a state banquet in honor of our delegation. One dish placed before me as the senior guest was an enormous sheep's head. Its size and distinctive, not to say pungent, smell took me aback. But of course it would have been unbecoming for me to reject the signal honor being bestowed on me. So I told His Excellency the president that my close comrade, Commander Chen, deserved the honor more than I did. He was sitting next to me, and as I glanced at him, I saw his face go quite pale. This man, who had never known fear in battle, was actually afraid of eating this smelly dead animal! But I must praise him for his great courage—he swallowed a few mouthfuls for me without turning a hair."

Then Chen Yi recounted how he in turn had decided to share the great gift with Liao. "I urged the president to please let me pass this honor on to him. And we must all pay tribute to his great courage. He polished off the entire dish!"

Liao was often the center of jokes about eating strange things: dog and cat meat, poisonous snakes, insects Cantonese style, Japanese raw fish, American steaks. He ate them all.

Liao got up next and made one of his spontaneous speeches, full of gracious wishes and sly jokes. Very few leaders gave speeches without a written text; Liao was one who did. As he finished, people urged him to sing.

"Sing us a beautiful German song." They all knew about his dirty German. Liao started to decline with elaborate formality, but we all knew that in the end he never refused to sing. We called him "China's Robeson" because of his deep, powerful voice. When Liao finished, he brought out the musicians, acrobats, and dancers despite his audience's protests that he had not yet sung enough.

That evening brought together most of the people who knew the real reason Wai and I were in China. But there were also officials from the foreign office, who, though they were directly responsible for the house and its expenses, did not know of the actual relations between Zhou and Father. They knew only that we were "the two children Zhou cared for." There were a few other officials involved in Thai affairs, but no overseas Thai. The nature of our presence was as much as ever a closely guarded matter of security.

As THE MONTHS PASSED, Liao continued to draw me into his family. On Sunday mornings he would ask me to come into his study with its beautiful Japanese decorations and tell me what I had been thinking about. As with his own children, he was funny and relaxed. When it came to explaining a problem, though, he liked to be organized. He'd make his points, one, two, three, and move on. When he traveled abroad, he never wrote home, but when he wrote to his oldest son in Harbin, he'd give instructions, "I want to sum up. One . . . two . . . three . . . four."

In this he was a little like my father, and I instinctively knew to come to him with my topics well prepared. If I was having a problem, I would ask him what to do. If I wanted to know about something that was happening in the country, he would explain that as well. And of course there was always the history of the Chinese revolution and the stories of the leaders. I'd tell him what I was reading, and that would launch him into various accounts of events and people.

Often when we talked he told me stories of his family's history, particularly that of his mother, whose memoirs he was working on. She was a real rebel, he'd say. "She was the lady who helped found the new China through her own courage and fortitude. When you look at the two subjects she most likes to paint—cherry blossoms and tigers—you see the two sides of her personality."

"She was the only person who ever called Jiang Jieshi a bastard to his face and lived to tell about it," he told me once with a mixture of pride and amusement. He gave me a copy of the poem she had written for Jiang, for many years the president of the Republic, as he faintheartedly pursued the war against Japan rather than prepare for the one with his feared enemies, the Communists:

> *Although he calls himself a man,*
> *He prefers to yield to the enemy.*
> *No fighting in the ancestorland,*
> *Ten thousand generations blushed for shame.*
> *Together with other women*
> *I'd rather die on the battlefield.*
> *I have brought one of my skirts*
> *For you to wear!*

"She wrapped the poem up in one of her skirts and handed it to Jiang that way. 'Take this skirt and wear it,' she told him. Jiang turned crimson. But you know, she had been his senior in the Guomindang, and Jiang at times still held to those mores."

Amah had her own version of things. "A rebel, indeed! I fought, I climbed trees, and I played rough games from very early on. I had three brothers and six sisters, and I had to rebel to get anything despite our high position in Hong Kong society. My mother insisted that I bind my feet. Necessary, she said, to be an 'elegant lady.' I knew about the women who had fought side by side with the men in the Taiping army. Some of my relatives had fought with the Taipings; I was determined to do as much. Every morning my mother would wrap my feet up. Every night I would cut the cloth bindings off with scissors. She'd angrily bind them again the next day. But I was more determined, and she finally had to yield. A disgrace to the family, but what could she do? She even gave me a fair amount of money as my dowry. 'You won't ever marry,' she sighed."

She pointed to her feet. "Big feet," she said, grinning. "I met my husband because of them, too. He was born in San Francisco, the son of a Guangdong laborer indentured to the owner of a California gold mine. By the time he was a teenager, his father had succeeded in becoming relatively well off. Liao decided to return to China to find a wife. He advertised in the local paper that he wanted to find someone to marry, but she had to have big feet. You can imagine how happy my parents were when they saw that. What an opportunity! So they set about arranging a marriage. They got as far as the meeting, but we happened to like each other anyway and remained together until he was killed."

Liao and his mother seemed very close. Every morning before dressing, he made her favorite Cantonese tea and kissed her before leaving for work. Every evening when he returned home, he'd go see her before turning in to his wing of the house. If she was painting, he would grind the ink for her. If she was resting, he would read her the newspaper or play mah-jongg with her. She, in turn, always had some special goody tucked away for him.

One Saturday night, Liao came to say goodnight, patting my nose as he always did. "Tomorrow will be Amah's birthday. So sleep well, and we will have a nice party tomorrow."

I had never been to a birthday celebration in China. Shanan had told me proudly that China's leaders were not glorified. No streets or cities were named after them—no Leningrad or Stalingrad. They didn't even celebrate their birthdays, he said, publicly or privately.

No birthday even for Chairman Mao. Shanan, I was learning, knew little about the world Liao lived in.

That morning Liao lined his daughters and me up and paraded us all into Amah's quarters to sing "Happy Birthday" and dance for her. We danced past a huge birthday cake, bigger than the one for Pibul, that sat on the far table. When we stopped, she sent her secretary over to open the cupboard where she kept her foreign sweets. She took the special tin box and gave each of us my favorite red and green British hard candy. Liao was busy with his camera.

Zhou and his wife, Deng Yingchao, arrived carrying the largest arrangement of fresh flowers I'd yet seen in China. Then came Chen Yi and his family, bringing live fish from the Yangtze—the particularly bony ones she so relished.

"I never dreamed that I would have such a happy old age," Amah said.

I heard them bantering about various things. Amah would complain to Zhou about how hard he was working Liao. "I want to see him home for dinner every night."

"I'll try to make sure he's here for dinner," Zhou said with a laughing look at Liao. Chen Yi showed off his new dark glasses. Amid the gaiety there was a more serious underside, the remembrances of the harsh times they had been through, the history they shared.

Zhu De came with his orchids. Amah greeted him warmly. "I always remember how you came to the station to receive me in Beijing," she said.

She had been invited by the Communists to come in April 1949, after Beijing was liberated. She had arrived by train with very few of her belongings, to be met by Zhu De and Zhou. "The years of uncertainty and suffering ended at that moment," she said. Zhu De's thick eyebrows knotted, and looking ever so much like an old Chinese peasant, he said, "It was so good to greet you then, to end those trials and pains. We just have to work hard to make sure we don't become the next Li Zicheng."

I knew that Li was an anti-Ming leader at the time of the Taiping rebellion who had entered the cities and become so corrupted that the Taiping rebellion was finally defeated.

"That is what we most hope," Amah agreed.

She reminisced with him, then the others. Zhou and Chen Yi left, others came. Madame Sun Yatsen came with delicious jams from abroad. The children were allowed to play freely among the adults, and I ran about with Liao's daughters and with the other children who arrived to celebrate.

Once people had met me in such a setting, even if they didn't know precisely why I was in China, I was accepted almost completely. In the future they would greet me warmly wherever we met—at a sporting event, on Tiananmen—and I gradually came to know their children as well and, through them, other children. Increasingly, I visited them in their homes, but few were permitted to visit mine.

ONE EVENING IN OCTOBER 1958, the beginning of our third school year in China, Liao came to our house on very short notice. Seeing his solemn face, we expected the worst. For some days we had been trying to follow what was happening in Thailand. General Sarit had proclaimed a one-party state and begun a massive martial law crackdown against all the other parties and all public opposition. The police were reported to have made sweeping arrests of opposition members of Parliament, liberal and radical editors, writers, teachers, students, and businessmen. Wai had followed events as closely as he could, and Zhou had told us that he was not optimistic about the outcome. The United States wanted a more dictatorial regime to complement its plans to escalate its military presence in Southeast Asia. Liao had told us earlier that a warrant for Father's arrest had been issued on Thai radio, along with a severe warning against anyone sheltering him. His pro-Beijing policies and his newspaper stories about China were being bitterly denounced, and many of the politicians, intellectuals, and writers who had been sympathetic to his views of China were being arrested.

"Your father has been arrested," Liao said.

I barely heard his words of comfort through my sobs. Wai and I had feared this or, worse, that he would be executed by the new regime. Wai wanted to return. In any case, there was now no point in our being here, he told Liao. Father was no longer a prominent politician, and our role was predicated on that. Our task here was finished. It would be better for Father if there were not rumors that we were in China. I'm a "political orphan," I thought to myself. I belonged nowhere.

Liao was uncharacteristically adamant. "You cannot go home now. Should you return, you might well be arrested or at least detained. This would only further complicate your father's position. The burden on your mother is already enormous, and we must think of her and your brother and sisters as well."

What were we to do? Wai wanted to know.

"In a grave and desperate situation," Liao said, "it is all the more necessary to think clearly and take a longer view. There is a long road ahead for Thailand and China, and you two are a great asset on this road."

Liao left shortly thereafter, but Shanan stayed that night. Wai discussed our alternatives. He did not want to stay, but he couldn't see what else to do. We had no idea what was happening to Father—or what had happened to Mother and our family. Sarit's White Terror, however sketchily known, left Wai in no doubt that the situation was bleak. "Life is up and down, like the waves," I heard Father saying. But it didn't sound the same with Father's world destroyed. My world in China was because of him; and now, from afar, he had taken my life away again.

For two days we stayed at home, Wai reading the Thai papers and I sunk in deep despair. I could barely move or talk. A few days later I talked with Zhou. Though I tried not to cry, I failed miserably.

"Be brave, my little girl," he said.

After some time I calmed down.

"We are very sorry about your father," Zhou said. "He and other Thai friends are friends of China. We respect them highly. Your father is a veteran, a staunch and heroic leader in the cause of opening up Thai-Chinese relations."

Zhou paused. "Now it is my duty to take good care of you for him and to fulfill his wish by bringing you up as successors in this cause. You are also the Chinese people's children now, and Deng Mama and I regard you as our own children. We Chinese people never forget our friends. We treasure them. This is a good test of our relations. Good relations can be made stronger, whatever the circumstances. You are reminders of your father's courage and devotion to our common cause. We have a saying in China, 'Turn grief into strength.' This applies to you, too. Your father has served the people's cause with his dedication; you must follow in his footsteps and carry the unfinished task through to the end."

I had never heard Zhou put our situation in quite such terms. He clearly believed them, and his tone and conviction echoed those of my Chinese heroes. This was Zhou's sphere, his emotional center, and in his own way he was inviting me into it. That had often been the thrust of his stories of the revolution, but never before had he made the point with such directness and forcefulness.

"Sometimes one has to pay a great price for one's motherland," Zhou said. "You remember what Yue Fei did in the thirteenth century, how honorably he acted? And for the victory of China today, thousands have paid with their lives. Your father has tried to bridge the gap between our two countries and to bring our two people closer—for that he fought, and now he has been put behind bars. They may lock up his body, but they cannot lock up his mind."

I couldn't think of anything to say.

"I will be in touch. Deng Mama and I will always be here for you," he said. Then he was gone.

I retreated to my room and stayed there for several days. I was cut off. The final threads had been snapped. I no longer sought to turn back or get away. I felt I had no other world but this. Zhou and Liao understood. They opened the door wide for me because they judged it was necessary to do so. I would go far, I would work hard at making China a part of me in the coming years precisely because I had been cast out and found myself so alone.

CHAPTER 8

Heroes of the Revolution

The great leap forward was in full fury when Father was arrested in 1958. The Party leaders hoped this gigantic mass campaign would galvanize people and the economy alike, overcoming the old distinctions of age, gender, and occupation while creating a new socialist world based on the communes in the rural areas. Everyone was expected to participate, and students were no exception. The older students in my school poured into the factories for part of each day to learn a few elementary practices from the workers. Nobody asked or told them to join in. For a few months the spirit of the people was palpable. In school large banners proclaimed, "We will teach the sun and moon to change places!" "We will create a new heaven on Earth!" Everyone wanted to join in "moving the mountain," to play a part in breaking the grip of poverty and backwardness on China.

At school, suddenly, all the talk was about steel—about its key role in modernizing China, the need to produce more, the need for all of us to help set new production records. The 1958 target was set at 10.7 million tons—double the 1956 record. This goal could hardly be met by normal methods; creative new ones were called for. The older students worked day and night to build steel furnaces on the old sports ground. Students, once so attentive, came to class only to fall asleep. Awakened, they spoke excitedly of their great revolutionary production tasks.

My school alone had three furnaces. The students dug a big hole in the ground to the lowest level of the soil, the yellow earth. The displaced soil was then carefully sieved until it was very fine, and the hole was refilled with it. Layer by layer the earth was pressed down until it was solid and hard. Then spoons were used to hollow it out, leaving two holes to the surface. An electric blower was placed at one hole and wood fed into the furnace through the other. As soon as the wood was ablaze, the blower was turned on. When the fire began to roar, I would join the younger students in tossing on the scrap iron and broken pots and pans we had collected. The older students, sweating profusely from the intense heat, carefully stirred this bubbling mix with large pokers. All day and all night the fires roared, filling the night skies with their reddish glare and smoke. The results looked like a spongy mush to me, but everyone hailed them nonetheless. Tests were solemnly performed as we assembled to watch in the courtyard, and our product was duly declared to be crude steel. This was our contribution to the steel quota for 1958.

At first our teachers opposed our participation: we were too young, the work was too hard. Some of them undoubtedly thought we should still be in the classroom. But they could no longer restrain us. I secretly joined with my classmates to run errands for the older kids, hiding as soon as we saw our teachers coming. I pushed my cart to the railway station to pick up scraps of iron and various other odds and ends that arrived by train from newly established communes.

In all my months in China, never before had I been without immediate adult supervision. Freed, I flung myself into my assigned tasks. My secret world still intruded, though. If my teachers couldn't supervise, my guardians still could. Shanan insisted that I keep to our daily schedule. Every day the car picked us up, a continuing reminder of our privileged status and now an even odder contrast to the collective spirit sweeping the school.

One day I spirited away a lump of our product and proudly carried it over for Zhou to see. His ready smile quickly disappeared when he saw what I'd brought.

"Is this what your school is working on day and night?" he said, his face taut.

"Of course," I replied. Something in his voice put me on guard.

Zhou took the mushy lump, turning it over and over in his hands. He was unusually preoccupied.

"Don't you like my joining in the steel campaign?" I asked.

At first he didn't answer. Then, looking at me but ignoring my question, he asked me to tell him exactly how the steel was made, how we had built the furnaces, and what else was happening at the school.

He listened intently to my account, although my excitement was rapidly diminishing as I sensed his displeasure. I concluded by saying how much steel our school had produced.

"I don't believe it," he said.

Zhou had never spoken quite like this.

"Now, I want you to remember to study your lessons. The children should get back to school. It is wrong for them to be pulled away from their classes like this." Then he abruptly changed the subject.

When I returned to school the next day, I gave no hint of his response. My enthusiasm was dampened, and thereafter I watched the progress of the steel campaign with mixed feelings. I knew, as I had known in my father's world, that public statements about events did not have to conform with private evaluations of them. In Zhou's comments I sensed something at odds with the publicly espoused line.

What Zhou said to me, or what was said in my presence, I never felt had to coincide with the rest of the world around me. Accepting the disjunction was by now second nature, part of the way I was raised to see the worlds in which I moved. I had all but come to expect that what was in public—the slogans, the propaganda—would be different from what was said privately. Although I was not unmoved by the simplistic public slogans, I rarely supposed that I would encounter such simplicity among the leaders. There the subtlety and complexity, the criticisms were much as I had always heard at home. The public propaganda ebbed and flowed, but the inner sanctum remained remarkably steadfast.

Wai did not join in the Great Leap Forward activities. He simply observed quietly, and occasionally in our conversations he would point out the contrast between the theory and the public statements on the one hand and the reality on the other. The reality, he argued in his careful, articulate way, was often found wanting. It was not logical to believe, he argued, that China could catch up with England in ten years and the United States in fifteen. Such arguments did not much move me. The feverish enthusiasm of the early months of the Great Leap Forward swept me along with countless others. When I paused to ask questions, I contrasted the inner and the outer realities and often found the inner quite sustaining and reassuring. Only behind the walls of Zhongnanhai, among the elite, did I hear criticisms expressed.

In the harsh aftermath of the Great Leap Forward, as the "three difficult years" began and famine spread, I watched Zhou say in public: "People, we must tighten our belts. We will fight and triumph over these adversities." In private he would say, "Look, people are starving. What are we going to do?" To me, this was not cynicism— it was normal.

I tucked away Zhou's disquieting signals and went happily on amid the euphoric atmosphere of the Great Leap Forward. In the fall of 1959, with the harvest results not yet in, my fellow students prepared to join in the enormous national celebration planned for the tenth anniversary of Liberation. For the occasion, ten large buildings were to be erected by the "masses" in ten months. The most famous of these is the one my school worked on, the Great Hall of the People that now stands so imposingly along one side of Tiananmen Square.

Each morning the older students assembled and marched off to work carrying buckets of earth for the workers. Day after day those of us left behind at school heard of their heroic efforts. We heard how they stayed up all night but still worked in school the next day. "The skies are lit up all night for the work," they told us excitedly. "The work never stops."

Posters announcing the surge of mass creativity were everywhere, and the efforts of my teachers to keep our attention flagged once again. This time the older students rebuffed us. We would only get in the way, they said. Outraged, my class mobilized and decided to write its own poster. Early one morning we added it to the school walls: "We can contribute our little buckets, our little legs and arms, and our little hearts for socialism!"

Our older classmates were chastened. Reluctantly they agreed to let us participate under their leadership. We would organize ourselves, we insisted.

We did, but that first day we got lost and never found the unit we were to hook up with. So the head of the Red Scarves in our class went to the student leader of the entire school, the seniormost person in the Red Scarves, and he put us in with one of the older teams. We had to return to school at lunchtime, but I loved the adventure. For the first time I was free of the car. I was allowed to go by bus. Evidently the class provided enough protection, and the image of our car driving up to the Great Hall construction site, assuming it could could even have made its way there, was simply too ludicrous in those fervent times. For several days I carried my little buckets of earth. Led by our team organizer, we sang songs as we worked, and when we rested, colorfully dressed dancers from the local dance academies entertained us and the other workers with skits praising our spirit.

From top to bottom, the whole nation seemed united in the tumultuous effort. Mao and Zhou, Zhu De and Liu Shaoqi, all appeared in the *People's Daily* visiting construction sites, carrying buckets, and shoveling dirt. Zhou was off to the Mi Yun reservoir construction site. All were to do what they could, contribute as they might. This was the aspect of my school life I enjoyed most of all. Like my reading of the history of the revolution, it directly connected my worlds.

Although it seemed as though everyone participated, I knew there were those who did not. In my own class some of the better students did not join in at all. Sometimes one of my teachers would say to them, "Look, Chang Yuan is a foreigner, and yet she supports the movements. Why don't you join in as enthusiastically?"

Some of the students said they were sick or had problems that prevented them from being actively involved. The Red Scarves criticized them, attacking them as "nonpolitical students." They wanted only to be "expert," not "Red." Two girls whose families were well off were particularly good at their studies, partly driven, perhaps, to prove themselves in the face of the liability of their bad class backgrounds. But their excelling only heightened the resentment of the rest of the class. Yet they were allowed to stand their ground; though not respected, they were not humiliated: it was clear that they were not the embodiment of the new spirit sweeping the country.

In China as in Thailand, I learned more outside school than I did in class. "If you want to understand China and the Chinese mentality," Zhou said, "you must see the Beijing Opera." The black face and the white face, he told me, stand in total contrast: the characters are either very happy or very sad, laughing or releasing a piercing whine. There is nothing in between, no middle.

Zhou's favorite Beijing Opera star was Mei Lanfang. "He is famous for his great grace," Zhou informed me as Wai and I settled into our seats for a performance of *The White Snake* in Zhongnanhai. I watched carefully, but the magnificent costumes and elaborate masks made it hard for me to be sure I'd spotted him. Where is he? I wondered as I pretended to Zhou that I had recognized him immediately. Zhou was undoubtedly amused, having neglected to tell me that Mei Lanfang was best known for playing the lead female part. By the time Zhou turned to explain, it was too late. Tired of trying to guess who Mei Lanfang was—and in spite of the loud banging that is so much a part of Beijing Opera performances—I had fallen asleep.

I next saw Mei Lanfang at Liao's, where he had come to visit Amah. He was a handsome man with very delicate features, graceful hands, and unusually expressive eyes.

"Are your eyes that way naturally?" I asked. As the "big-eyed" granddaughter, I knew how some Chinese admired such eyes.

"By no means," he replied with utmost seriousness. "When I was a little boy, my eyes were quite ordinary. But since my family had been actors for three generations, I knew the importance of good training. So every day I gazed at the flame of a burning incense stick in a dark room."

"And that was how you learned?" I asked excitedly.

"Oh, yes," he smiled. "And then I would go outside and fly kites and watch them drift in a clear sky. That helped too, along with the pigeons I'd release so I could watch them as they flew higher and farther away."

I couldn't decide if he was telling me the secret of his success or not, though Liao's laughter suggested something was up.

He was one of a number of performers I was introduced to by Zhou, who took a special interest in actors, dancers, and athletes. If I expressed a wish to meet a famous actor, several weeks later Zhou might surprise me by arranging it. I had loved movies in Thailand, where my friends and I would dress up as though going to a party and then stuff ourselves with chocolate balls and cookies as we sat in the plush seats.

In China, of course, the theaters were plain. Still, I loved the emphasis on heroism in the films. Korean War films reminded me vividly of those I had seen with Father and vaguely of why Wai and I had been sent to China. The Chinese hero Dong Chun Rui was incredibly handsome and brave, fighting not only against the terrible enemy but against hunger and hardship; at the end, death gave him a revolutionary immortality. I remember one hero rushing forward with a pack of explosives toward the bridge from which the enemy was firing on the Chinese troops and blocking their advance. As he sacrificed his life, I burst into tears. The bridge was destroyed, his mission a success. How noble and selfless, I thought, eager to identify with the act.

Zhou and Liao knew how much I liked Zhao Dan, then starring in many films. Zhao had played Lin Zexu, the national hero who had bombarded the English ships that had carried opium to China. On a trip to Shanghai, Wai and I were taken to a film studio to watch the shooting of one of Zhao Dan's war sagas and have lunch with him. Wai asked him how the old and new Chinas differed from each other. "A bad society turns human beings into demons, a good society turns them into human beings," Zhao said. He spent the rest of the day with us, inviting us to his home, which was tastefully decorated with old paintings and antiques and strewn with movie magazines. He told us of his meetings with Zhou and what Zhou's support meant.

This was more and more my world—doors opened, people were communicative and friendly. And always Zhou was the connection. My school, he knew, was hardly able to absorb my time fully, nor could I learn enough about China there. I was therefore introduced to whatever people and places interested me.

In these early years, given my fascination with the heroes of the Chinese revolution, I asked that our trips and vacations focus on their exploits. Often, upon returning, I'd see the leaders and tell them what I had seen. Initially, I was surprised to find that many of them had never returned to the scenes of some of their most renowned exploits. Some found it too painful to do so. When I asked Zhu De about crossing the marshlands in the Long March, his normally cheerful face looked stricken with great pain.

"My comrades in arms," he'd say, "our soldiers," but never "the soldiers I led." The trip, he told me, was the worst time of his life. "You could do nothing for those who got ensnared or lost. You could do nothing for them even though you knew that left there, they would die."

His enormous shoulders slumped. "So many fell into the marsh and were finished. So many were sick; they couldn't make it. I'm sure almost all those left behind died. Sometimes you could see them and not help. It was horrible."

Zhu De never forgot those who died. "We live in their debt," he said. "Without their sacrifice we would not be here today." They had made the revolution possible for him, and if their acts seemed less glorious then blowing up a bridge, I was still deeply moved. Zhu's commitment was born out of suffering; somehow he had endured with it.

I was enthralled by our visit to Mao's birthplace in Hunan province, and on returning I was filled with questions for Zhou and Liao. What I had seen in the Museum of the Chinese Revolution in Beijing and read in my textbooks was not exactly in accord with what I saw there. Quite a large house for a poor peasant, I thought. But what came through was the sense of sacrifice: people in the village talked about Mao's brother's being executed, about the deaths of his uncle and aunt. In school Mao's role was lauded, but the details of his early life were barely discussed. Mao's more detailed account of his life in Edgar Snow's *Red Star over China* was not read in school; no one knew what it said, and I myself read it only many years later.

Liao and Zhou both told me about Mao's personal history. The leaders knew its details well but didn't pass on more than the broadest outline even to their children. About Mao's wife, Jiang Qing, I knew little; she was rarely mentioned. Liao had no pictures of her to show me, and she was never at the pool in Zhongnanhai or at the dances. I knew I should not ask why.

Of Mao's tragic marriage to Yang Kaihui I heard many times. That she was tortured for her revolutionary activities and then executed in 1930 was well known in China. Zhou told how Mao's eldest son, Mao Anying, had been forced to watch as his mother was tortured and then dragged off to her execution. She was beheaded, her head stuck in the center of one of Changsha's main public places. Though cast out, Anying was found by the Communist party's underground organization, and he and his two younger brothers, Anqing and Antong, were placed in a Shanghai nursery run by the Party.

For a few years they had some peace; their uncle Mao Zeming visited them regularly. But then he disappeared as the counterrevolutionary terror against the Shanghai party struck yet again. Anying remembered the morning that a teacher rushed up to him and his brothers, pushing them into a room where a friend of Uncle Mao Zeming's awaited them impatiently.

They fled as the Guomindang troops and police began to break into the building, shooting. In the confusion, Antong was lost. Despite countless searches through the years, he was never found.

The two remaining boys became homeless wanderers and beggars on the streets of Shanghai, sometimes selling newspapers. At one point, Anqing sustained a severe concussion when he was bashed over the head with a police baton. Anying and Anqing lived this way for five years.

In 1936 the Party made contact with them, and they were sent to Moscow under false names. They both learned Russian, and in 1938 Anying, the better student, was sent to a school for foreign children in Moscow. In 1940 Zhou, having gone to Moscow for medical treatment for his right arm, met the two children whom Mao had yet to meet. Anying was doing well, but Anqing was still showing the results of his concussion, from which he was never really to recover. It was Zhou's first contact with the children, whom he tried to help in the years ahead. Jiang Qing, who married Mao in the late 1930s, was not pleased by the prospect of their return. Protecting them from her would tax Zhou's diplomatic skills in the years to come.

Anying joined the Russian army, becoming an artillery lieutenant.

In 1946 he returned with Anqing to China, where they met their father for the first time in Yan'an. Mao, Zhou said, seemed quite fond of Anying, though he said little of the personal relationship that developed in the next few years. Anying, a toughened Communist, was sent by his father to the rural areas. "You have learned about Russia," his father said. "Now you need to learn about China."

When Chinese troops entered the Korean War in late 1950, Anying asked Mao to let him go. Zhou strongly opposed the idea. Anqing was not normal, and Anying was Mao's only heir of sound mind. But Anying persisted and Mao agreed, telling Zhou that the very fact he was Mao's son was the most powerful reason why he should serve at the front.

After visiting his mother's tomb in Hunan, Anying left for Korea and in November 1950 was killed in a bombing attack. He was twenty-eight. Zhou was with Mao when the news arrived. Mao told Zhou that Anying was an ordinary soldier who died doing his duty protecting China. And then he shut himself up in his room to mourn.

Anying had not gotten along well with Jiang Qing. "You don't love my father, you love his position," he had once said. But he could protect himself; he was strong and very able. Anqing was not. He suffered from severe headaches, vomiting, blurred vision, and loss of memory. Zhou, I knew, had arranged for Anqing to be cared for at a seaside resort outside Dalian. There he married a nurse, and he seemed to improve. Jiang Qing was kept clear of him until she herself went to Dalian and encouraged Mao to seek further treatment for him in Russia—apart from his wife. In 1953 he left for Russia again.

Exactly what Jiang Qing did in those years, I never knew for sure. The rumors were that she had written Anqing to tell him his wife was having an affair with another man, that she had written to Anqing's wife that he had become involved with a Russian nurse. She had intercepted all their letters to each other as well. Zhou had sought to arrange for Anqing's wife to go to Russia, but the intricate intrigue was protracted and unsuccessful; no one, I gathered, wished to speak too directly to Mao about his domestic situation. In frustration and despair Anqing's wife demanded a divorce, and she remarried in 1955.

Jiang Qing herself saw Anqing in Moscow in 1955. Despite Jiang Qing's desire that he remain in the Soviet Union, he refused to marry his Russian nurse. His condition continued to deteriorate until his deplorable condition was reported to Zhou. He was brought back to Dalian, and this time Mao entrusted his care directly to Zhou. Later Anqing married his ex-wife's sister and was protected in the years that followed.

Before the Cultural Revolution Zhou never said a negative word about Mao's wife. Only afterward did I learn of the anger she bore him. That the marriage between Mao and Jiang Qing was bitterly opposed by many of the old guard was no secret by the early 1970s. But until Liao told me, I had not known that it was Zhou who had been picked by his colleagues for the task of imparting to Mao their instructions for his wife:

> Not appear as his wife in an official capacity.
> Not to participate in politics.
> Not to be a "Danji"—the name of the last Zhou emperor's concubine, regarded as having brought about the ruin of the state.

AFTER TWO AND A HALF YEARS in the middle school, I spoke fluent Chinese and could write well. The question arose as to what Wai and I should do next. My class was being divided up: some would now go to high school, others to technical school, and Liao was unsure where we should go. At eleven I was too young for high school, and for Wai it would be more of the same; he had long since tired of mastering, in Chinese, the intricacies of modern science and still preferred Thai language and literature.

In the midst of this dilemma, Wai and I saw a stirring Chinese movie about Nie Er, the composer of the Chinese national anthem. Maybe I could write a new Thai national anthem someday, I told Wai.

Wai laughed but seemed to like the idea. "Let's study music," he suggested. He had always wanted to play the violin, and perhaps I could dance or sing or find some instrument to learn. In any case, studying music would get us out of having to go to regular school. In

Thailand one learned music for enjoyment, not as a career: professional musicians were strictly of the lower class. Music, we concluded, might be fun.

The music academies turned out to be anything but frivolous. Chinese students from across the country competed fiercely to get in. Those who passed the arduous exams almost always listed the Beijing Conservatory as their first choice, and that meant further tests and interviews. Once in, one was treated with great respect. I didn't know any of that when Wai and I, entirely unschooled in music, began our studies there in 1960. Zhou had simply arranged for us to be accepted in the middle school attached to this conservatory.

The routine was radically different from that of our old middle school. Students were expected to set their own schedules, and this I found difficult. In the morning the routine was clear enough. One studied literature and history, and I started studying Russian. But in the afternoon one was to listen to music in private or arrange times to practice one's instrument. The Chinese students had no choice in selecting their instruments; the school did this for them. Half were chosen to study Western instruments like piano, oboe, or clarinet and half Chinese instruments, like the Chinese violin or the *zeng*, a long stringed instrument once played by the ladies in the imperial court. Each student was assigned a teacher, who gave private lessons once a week. As usual Wai and I followed different rules. We picked the instruments we wanted. Wai picked the violin. I chose the piano.

I found I could listen for hours to Mozart and Beethoven, but once I started practicing Bach's basic chords, I couldn't stand to listen to him. Practically no one in the school knew who I was; only the headmaster and the Party secretary of the conservatory knew of our connections.

None of my old school friends had gone on to conservatory, and once again my classmates were at least two years older than I. They spoke of their first loves, of things I had never heard spoken of in China before. It was a much freer atmosphere, less moralistic and definitely more relaxed as far as manners and behavior went. "Artistic people are like that," Zhou had said. "Try to understand them."

Wai found a teacher he really liked, a gentle, freckle-faced man from a Shanghai family that had been well to do before Liberation. If Wai wanted to continue his neat, well-dressed Thai ways, that was all right with his teacher. There were no pointed comments, no looks of disapproval. If Wai wanted to drink beer, that was all right, too. Wai also fell in love with a violinist, a Chinese girl two years younger than he. She had a pure, innocent look and, when she smiled, big dimples in both cheeks. I saw less of Wai than before; we sometimes stayed in our conservatory dormitories, and he was now busy with his girlfriend.

One day while I was practicing the piano, a man came up and told me he had been watching me and thinking about me for a week, waiting for a chance to tell me he loved me. I froze for a moment, then ran. Wai was ready to go knock the man's head off but settled for asking Zhou to install a piano in our house. Soon I had one in our sitting room so I could practice at home.

The conservatory had none of the spirit I had come to enjoy at the middle school. There, people had been open-hearted and supportive. Here they seemed intensely competitive, almost selfish. Knowledge seemed to be something to show off; these lovers of music listened to it for hours so as to tell others about what they had not yet had a chance to listen to. I felt lost.

WITH PIBUL GONE AND FATHER IN JAIL, Wai and I had no contact whatever with our family. Returning to Thailand was now an impossibility. I began to think more about who my father was and why he had done what he had, not just in our lives but in a larger sense.

After Father's arrest, Zhou, Liao, and others who knew him spoke of him as a fighter, a hero, someone who had suffered greatly and sacrificed much in the cause of better Chinese-Thai relations. I liked thinking of him there in the great pantheon of persecuted figures, suffering, holding steadfast to their principles. Out of power and in jail, he seemed to have even higher status in their eyes. The longer we stayed, the higher our status, too—and the harsher the contrast to Father locked away in prison. Thinking of him was inherently difficult.

But he was not a Communist, and in the lexicon of the Chinese Communists he had collaborated with the Japanese. In one of my rare letters to Father I had been critical of his role in the war. "Why," I had asked, "did you surrender to the Japanese? History will not forgive you."

His answer had come back quickly. "I am very happy that you are so advanced and starting to analyze history," he wrote. "But take some time to see the reality, try to understand why we had to do what we did."

Once I asked Zhou, "Could it be that Father was right to seek the balance he did in the Second World War? Could it be that it was not altogether bad of my father to surrender to the Japanese?"

"It could," Zhou replied. "But you must study this carefully. Each country's history has its own pattern. You must try to use what you've learned here and then analyze your history. Don't just read the history analyzed for you by the West. Find your own way. You can study our revolution and our history here. But you will have to apply it to your own land; that is up to you. You must learn to do this independently."

Zhou was a dedicated Communist; he believed deeply. But he combined this with a sense that I had to find my own independent way. "Don't copy," he said repeatedly. "Learn to assess the situation objectively, accommodate where you can, give way where you must. Be firm and flexible."

In the early 1960s this is very much what Wai chose to do. Zhou knew Wai liked to sit and read and write, and he encouraged that. He arranged for tutors, for books, however hard to get; whatever materials Wai wanted were his for the asking—about the history of the Chinese revolution and about Thailand. Leading cadres from the Party school came to tutor him and discuss issues with him. He could ask whatever questions he wished. At night he stayed up late reading and writing, thinking through things about Thailand and Father.

Sometimes Shanan would slip and his opinions of Pibul's working under the Japanese would come out. He might say, "Pridi, in contrast to Pibul, carried on the fight against the Japanese; he did not surrender. Of course, I'm not talking about your father," he would quickly add.

Who, I often asked myself, was this man who had sent us here? My ability to move easily between public propaganda and private assessments did not serve me well here. China's leaders were quite proud of their successful struggle against the Japanese, and publicly they extolled many other countries for thier role in it—the Laotians, the Cambodians, but never the Thais.

Often bored at music school, I spent even more time at Liao's, and our long Sunday talks almost invariably centered on my favorite subject, the revolution, also became occasions for assessing my background and its relation to the ideals I had come to admire. Sometimes Liao suggested books to read, and the next week I would come prepared. "Read *The Red Cliffs*," he said one day after I asked about women in the Chinese revolution. I was enthralled by its account of Hong Yen, a woman working in the Shanghai underground to assist the Communists. She had great wit and courage, moving supplely within the elite circles of corrupt Shanghai society and unraveling one complex situation after another. Against enormous odds, she survived and flourished, using her many talents to aid the Party.

Liao listened to my romanticized version of the book. Then he told me what life in Shanghai was really like.

"I, too," he said, "was in the underground Communist party. I joined in 1928. I didn't tell my mother. She was still prominent in the Guomindang, and I was not sure what her reaction would be. Party discipline was very strict. No one was to be told of your membership."

Keeping secrets from one's parents was a degree of secrecy beyond what even I was used to.

"Not until later did she learn, and then only because she had become involved in trying to protect me against the White Terror of Jiang Jieshi."

Didn't I come from the bourgeois class? If Father wasn't a Communist, how could he be a courageous and good person? The bourgeoisie are selfish; they think first of themselves and oppress other people—Chinese propaganda relentlessly carried such messages.

Perhaps no family could have provided as suitable a context for answering my questions as did Liao's. His family and the history of Sun Yatsen, the leader of China's bourgeois revolution, were intricately interconnected, and in response to my misgivings Liao often evoked Sun. "Sun was like your father," he'd say. He, too, came from a bourgeois background, and he represented some of their interests, but he did so in a way sympathetic to the Communists, who had their own discipline and ideas. Both Sun and Father wanted their countries to be able to develop and be independent.

"It is too simplistic to talk about people being bad or good according to whether they are Communists or bourgeois. Some very bad people are Communists, some very good people are of the bourgeoisie."

I wondered, though, if there might not be a way to study what a Communist was. Liao suggested I carefully study Liu Shaoqi's *How to Be a Good Communist*. I tried repeatedly, but it was too dry and theoretical for me. As he often did when my limited capacity for theory became all to evident, he illustrated what he meant by stories. Liao respected Liu greatly, and the discipline Liu wrote of, Liao said, reflected the dark suffering he and his comrades had gone through. "To be able to forget such a past is not quite human," he'd say.

Liu had paid dearly for becoming a Communist, Zhou once said, telling me the story of Liu's two sons by his first wife, He Baozhan, a Communist and a respected leader since the early 1920s. Mao Mao, the younger son, was only three when his mother was arrested. Two months later she was executed.

Mao Mao, his sister, Aiqin, and his brother, Yunbin, spent several years in a Shanghai orphanage and on the streets. Finally Yunbin was found and secretly sent to Yan'an and then, in the early 1940s, to the Children's International Educational Center in Moscow. Liu Yunbin did well in school, eventually completing a master's degree in science at Moscow University. He married the daughter of a Bolshevik, had two children, and for the first time led a settled life. But as relations between China and the Soviet Union rapidly deteriorated in the late 1950s, Yunbin, as the son of China's president, was expected to return to China. He returned, but unhappily: his wife, a dedicated Russian Communist, had decided to stay. He killed himself during the Cultural Revolution.

Mao Mao's case was even sadder. He was found in Shanghai in 1946, having somehow survived alone on the streets all those years despite beatings and other punishing physical abuse. When the Party located him he was eking out an existence selling newspapers. He was sent to school in Yan'an, where he was a morose and difficult loner.

In 1952, though, he entered the Middle School Number One attached to the Beijing Normal College and in 1955, having done well, went to the Soviet Union for further study. Friendless as always, he finally met a young Russian woman and fell in love. After courting her for a year, he wrote to Liu for permission to marry her.

What was Liu to do? His disturbed son was clearly quite happy with the girl. She had made him more gentle and tractable, and the relationship was the first really good thing that had happened to the young man in his entire life. But Liu also knew that a rift between China and the Soviet Union was coming. Liu asked him to postpone his decision and return. Mao Mao came back in June 1960, thinking it was only for a vacation, but he was not allowed to return to Moscow and remained permanently distraught and embittered. When Liu led the Chinese delegation to Moscow for an international conference of Communist parties that November, Mao Mao begged to go. But again Liu felt he had to refuse. Mao Mao, hating his father for destroying his love, collapsed. In the Cultural Revolution he would be imprisoned as a Russian spy and tortured to death.

From all this suffering and loss, it seemed, arose the iron discipline of the "heroes" I read about and met. "When in the dark," Zhou often said, "you must think of the morning dawn." Was this, I wondered, what being a Communist was about? It seemed quite the opposite of the sometimes blinding optimism expressed in public.

"COME WITH US," Liao said a few weeks later. "Mother is going to Nanjing to pay a final tribute to my father. We are all going."

I had come only for the weekend, but by now I knew that some of the most interesting events occurred abruptly. I was happy to go. There were twelve of us: Liao, his wife, and their seven children; his sister, Liao Mengxing, and her only daughter; and me. It was the winter holiday of February 1959, so Liao's eldest son, Liao Kaisun, and his eldest daughter, Liao Jian, were home from school, he from the Harbin Military Academy and she from Nankai University. Amah had brought them up herself in the most difficult years, selling her paintings to feed them while Liao was in jail and their mother in hiding. They had accompanied her when she took the train to Beijing after liberation.

Anyone seeing this tiny lady in her wheelchair and her stylish black-collared dress would certainly have sensed her status. We traveled on a special train; she had a sleeper, her own cook, and a room for playing mah-jongg. All the regular seats had been taken out, and a plush red-and-blue carpet had been laid so we could sit on the floor to play games or read the books placed all about. The bed was enormous. Because Liao was not of his mother's status, he and the rest of us slept in another car. In Nanjing, where we were put up at a special retreat built for Chairman Mao, she lived in the main building, we in a side one.

The rules of this elite world were different from those in Thailand. Liao's house staff always called him *Liao Gong*, or "Director Liao," not "Your Excellency." The tone was different; the respect genuine. But the deference shown to Liao did not automatically extend to the rest of the family, as it would have in Thailand, particularly to the wives. The staff was there because of Liao's and his mother's positions. The status of the husband was not automatically conferred on the wife.

This was evident in the smallest ways. When we traveled on the train, everyone was expected to pay for the food allotted them. Even a minister was to pay—that was the Communist way, I was told. Liao's wife explained that she had paid the five yuan each for her children and me, handing it over to the man who worked in her husband's office. On these occasions Liao and his mother were each charged fifteen, but the assessment was paid by the state. At the guest house it worked the same way.

In this world the children's privileges were a source of continuous contention. The staff would serve them, the driver would drive them, but everything depended, at least in part, on these people's view of what was required for Liao and his mother. The children could not simply order the driver to take them somewhere, yet the driver could not simply dismiss their request either. It had to be carefully evaluated as to its appropriateness. The line between official and merely personal concerns was often a thin one. Implicit in the distinction was the perennial reminder about corruption and privilege; often it was fraught with resentment.

I shared a train compartment with Liao Kaisun and Du Du, the second daughter, who was closest to my age and whom I knew well. This serious older brother, however, I barely knew. He was then around twenty, and Du Du was happily planning her role as matchmaker for him. She had brought along lots of photos of her friends to show him, and all along the journey, through the night, we discussed suitable candidates for him to date back in Beijing before returning to the academy. He himself spent a good deal of the day with his grandmother, for he spoke her Cantonese dialect and knew her smallest needs from having grown up with her.

She seemed content to be surrounded by her family. "I am grateful to Premier Zhou and the Party for this occasion," she said several times. "I am so happy. Please give my deepest thanks to the premier," she said to her son. It was both an intimate and an official request. Politics crossed right through the center of the family dynamic. For he was a Communist representative, while she was the chairman of the Guomindang party in China. She never crossed this line either, and the delicate playing out of their roles was part of their closeness. Sometimes when Zhou came to her birthday party, he would first talk with her and then take Liao aside to ask him to make a request of her officially. "There would have been no fighting in China," Wai used to joke, "if the relationship between the Communist party and the Guomindang party were as harmonious as that between Amah and her son."

As we traveled, Amah dictated to her secretary a speech for one of the upcoming national congresses, while Liao sat near her, pouring tea and helping her remember names and organizations that would need to be mentioned. After lunch, she napped, and then she and the grown-ups played mah-jongg while we, in her sitting room, played baccarat.

It was a chilly February morning when we at last stood before Liao Zhongkai's tomb, next to Sun Yatsen's. For Amah it was an emotional farewell. It was the anniversary of her husband's assassination, and she wept as she approached the tomb in her wheelchair, flowers resting in her lap. We all stood in a straight row and bowed three times. Amah moved her lips and said something that we could not understand or that she did not want want us to hear. Liao and Kaisun came up to her then, lifting her so she could lay down her flowers. We bowed three times again as we left.

She turned to me and in her Cantonese accent softly said, "Next time I will be here lying with him. I will not come again."

As Liao had observed, she was gentle yet ferocious. "Amah will never take you to the zoo to see real lions and tigers," Liao said one day. "She is too scared of them."

"I like mine better," she quipped, but with a fierce determination in her eye as she paused before unleashing her next brushstroke. "I didn't go to the Berlin zoo in 1928, when I first could have seen real ones. No need."

Partly because she had been born to such privilege, it was easier for me to identify with her than with the other women I knew in China. Perhaps it was also the way she seemed to balance so many opposites: frail in appearance but strong inside, soft-spoken yet capable of erupting in fury, kind but capable of merciless scorn; although she complained incessantly about Liao's absences, there were no tears at all if the parting was judged necessary.

Her favorite stories were about Sun Yatsen, whom she adored, and Jiang Jieshi, whom she disdained. She and her husband had met Sun in Japan and had been quick converts to his political faith. As Qing Dynasty spies were everywhere, Sun often held meetings in their home in Tokyo. Having survived various attempts on his life, Sun trusted few people. Amah had to take over her maid's tasks when Sun was there; he wanted no one in the house who might overhear what was said. Consequently, this most privileged lady had to learn to cook while coping with her infant daughter. She had never even learned how to boil water—each time she would spill some and extinguish the gas fire. Sun was enormously amused, calling her *Ah Ba Sang*, "Old Mama" in Japanese.

Eventually she learned to perform the cooking, the cleaning, the organizing of the daily details of life, as well as the revolutionary work. "We can change," she would say. "We can all change."

Memories came flooding back on that trip. "There was Chen Jiunming," she said when I asked about some of her conflicts with the Guomindang.

Liao stepped in to tell the story. "Chen Jiunming was a leading southern warlord who had been an earlier supporter of Sun," Liao said. "But he turned and dispatched several thousand troops to shell the palace in Guangzhou where Sun and his wife were staying. When they escaped Chen, in his disappointment, had my father arrested."

Liao's mother listened quietly.

"Then the news came that Chen's own brother had been killed in Hong Kong, and Chen suspected that it was in reprisal for my father's arrest. He invited Mother to see her husband and she went, though expecting it to be a trap. When she arrived she was allowed to see Father for only a second, during which time he tried to thrust two farewell poems, one written for me, the other for my sister Mengxing, into her hands. The five guards immediately rushed them, pistols drawn, prepared to shoot.

"I asked them," Amah interjected, " 'What are you waiting for? Go ahead and shoot me.' "

Liao went on. "The guards were taken aback, and Amah snatched the poems from his hand and walked back to the waiting area outside Chen's office. She had gotten soaked in the rain, and Chen appeared with a glass of brandy, asking her into his office. She took the glass, drank it at one gulp, but refused to enter. So Chen suggested she change out of her wet clothes."

"I told him that was not what I had come for," Amah said.

"You can imagine how ferocious and angry she was," Liao continued. " 'What crimes has my husband committed? You have arrested him because he has raised funds for Dr. Sun. Didn't Zhongkai also raise funds for you in the past? I have no intention of leaving here. You can chop me into a thousand pieces, but I'll stay until I get a clear answer from you. Are you going to kill Zhongkai, or are you going to release him? If you want to kill us, all right, go ahead!' "

Liao looked at his mother before he went on. "Chen's guards rushed forward, trying to calm her. But of course she did not stop. 'If you want to release him, let him go home with me now. If not, shoot him here in my presence. But don't play any games with me and pretend you are going to release him when you plan to shoot him in the back.' "

I knew the story's end. Chen had released Liao's father. She had shamed him, and in front of others. Because he knew that she and Liao had helped him on the way up, for a brief moment he had relented. Amah had had the sense to arrange for their immediate flight to Hong Kong. Sure enough, that night, Chen had sent his troops to seize them once again.

The story Amah told the most was not this one. It was of Sun Yatsen's death in 1925. He had gone to Beijing to negotiate a new alliance and there had fallen ill with cancer. She went to be with him as he lay dying. He had summoned her, calling for her officially as Madame Liao Zhongkai in a way he had never done before. She and Sun's wife came to his bedside.

"He took my hand, shook it, then held it for several minutes," Amah said. "I've always remembered what I promised him. 'Although my faculties are limited, I understand your spirit and the revolutionary goals you have set for the Guomindang. I vow to adhere to your principles and will do my best to look after Madame Sun.' "

Sun was quiet for some time. Then he rallied. "Madame Liao Zhongkai, I thank you—peace. Struggle to save China."

Those were his last words to her; he died early the next morning. She wept as she told the story now, as she did each time she told it. For her it was the beginning of an even more terrifying unfolding of events—the murder of her husband, the struggles to save her children, the staggering suffering involved in finding some way out of China's deepening darkness.

She never told me the story of her husband's murder. That was too painful. However, Liao, whose life had been shaped by it, spoke of it often.

His mother and father had gone together to attend a Guomindang Central Committee meeting in Guangzhou. As they got out of the car, Amah had gone to greet a woman leader. She heard two shots, turned around, and saw her husband lying in a growing pool of blood. The shots continued, bullets flying over her head as she ran to him. He died minutes later, on the way to the hospital. It had been a trap; none of the key right-wing members had appeared—not Hu Hanmin, the leader of the Western Hills faction of the Guomindang rightists, nor Generalissimo Jiang Jieshi. Neither had Wang Jingwei, nominally in the Left Guomindang.

"I was determined from then on to avenge my father's death," Liao told me. "Mingxing and I led her up to the coffin, where she dried her tears and said her farewell."

Her life had seen little peace in the years that followed. Liao told me of his own deepening commitment, his joining of the Communist party, and his years in and out of prison. Neither he nor his mother held Jiang directly responsible for the assassination of his father. Jiang knew of the intention to do the deed, Liao said, but he was not directly involved in the murder. He could have prevented it, but only in that way was he responsible.

Amah had no respect for Jiang, who had "dared" to put her son in prison and prevented her from visiting him. She often spoke of the times she had gone to see Jiang. "I am here to see Jiang Jieshi," she'd announce—not President Jiang or Generalissimo, no title at all, just his name. When the guard became threatening, she'd say, "Go and tell him who I am before you do anything to me you will regret."

In this world of Chinese politics, I was learning, Jiang had been shamed. Not because he was indirectly tied to Liao Zhongkai's death, but because he had wronged this woman who had help him in the past and even raised funds for him.

"How dare you?" she had said to Jiang. "How dare you betray me and take my child away! Give him back to me!"

Jiang towered above her; she was just over four feet.

"Look into my eye!" she said to Jiang as he glanced away. With that forceful fury she had triumphed. But it was the way she successfully combined it with classical Chinese elegance and gentleness that moved me most.

CHAPTER 9

A Family Reunion

"I HAVE NEWS ABOUT YOUR FATHER," Liao said. He arrived unannounced late one night in the fall of 1963, just as we were going to sleep.

"Premier Zhou was finally able to have friends in Thailand visit him in prison. He is doing well. Zhou told your father that you are fine, and he sent his own warm greetings from the Chinese government."

His smile grew even wider as he handed us a letter. "It's from your father."

Wai and I read it again and again. We had waited five years to hear from him. The note was brief, but his good spirits came through.

"That you are doing so well pleases me no end and is a great solace to me," he wrote. "I have been deeply touched by Premier Zhou's friendship. Such steadfast friends have been hard to find even among my compatriots."

Liao gave Wai and me a big hug. "Your father is a true friend of China. We shall help him. Premier Zhou told your father through our intermediary that he will do all he can to help your family keep its head above water."

"Will you be able to continue to reach Father?" Wai asked.

"From now on we shall be able to take notes back and forth. You may write to him now."

More than notes followed. No longer totally cut off in his prison cell, Father was becoming politically active once again. Neither Wai nor I fully sensed the immediate reverberations of Father's being back in touch until Chareon Kanokratana stopped by. We had not seen him since those early days when he had brought us to China and occasionally visited before Father's fall from power. He had fled Thailand after the coup; his name was on the proscribed list, and he had been a political refugee in India for five years. Wai and he had kept in touch. Until now, though, his letters had been little more than friendly communications.

Chareon marveled at how grown up we seemed, and yet our house, the staff, it all seemed the same. He admitted how anxious he had been bringing us from Thailand. "Your father entrusted me with you. I dreaded that I might fail or something would happen to you. I was so relieved when we reached China."

Wai and I both laughed, although not without embarrassment, about our first few months in Beijing.

"What difficult children you were," Chareon said. "When your Chinese teacher used to come to me and weep over her inability to manage you, it was hard to know what to do. Not easy for her, not easy for you. Every day she came. I'm glad to see so many of your father's hopes have been realized and that this work has gone on." And he told us the details of Aree's first visit and of his early trips back and forth between Rangoon and Bangkok.

Chareon came to the point. "Your father has had many years in jail to think over the political events that have shaped recent Thai history." One great problem, he said, was the bitter struggles that had kept apart the two great leaders, Marshal Pibul and Dr. Pridi. Why not, at last, a reconciliation? This, he said, was my Father's hope.

It was a jarring thought. We had grown up in a world defined by the division between these two men.

We discussed the implications of Father's ideas for hours, and Wai and I continued on into the night after he left. Wai, of course, had followed Thai politics more closely than I. I knew Pridi's daughter from the music conservatory, but though Pridi had been living in exile in Guangzhou, we had not met him. I thought of him as an old statesman, part of Thailand's history. Now Father was saying to Pridi that it was time to overcome his differences with Pibul for the sake of Thailand's future. Pibul himself was in exile in Japan. Since Father was Pibul's closest political associate, his proposal would be seen as a clear initiative from Pibul himself.

Following appropriate protocol, Chareon informed Liao's office that he would like to go to Guangzhou to meet, and pay his respects to, Dr. Pridi. I talked with Zhou as well. The Chinese had no objections; such a reconciliation was a question of Thailand's internal politics. Chareon left a few days later for the south. He returned several weeks later full of news of his discussions with Pridi. The years had dealt kindly with Pridi. Alert and vigorous, he spent much of his time keeping well informed on Thai affairs. His years of exile had not embittered him, and despite having been forced into exile, he was open to an approach from Father and Pibul. For three days and nights Pridi had asked Chareon questions. He had weighed the pros and cons very carefully, and finally he had accepted. He agreed to wipe the slate clean and work with Pibul.

Chareon told us he himself was off to Hong Kong. He would contact our mother and wait for Father's response. Back came the message: Mother herself would speak to Pibul on Father's behalf. She would take my middle sister, Pongsri, to continue her studies in Japan under Pibul's care. As a businesswoman, she had once again resumed her travels, working to provide for the family as best she could. If anyone could reach Pibul, Father had reasoned, Mother could.

"Your mother will be coming to Hong Kong," Liao called to say one day. "Why don't you go down and see her?"

I cried for joy. We had not been out of China for seven years, and Wai and I had not seen Mother for almost as long. Wai was delighted, perhaps hoping this might be a step toward our eventual return home.

Along with the joy, though, I felt a growing uneasiness. Hong Kong loomed as a frightening world of thieves and pickpockets.

Spies and gangsters lurked in evrey dark corner, I feared. Someone would surely try to take us and drag us away. The various degradations of the outside capitalist world had been repeatedly depicted in movies I had seen and stories I had heard.

I had no passport; it had long since expired. I would be traveling without its protection.

I kept such fears to myself, saying nothing to Liao. When Zhou's office called to say we should be ready to leave in the morning, I was truly frightened. At breakfast at Liao's house the next day, Liao was clearly oblivious to my worries.

Putting his hand on my shoulder, Liao explained that Uncle Shanan would take us down to Guangzhou, arrange all the necessary documents, and then accompany us to the border at Shenzhen. "Simply follow his instructions, and all will go well. Nothing to worry about."

What were these necessary documents? I wondered.

"I have told people in Hong Kong to look after you and to provide you and your mother with protection. But you still have to be very careful and avoid arousing any suspicion."

I was excited but not convinced.

When I returned home, Wai and Shanan were waiting. I had not seen Shanan for several months. It had been a long time since we had needed him to shepherd us through our domestic crises and adjustments to Chinese society. We saw him now mostly on special occasions. His reappearance indicated how seriously Zhou took the implications of a reconciliation between Pibul and Pridi for the future of Thai politics.

Once off the plane, we were taken to a secluded guest house set beside a quiet lake and surrounded by trees. It had once been Jiang Jieshi's local headquarters, Shanan told us, pointing out the rooms Jiang had used. Final arrangements for us to cross the border would take a few days. In the meantime we would pay our respects to Dr. Pridi and his family.

We were driven to Pridi's villa the next day. Once the residence of the British consul general, it had a decidedly Western feel to it. It was located among other villas along the shore of the island of Shamien, where the Western elite had once thrived. The area was quiet and secluded, with huge banyan trees shading the water's edge where Pridi's house was perched.

His wife, Lady Poonsuk, was at the door to welcome us. She was warm and vivacious, and upon receiving our Thai greeting, she took us in to see Pridi in his sitting room. His room was cluttered with newspapers and books—they lay on the tables and chairs, even spread out on the floor. In the middle of it all, in a large chair, sat Pridi. He rose as we entered. I had seen his pictures over the years but never met him, of course. He was striking in person and a very fit sixty-three-year-old. He exuded both a certain reserve and a kind of wisdom. Wai was excited to meet him; he had by now read a good deal of Pridi's writings and knew his role in Thai history well. His wife came from a very old and wealthy aristocratic family in Thailand; Pridi, by contrast, had been a poor boy from Ayudthaya Province. They seemed devoted to each other, as though the fifteen-year exile in China had served only to bring them closer.

In the following days, Wai and I dropped over every afternoon to talk. Pridi asked us for all the news about Father and what his life was like in jail. He was grieved by what had happened to Father and other Thai intellectuals, many of whom were his old friends. He was also uneasy about the escalating war in Vietnam.

Pridi spoke with great precision. He never expressed the slightest hostility to Pibul. When Pibul's name came up, he always referred to him by his proper name or as "His Excellency." From his own experience, he undoubtedly knew the toll Pibul's exile was taking.

Our discussions ranged widely. Pridi and Wai discussed the Great Leap Forward. Pridi looked at what had happened from the perspective of a technical economist, which he was; the enormous problems had not surprised him. He was grateful to the Chinese, who had provided for him for so long. His spirit, though, remained in Thailand. He knew about us and about our trip to see our mother. He had carefully weighed the full implications of my father's proposal.

"Let bygones be bygones," he finally said. "Would your mother tell His Excellency that?"

Between the talks we toured the city, sometimes with Madame Pridi. We also took a crash course in Cantonese.

"You have to be able to answer a few basic questions in Cantonese," Shanan warned us. "The Hong Kong passport control at the border will interview you in Cantonese."

China and England, I learned, had a special agreement so that Guangzhou residents approved by Chinese authorities could visit relatives in Hong Kong. Minimal Cantonese was required for anyone going this route. So after a few more days, and in possession of some Cantonese words, we said good-bye to Pridi and his wife, boarded the train with Shanan, and arrived in Shenzhen to spend the night.

The next morning Shanan introduced us to a "Mr. Liu," who wore the white uniform of the China Travel Service. He greeted us warmly and explained, as had Shanan, that he was to walk us over the bridge that constituted the border. There we would pass through British passport control.

I peered at the soldiers and police on the other side. They were dressed differently; their weapons protruded ominously. "You will have no problems," Shanan had said.

Though Mr. Liu walked by my side, I couldn't stay calm. With each step I felt more panicked and disconcerted. I wasn't sure why; I knew that the Hong Kong officials had been taken care of—they would simply pass us through.

On the other side, I was separated from Wai and Mr. Liu and taken into a small room. A border official asked me something. I assumed it was my name. "Lim Fantan," I answered. As I did, a man in civilian clothes entered and helped me with the questions. I breathed more easily. I explained in my broken Cantonese that my grandmother was seriously ill and that I wanted to visit her. They let me go.

As I walked out, a voice said, "Come back."

I turned. Someone else had emerged—a huge, stern-faced British official stood there, eyes unflinching, face set, just staring at me. He asked me my name and age and my reasons for visiting Hong Kong.

I could make only the briefest answers with my few Cantonese phrases. No sooner had I finished answering one question than he asked me all over again. Again and again. He didn't seem interested in ending the all-but-incoherent discussion.

He was not the friendly Hong Kong official I'd been promised. As I stuttered on, though, I noticed that the translator had now stepped in and was effortlessly passing on my broken Cantonese into seemingly fluent English. As he did, the English official's face slowly relaxed. I knew I couldn't be silent, but freed from the need to speak Cantonese I went on in a jumble of Mandarin and Cantonese. The translator talked smoothly after each of my nonsensical recitations.

The English official finally waved me on and I crossed the bridge.

Wai was waiting anxiously. "Hard, very hard," I mumbled, as Mr. Liu whisked us to a train for the journey to Kowloon. I said little. On the train I sat gazing out the window, memories flooding back as I saw the peddlers selling sweets I'd had as a child. Mr. Liu bought us some and a Coke. We had no money of our own. I ate and drank quietly until the train pulled into the Kowloon station.

Immediately upon leaving the station, one sees the skyscrapers of Hong Kong. Wai was thrilled; I was intimidated but curious. Mr. Liu, however, didn't stop for a moment. He took us straight to a nondescript building that seemed modest but adequate as a place to stay. He introduced us to a short, middle-aged "Mr. Wong," who wore a perpetual smile. In the days that followed I found it hard to remember his name, probably because I knew that, like Mr. Liu's, it was fake. Wong, I sensed immediately, was a senior cadre from Beijing: he said little except that Liao Gong had asked him to take care of us. "It is a very great honor to do so," he said. He mentioned Liao with great respect and seemed to know I had somehow grown up in his family. "You are very fortunate to be under his care and guidance," he said in one of his brief comments.

For five days we stayed in our room. We were not allowed to go out by ourselves for any reason. Carefully chaperoned, we went shopping a few times and bought some clothes, though Mother, I felt sure, would be loaded with Thai outfits for us. The streets of Hong Kong intimidated me with their signs and their noisy bustle. I preferred to wait in the room. Boring but safe, I thought. Wai, however, felt at home instantly.

When I opened the door to a knock on the fifth morning, Mother stood there, looking much the same as I remembered her. Wai and I, now nineteen and fifteen, could not have looked like the children she had left seven years earlier. She hugged us each for a long time, then took us by the hand and led us to the room she had taken down the hall. As we entered, from out of the closet leaped my two sisters, shrieking and laughing with delight. There stood Tukta, though I would not have recognized her if we had passed on a Hong Kong street. Pongsri was much bigger, of course, but otherwise not so changed. We hugged and hugged, and the four of us danced in a circle as Mother stood to the side, smiling tearfully.

We talked in her room, catching up, for the next four days. Wai hungered for news about all that was happening with his old friends. I liked snuggling up with Mother and my sisters, avoiding any thought of our having to separate in a few days. As I expected, Mother had come with bags full of Thai clothes, books, food—anything she could think of to please us. She didn't say much about the hardships of the last five years. She preferred, as she so often did, to talk about small things, to hear about our daily life.

It was Pongsri who told me how soldiers had broken into our house and ransacked the place, and how shortly thereafter Father had turned himself in and been sent to prison. Pongsri described how Mother had gone to the prison almost every day, taking food for Father and other political prisoners. Man often went with her—it was the second time he had lived through this, having been old enough to remember visiting Father in his "school for politicians" after the war.

Mother was more spirited than I had remembered. "I am used to life with your father. It was always up and down since I married him. Perhaps now we are on the way up. Who would have dreamed that all of us would be meeting this way?

"Our family survives," she said sadly, "but we must remain apart. You and Wai are to stay in China. Man is now in America. And Pongsri I am taking to study in Japan; Pibul assures me she will be well taken care of.

"Children," she said late one night, "I have never cried in front of your father—and I do not want to do so in front of you." She found it hard to speak of our past, and she did not wish to hear of the difficulties of our years in China. Repeatedly she spoke of her relief at hearing how Zhou had taken care of us; that had kept Father going in his darkest moments.

She gave Wai and me two letters from Father—one for us, one for Zhou. In ours Father stressed how important our role in China was to him and how proud he was of us. There was no question in his mind but that we would remain there.

"For all those long years your father was cut off in prison. I could visit, but we had no way to contact you, no one to turn to in Thailand to help us. We had no idea whom to trust. Even your father's closest foreign friends didn't make efforts to see him. But one day when I came he was transformed with excitment. He had to speak quietly, but he told me someone had just been there. He didn't even know the visitor's name. The man had appeared at the cell door without any announcement. 'I have come on behalf of Premier Zhou,' he said.

"Your father must have looked astonished; he still did when I saw him. 'The premier has great admiration for your fighting spirit,' this man told Father. 'He is very sorry that it has taken us so long to get in touch with you. Your family must have been in great difficulty. Your children in China are doing well. If I can do anything to help, please let me know. I will contact you when I can.' "

The man, it seems, had said little more than that and had left soon after, but he had returned several times and had promised to continue to do so regularly. Father would be able to send us letters through this man, who remained unnamed.

Mother, as we knew, was on her way to talk with Pibul about a reconciliation with Pridi. Father was confident that the old compatriots could become friends again. I understood what bringing Pridi and Pibul together meant; the two halves of the political world I had grown up in would at last be reunited. They agreed far more than they disagreed about what policies were in Thailand's true interests.

We discussed Pridi's past, his anti-Japanese, antifascist stance, and the question of Father's role in the Japanese war inevitably came up.

Why, I asked Mother, was Father pro-Japanese?

"We were not pro-Japanese," she said firmly. "Your father hated the Japanese. But what could we have done? They had infiltrated everywhere. If we had taken up arms, it would have been a disaster. There would have been too many lives wasted. Thailand was harmed far less than its neighbors. It was a life under shame—that is what it was, a life under shame. But we preserved ourselves. Your father is as committed today to retaining Thailand's independence from any foreign power as he was then. That is why he is so committed to reconciling Pibul and Pridi. Both men embody that independence."

I was quieted by this. This was a much more politically articulate mother than I had grown up with.

For the next few days, we took excursions in Hong Kong, going to the Tiger Balm Park and the dolphin show and hunting for books for Father. But mostly I just enjoyed being part of a family again. As Mother began making preparations to leave, I remained outwardly cheerful in imitation of her. She had told us her cheerfulness was partially an act, but she expected it of us now as well. Most of the time I managed, but at night, cuddled up next to her, I fought back the tears. "There's one less day for us to be together."

"But soon we will be together again, believe me," she said with a strong voice. "We'll meet again, children." My heart sank each time I heard this.

To say good-bye alone would have been too painful, so in the end we did it in front of our Chinese hosts. Mother asked them to thank Premier Zhou and Liao for making the reunion possible, as well as for all that they were doing. They assured her they would.

"Father puts all his hopes in you because you have grown up in China," she said. Then she was gone.

Wai and I returned, subdued, to Guangzhou the next day. Mr. Wong wished us well, and Mr. Liu of the Travel Service reappeared to take us back. This time there was no imperious British official. Wai forgot to respond to his Cantonese name, but Mr. Liu simply nudged him and a minimal response was all that was needed. Mr. Liu left us then, saying we should "pick up a message upstairs." The Chinese customs officers took us into a room where Shanan and a few local officials awaited us.

It was strange to be back in China, disorienting to have lived in my family only to be cut off again. At first I had trouble telling Shanan about our trip. Wai did far more of the talking. This was official business, and that he always handled well.

That night Wai and Pridi discussed Mother's trip. Wai relayed Father's best wishes to him from Mother and told him that she was shortly to see Pibul in Japan. Pridi listened attentively, nodding approval. He and Pibul were consummate politicians; they understood each other very well.

"And how did you like capitalist society?" he asked with a laugh. Wai had loved it, and while he spoke of its attractions, I thought of the family warmth we had left behind.

When we returned to Beijing, I took Father's letter to Zhou.

"Many of my close friends," he wrote to Zhou, "have ignored me in these years. But you came to me and helped. Your help has sustained my spirit and determination. I thank you as a younger brother to the elder. My children have grown up well with your care. My heart is filled with gratitude to you and your government. In my gloomy days, they are my source of strength; your support has become my courage. Thank you with all my heart."

Zhou read Father's letter, then patted my hand, saying, "He is a man of great courage. I hope he will soon be out and contributing more to his country."

For a month we heard nothing. Then Chareon called—he was back in Beijing. He had gone to Japan via Hong Kong, and now he was full of excitement. He and Mother had spent four days talking with Pibul and his wife. Pibul evidently looked very fit and relaxed from his years of exile in Japan.

Chareon told us the details of what had happened to Pibul since he fled Thailand in September 1957. He had gone first to Cambodia, where Prince Sihanouk and his wife, Monique, had greeted him as an old friend. He had stayed there for three months, then gone on to Tokyo, where he established a residence, and to the United States, a country he had long wanted to understand better. After a year of traveling there, he returned to Japan, settling into a permanent residence in Sagamihara. He and his wife had learned Japanese together. Pibul still played golf, indulged his fascination with fast cars, and, all in all, seemed to be enjoying his retirement, spending his afternoons in his beautiful Japanese garden and his evenings listening to the world radio services.

Father had been right, though. Mother's visit aroused Pibul from his political lethargy. He had known her well, and the old tie with Father seemed to galvanize him once again. Pibul was deeply distressed about what was happening in Thailand and neighboring Indochina. After many days of talk, Pibul said he, too, wanted to put the bitterness of the past with Pridi behind him. "Let us start afresh," he told Mother. Pibul had asked Chareon to convey a message to Pridi, recalling their days together in France and urging that they set aside their past disagreements.

Over the next nine months or so, Chareon came and went. Pridi was elated by Pibul's message, and as Father's letters increased, so did Chareon's trips between Guangzhou and Tokyo. Mother traveled back and forth frequently now. The upshot was the electrifying news that Pibul himself would come to China and see Pridi.

We waited excitedly for word of the final details. It was June, and he would be arriving soon. Wai and I were in China because of Pibul; some of my happiest moments were associated with him. He had asked Mother all about us, and it was likely that we would see him.

The news came with shattering abruptness. Pibul was dead. The death was quick, its cause unclear. Few Chinese officials thought it was natural; nor, as I later learned, did Pibul's family. A reconciliation of Pibul and Pridi threatened the status quo of Thai politics.

The days of the Bangkok-Tokyo-Guangzhou triangle came to an abrupt end. Pibul's stature and his continued hold on Thai politics were evident in the royal reception when his casket arrived back in Bangkok: there was a three-army salute, and an honor guard accompanied it from the airport. Now that Pibul was dead, the question of what to do with Pongsri arose. Without a guardian in Japan, she and Mother decided that for the time being Pongsri should go to China if Zhou agreed. He did so readily. Late in 1964 she came, and shortly thereafter Tukta did as well.

My sisters moved into our house with us and entered Chinese schools, studying as we had. Indeed, as I watched them struggling to cope, I came to understand better the distance I had traveled into China. With few of their old amusements at hand, they were bored. They missed their pretty little things, and the weather seemed to them mercilessly cold. They hated the heavy padded jackets. Wai and I laughed when we saw how unimpressed they were by what we had come to like. My favorite Dongsi market they found uninteresting; I now loved its Chinese art and the countless things that could be transformed into something of use. I enjoyed the challenge of going to the department store and figuring out how to get what I needed; Tukta was baffled by my enthusiasms—having seen the big department stores in Japan, she found those in China wanting. She and Pongsri did not regard the movies as entertainment. They couldn't eat the food; they missed their sweets and snacks. There was no rice ice cream, Tukta's favorite. They found it hard to eat the food in the canteen, so they took their own lunches to school, and often Tukta joined Pongsri at the Friendship Hotel, where the food was more to their taste.

Most of all, they felt differently than Wai and I did about being in China. They were not a bridge; they were merely privileged foreign students. They moved far more in the world of foreigners than we ever had. The Chinese had less reason to worry over their security, and in any case our being in China was no longer considered quite such a secret, though our relation to Zhou was always a matter of great discretion.

CHAPTER 10

Prince Kazu

"LIAO IS PLANNING TO TAKE a foreign friend to a private meeting with Chairman Mao," Zhou said. He had taken me aside at Amah's birthday party. "If the meeting takes place," Zhou continued, "I will ask Liao to bring you along. It will probably be shortly before National Day."

Zhou sometimes told me the most important things in the briefest, most casual way.

The visitor's trip was secret, he stressed. But I would find the talk revealing of the way China wished to deal with its neighbors. "I want you to listen carefully. We can discuss it afterward. I think you'll find it interesting."

The children of the Chinese leaders saw Mao on various formal occasions and sometimes, in earlier years, informally, around the pool or on the reviewing stand in Tiananmen Square. He was "Uncle Mao." None that I knew, however, had sat in on one of his discussions. I spoke to no one about it, and nothing more was said to me for weeks.

Liao simply called one morning and asked me to come to his house. We left immediately in his limousine, curtains drawn.

"We are going to Chairman Mao's residence," he said.

"You should have warned me earlier," I said excitedly. Even the name of the building where Mao lived was intriguing: the Library of Chrysanthemum Scent.

"No, I couldn't. The time of the meeting was only fixed two hours ago."

The top meetings were always planned this way.

"Premier Zhou will not be at the meeting," Liao continued. "Only our foreign guest, the translator, you, and I."

I had seen Mao relaxing—swimming in the pool, dancing at the parties, standing on Tiananmen Square to review proceedings. And of course I saw his picture everywhere, Mao the great revolutionary leader. But Mao in his official role, Mao sitting among all his books talking with visitors, I saw only in the *People's Daily*.

I calmed myself by gazing at the familiar settings as the car wound its way slowly past the lake and the beautiful hanging willows Zhou so loved. Then it turned in a new direction, toward Mao's house. As the car pulled up to the stairs, two men ran down to open the door. We were led inside and quietly ushered into Mao's giant study, where we met the interpreter. Mao, it seemed, loved space; the room, with its high ceilings, had something mysterious and awesome about it. A gigantic table was piled high with documents and old Chinese books lying half open. A few boxes of ink were next to a cluster of Chinese brushes, and everywhere there were fine Chinese books. Like the home of a court official, it seemed a part of old China, its books suggestive of ancient wisdom.

The foreign guest arrived, and we spoke quietly as we waited for Mao. Then I heard his slow, steady, heavy footsteps. He entered flanked by protocol people, who discreetly assisted him to his big settee; and then disappeared behind a closed door. Even in so huge a space, it was impossible not to perceive the enormity of his presence. He was simply dressed in the most ordinary Zhongshan clothes and cloth shoes. For the next few hours, he was rarely without a cigarette.

Mao and Zhou were an extraordinary contrast. Zhou was all charm, his movements as elegant as those of a Beijing Opera performer. He knew just where to put his feet, his hands. Mao was a block of iron; he simply sat there, stolid. He would inhale deeply, apparently in profound thought, and blow out as though the thoughts themselves were emerging on his breath. When he spoke in his deep voice, with its Hunan accent, his words seemed almost caught inside his mouth, so that his interpreter had to reach down and pull out one by one. He didn't speak very loudly; perhaps that was why as a child I had noticed his black teeth, watching as I did to see how his words could be coming from so deep inside. He would observe as his words were translated, as though thinking with his eyes.

Although he was soft spoken, he used graphic, earthy expressions. For several hours his ideas and comments seemed to pour forth endlessly, mesmerizing me as much as the guest. His brain, I began to think, seemed a presence all its own—as if he had already become the Lord Buddha, somehow above the world, always seeing something in its widest scope, seeing problems as minor ones in the great cosmic scheme of things.

The Mao I knew of was Mao the great leader, the great theorist of the revolution, the great Communist theoretician. In private, I thought, he must surely be a serious man who spoke big words and big theory. But this Mao was nowhere in sight. In two hours he never mentioned a single theory, a single article of dogma. He seemed totally unconfined in his thinking—entertaining first one thought, then another. His calmness was extraordinary; and somehow I sensed in it an awesome ability to make people yield to him. One immediately perceived the power Mao had to rule over people. In this meeting he seemed entirely in his element, at ease with himself and his world.

When the visitor asked, not disinterestedly, if there were any chance for improved relations between the United States and China, I wondered if Mao would respond as had everyone else: the problems in the relationship, the character of American imperialism. That was the public message reiterated day after day and almost always heard in private as well.

Mao closed his eyes for a second, exhaled, then said, "If it were not possible, I wouldn't be sending my ambassador to talk with them every year in Warsaw."

He inhaled as his words were translated. "We are playing hide-

and-seek with America," he continued. "But we are not worried. We exist even without them. They're the ones who are worried."

The discussion turned to whether communism was on the agenda for the visitor's country.

"Why worry about it?" Mao said. "We certainly didn't want communism in China. We tried everything else. We tried peasant uprisings; they failed. We tried a bourgeois revolution with Sun Yatsen. But that didn't work either. So what to do? We tried various kinds of communism, too, various strategies. None worked. There really is no theory at all of what to do, no special theory at all. You have to think about the specifics of your own country. There is nowhere else to go."

The visitor commented on all the wonderful changes he had seen in China, but Mao waved his hand dismissively.

"We are not so clever," he said in a cheerful but slightly mocking tone. "Don't listen to all those people. They just trot out the good figures to impress you. When they ask you to go with them to visit someplace, believe me, they're putting their best foot forward. The achievement is not as great as you think. It's all been arranged beforehand for your benefit. Don't believe it for a minute."

And on he talked. He reminisced about the revolution and about the harsh times China had lived though—"those times when our troops had nothing to eat for days and days, and we had to boil shoes. Not like in the Charlie Chaplin movies you all laugh about. This was real life."

Mao never once spoke about his own personal history; there was nothing about his family or his hardships. "We" had been through this; "we" had struggled. Only once did he use the personal "I." "When I go to see Marx and Engels," he said simply, with a smile, "I will go with nothing."

Afterward, I recounted the conversation to Zhou. Mao had seemed so serene, so calm, floating over everything—no theory at all.

"That is what makes him such a good theorist," Zhou said.

As WE FINISHED OUR THIRD YEAR at the conservatory in the spring of 1963, it had become evident that Wai and I were not destined for great musical triumphs. Wai was increasingly interested in the study of philosophy, especially the translation of Chinese philosophy into Thai. I was not sure what to do. Liao said only that it was time to specialize a little more.

For Wai going on to Peking University made sense. But I had no particular ability as a scholar or interest in pursuing academic subjects. Zhou suggested another foreign language. I had already been studying Russian. What did he have in mind?

"English.. You should study English," he said. "The university's English department is extremely good." At a time when Russian was widely studied in China, Zhou urged me to put my energies elsewhere. "English will serve you better whatever you do with the rest of your life," he said.

Instructions were given to officials of the university, and Wai and I were admitted for the fall 1963 term. As with all my schooling, I was thrown into an environment where I was a complete novice. Those in the first-year English program at Peking University had already had three years of English at the middle school. So Zhou's office arranged for me to be tutored by one of the instructors, Teacher Meng, as I called him. For a month and a half, seven days a week, he taught me English every morning, giving up his summer holiday to do so. He was the son of a famous old capitalist who was a member of the Political Consultative Conference. Although he looked very much the part of the formidable old-style Chinese intellectual, his study was lined with pictures from his family travels in America and Europe. Within a few months I had at least a beginner's knowledge, and for the entire first year he nursed me through my courses.

Peking University was an enormous change for Wai and me. Neither the middle school nor the conservatory had many foreign students; at the university there were over two hundred foreign students. There were students from Vietnam, North Korea, the Soviet Union, Poland, Hungary, Bulgaria, Sudan, Sri Lanka, Nepal, Laos, and Cambodia, along with some from the former British, French, and Belgian colonies in Africa. Wai and I were the only students from Thailand, and some of the most politically astute students were astonished by our presence, given the hostility between China and Thailand. Their puzzlement was shared by others when they learned we came and went by private car and were seated next to Lu Ping, the president of the university, at receptions.

Wai and I lived in dormitories separate from the regular Chinese students' housing. By now we knew the explanation. The Chinese students were expected to be able to live a more spartan existence; our dorms had Western and Chinese food and fairly modern washrooms. Liao and others wanted us to live in relative comfort; they felt we could not easily forgo it. But foreigners were separated from Chinese students for other reasons. The Chinese authorities did not believe that foreigners could or should conform to the Chinese way of life. Further, they did not want to expose Chinese students to the way of life of the foreigners, some of whom smoked and drank and listened to rock and roll.

The foreign men lived in Dormitory Number 26, the women in Number 27. Each foreign student had a Chinese roommate, selected by the authorities for his or her political reliability and strength of character. These students were all members of either the Youth League or the Party—they were expected to help their foreign roommates understand China. I shared my room with only one other person. Ordinarily, there were three or four students to a room.

At nineteen, Wang Mei was four years my senior. She was protective and kind, treating me as though I were a younger sister. Her parents worked in a textile factory in Shanghai, and she had passed her entrance examinations (which Wei and I had been excused from) with high honors. Having already studied English for three years, she was picked in part so she could help me with my studies.

Wang Mei told me about her working-class family and her past, but she never asked a word about mine. She knew I was from Thailand; she knew I had connections. She did not know why, and she showed no curiosity about it. That, in those days, was the discipline Party members felt so proud to possess.

YEARS BEFORE, at the Bangkok airport, as I had boarded the plane that would take me to China, I had heard my aunt's voice in the background muttering with great concerns, "But who will tell her about her period?" She was right to wonder—no one ever spoke to me about reaching puberty. I had heard some talk by Shanan's wife and our cook's wife about women needing to have a checkup after they turned fifty so that they wouldn't have to worry about getting cancer of the womb. It was hard to get the facts straight, and in any case the wives were very discreet. So when my first period came, when I was twelve, I had no idea what was happening. It was the Chinese New Year, and I was at Liao's. As the festivities went on, I felt increasingly nauseated and peculiar. Everyone else was sitting around joking and drinking. Feeling sick, I went to the bathroom and was shocked by what I saw. I'm dying of cancer, I thought.

As I staggered out, Liao's wife saw me. What, she wanted to know, was wrong? I looked so pale, she said, taking me into another room. I said I had to go to the hospital right away. "I have cancer in the womb or, if not here, in the stomach," I sobbed.

"Nonsense," she said. "Whyever do you think that?"

I told her what had happened. She burst into great gales of laughter and assured me I shouldn't worry—she would explain as soon as she could stop laughing. Then Liao came in.

"What's the joke?" Liao asked. He loved hearing one almost as much as he loved telling one. At first he thought his wife was drunk, she was laughing so hard. He tried to calm her. When she uttered a few words in Cantonese, he started laughing as well but left quickly.

Finally, she took hold of herself and got some cotton. What had happened, she told me, was something that would happen every month from now on. That was about all she said; the rest was left unexplained. Except for the reassurance about the cancer, the news was not very comforting.

I told Wai. He immediately said that it was long past time for me to start observing certain rules of appropriate behavior between men and women.

"You must never touch a man's hand now," Wai said. "You must not do so, even playfully, or go too near men."

Evidently, this is how he thought girls in Thailand were meant to act. His idea was utterly foreign to the informal but nonsexual relations that existed between men and women in China. In Liao's circle it would have been odd to do as he suggested. Since Wai was seldom there, however, that was no problem.

At Peking University it was not difficult either, initially. I was too conflicted to show any interest in the other foreign students. If men smiled at me, I kept a straight face and walked by. Still, I began to dress more stylishly after years of opting for a more simple appearance. I let my hair grow longer. At the annual college gathering and dance, I sat at the head table but completely ignored any foreign students who came and asked for a dance. Wai had become quite possessive, and we usually had lunch and dinner together. His earnestness was matched by an unfailing capacity to make me—and others—laugh, and in his presence I felt less awkward. Weekends I liked to go home or to Liao's, where I could be affectionately called "little devil" again.

That winter Wai and I spent our vacation in Guangzhou to get away from the Beijing cold and to see Pridi. On the long flight back, Wai took his seat next to a stunningly beautiful Japanese lady. She was taller than most Japanese women I had seen and slim, with extraordinarily delicate features and a serene look.

As though I wouldn't have noticed, Wai whispered to me how beautiful she was. He had already said hello to her in Chinese, and she had smiled and responded in Japanese. I watched as she took out a letter to read, and I saw the name Saionji in Chinese. Liao had a friend named Saionji. His name appeared in the Chinese newspapers every time important Japanese visitors came to China and were received by Zhou or Liao. I was sure she was related to him. "He's a prince," Liao once said gaily. "I call him His Royal Highness."

When the plane went down in Zhengzhou, the three of us got off together to have lunch. Wai always liked to talk with good-looking women, and now he communicated with extravagant hand gestures. She laughed and did the same. She spoke not a word of Chinese, but Wai and I made ourselves understood by writing simple Chinese characters. That part was fun, and it broke up the monotony of the subsequent flight. We told her we had just begun studying at Peking University. Her son Kazu, she replied, was there studying economics. I said nothing about Liao.

At the airport in Beijing, I saw her in the arms of a young man who was the exact masculine replica of his mother: taller but delicate, handsome, gentle mannered. When he looked up and caught my eye, I blushed, embarrassed, and quickly truned my head away. He kept looking, and in my confusion, I walked to our car, which was waiting nearby, without even saying good-bye to his mother.

Wai hadn't noticed.

"What a coincidence," Wai said when he got into the car. "That's her son who's at Peking University. I thought he looked familiar when we got off the plane, but I couldn't quite place him."

I shrugged, as though indifferent, but that was not how I felt. Something about his demeanor—not just his appearance—was very attractive. And the person he most reminded me of in his elegance and bearing was Zhou.

What would I do if I bumped into him at school? Surely his mother had told him about her plane flight. But if he spoke to me, what would I say? I still barely spoke to any of the foreign young men. My reputation for coldness had been well established in Dormitory Number 26 in the three short months I had been at the university.

Wai and I noticed Kazu in the canteen the next day. He seemed to be looking our way, but he said nothing. Over the next few days, though, he started eating at our table and talking with Wai. Wai liked him, and they became more friendly in the weeks that followed, but there was no communication between Kazu and me. Wai evidently did not find this all that odd. He knew I always waited for foreigners to take the initiative. With the Chinese I did the opposite: I could easily be the first to start a conversation, to make a social overture.

Like Wai, Kazu loved sports, especially basketball, and he and Wai played for hours. At the school sports meet Wai competed in a foot-race, and Kazu was there to cheer him on. Together they played Ping-Pong, at which Kazu was particularly adept.

I'd watch the games and the Ping-Pong, but still nothing was said. He'd glance at me between serves, perhaps to see if I would smile, but I always looked away. At meals Wai relieved the tension with light conversation and his ready supply of jokes.

By now I knew who Kazu was. He came from a famous Japanese family whose head was the *genro*, the hereditary adviser to the emperor. Prince Saionji, Kazu's father, had been Liao's closest Japanese friend for many years; Liao loved talking with him in Japanese at their frequent breakfasts together. Prince Saionji's grandfather, Kazu's great-grandfather, had twice been prime minister of Japan.

Prince Saionji himself had been educated at Oxford. He had bitterly defied his father, openly rebelling against the strict Japanese social code by marrying an extraordianarily beautiful geisha from the lowest social class. The family never accepted the marriage. He served in the Japanese government, visiting Nazi Germany and Soviet Russia as a member of a delegation headed by Foreign Minister Yosuke Matsuoka, and met both Hitler and Stalin. He later joined the peace movement and become involved in the historic Sorge case, in which a spy ring succeeded in informing Stalin (who ignored the information) of the exact plans for the German invasion of Russia. Because he was the only son of such a lofty family, he was the only one not executed for his alleged part in the Sorge affair. In the early 1950s he won the World Peace Movement gold medal. As the domestic political situation made his position in Japan difficult, he asked Zhou if he could come to China. Zhou and Liao warmly welcomed him, and he and his family came in 1958. They had remained ever since, although Madame Saionji spent half her time in China and half in Tokyo, where she kept an antiques shop.

I decided that Kazu was shy. I knew I certainly wasn't going to be the first to talk. If he took the initiative, though, I was going to respond.

A month passed, and I signed up for the annual Ping-Pong tournament between the Chinese and the foreign team. For many years Wai and I had played together at home. I often played at Liao's, too, Ping-Pong then being all the rage. Many of the old veterans, like Chen Yi and He Lung, loved to play. On Amah's birthday we had once organized tournaments, one for the veterans and one for the younger generation. Even Zhou had participated; though he could never straighten his right arm, he still managed. Zhu De and Chen Yi battled it out with He Lung, who emerged the champion.

Kazu came whenever I was scheduled to play. By the final match, the number of spectators had grown considerably. My Chinese opponent was very skilled. The game started, and I found myself looking around for Kazu in the dense crowd. He was standing with Wai; our eyes met. I was determined to do well.

When I won the first game, my brother ran up and kissed me. I was so surprised by winning that I was too nervous to win the second game. The audience was roaring its support—the foreigners, of course, for me, the Chinese for my opponent. While waiting for the last game to begin, I looked over at Kazu again, and he made a gesture to indicate that I should be hitting the ball to my opponent's left side. I decided to follow his advice. I played all the tricks Wai had taught me but aimed them to the left. I won.

To great applause I was declared the champion, the first foreigner ever to win. My brother walked up to me with Kazu a few steps behind. For the first time I smiled at him. Now he was the one who blushed, and when I turned back to look a moment later he was gone.

I rushed back to the dormitory to shower and dress so I could meet Wai and Kazu at our usual dinner table. People were shouting their congratulations as I entered the dining room. Kazu wasn't there. Every day for a month he had turned up, and yet now he had not. I forced myself to eat while Wai, ebullient, went on about my victory. I heard him ask someone where Kazu was. I sat quietly, not really understanding why my feelings should be so hurt—we had not even been formally introduced.

The next morning, having barely slept, I was at the canteen by dawn. Kazu was never up early, that I knew. After picking up my breakfast, I walked back to the table. There at my place was a small package addressed to Chang Yuan.

I opened it to find a finely carved silver box. "For the champion," the attached card said. With it was another congratulatory card with a large picture of a red rose and a bee. And inside the box, another note: "Sorry I could not join you at dinner last night. I went back home to tell my mother about the match and to get you this small souvenir. Kazu."

I sat through several classes that morning, but instead of taking notes I wrote Kazu's name over and over again. When would lunch finally come?

I rushed back to the canteen. Kazu was there, chatting animatedly with Wai. And yet I could think of nothing to say. Embarrassed, I sat and listened to Wai, who was still going on about the match. Finally I left—perhaps, I thought, that would offend Kazu and would end everything.

As I walked out of the dormitory a little later for my afternoon class, I almost bumped into him. He asked, "Going to class?"

"Yes," I replied. Then, with all my courage, I thanked him for the present.

He had to speak fast in the short distance we walked together. What time, he wanted to know, did I eat breakfast? When he came into the canteen the next morning, he barely looked up. We had a quick breakfast, and he asked to walk me to class. Walking through the door ahead of him, into the open, I saw out of the corner of my eye a smile of triumph on Kazu's well-shaped lips.

"The cherry blossoms in Tokyo are as beautiful as this," he said in a very serious tone of voice. It was one of the handful of days when the cherries were in full bloom, brightening the often drab Beijing landscape.

From then on he walked me every morning.

JUST AFTER SPRING FESTIVAL in 1964, the university held a dance for the foreign students. Knowing that I had never bothered to attend one in the past, Kazu asked me specially to come.

On the evening of the dance the dining room was turned into a glittering ballroom. Wai and I were seated at the head table where the president of the university and the leading faculty members sat. As soon as the music began, I looked up to see Kazu in front of me bowing and asking me to dance. I froze.

Then I heard Wai saying, "Why don't you give it a try? I feel like dancing, too."

Kazu led me out onto the dance floor. It was the first time we had touched, and I found the feel of his hands warm and reassuring. But I didn't dare look into his eyes. He held me tighter. My heart was pounding—hard enough, it seemed, that I couldn't hear the music or keep the beat.

"Like it?" he whispered in my ear.

I looked away but nodded. Then the music stopped and there was a chill as we drew apart. I felt unwell, and instead of returning to the table I headed for the cloakroom for my coat and left quietly by the back door. The cold night air helped; I tried to pull myself together as I walked. When I heard footsteps behind me, I hurried on, too fearful to look back. Then I heard his low voice calling me. I didn't say anything, but I slowed down and let him catch up to me. He stopped me, gently pulled me close to him, and told me he loved me, loved me more than anything else in the world. Did I love him? he wanted to know.

In the preceding weeks, we had begun to talk regularly on the phone. But the next day he did not call. I finally called him, but his mother answered and I couldn't understand anything she said. I didn't dare try again. Days passed. No news.

When Liao called and asked me to come right over, I was glad for the distraction. I had said nothing to him about Kazu, though, knowing Liao, I was sure he sensed something already.

"My little girl has grown up," he had joked one day. But he didn't push, and I felt uneasy about speaking about Kazu with anyone.

Liao was waiting in the entrance of the house when I arrived. "I want you to meet the wife of my best friend," he said with a broad smile.

He led me into the sitting room. There sat Kazu's mother, whom I had not seen since our plane ride. Liao introduced me to her in Japanese. She held out her hand, all smiles, and told Liao she had met me on the plane before.

"She would like you to go to her house with her," Liao said.

She led me out to the waiting car, and off we went. She tried to put me at ease with her friendly smile and gentle gestures, but I was very nervous. We drove to the old colonial section of Beijing and pulled into a quiet street. Passing through a large gate marked "World Peace Committee," we entered a large residential area where well-known foreigners like Anna Louise Strong and Rewi Alley lived. As the car drove up to the house, I kept wondering how much she knew of my relationship with her son. Neither Liao nor she had mentioned Kazu. Nor had Liao given me any idea why she had gone to the trouble of inviting me through him.

The house was decorated in a blend of Japanese and Chinese styles, except for the dining room, which was totally Japanese, with a mat and a low table. We passed Saionji's study; his books were neatly shelved. Without pausing, she led me straight to Kazu's room, where he was in bed, looking very sick. I hung back for a moment, but his mother led me forward. Then she turned and quietly left the room. I was no longer anxious, and when Kazu reached out and brought my hands up to his burning face, I felt happy but confused.

Kazu spoke shakily. "I'm going crazy. I can't think of anyone or anything else except you!"

I tried to pull away, but he begged me to stay close. "Tell me if you don't love me," he whispered.

I could say nothing. Certainly I could not say I didn't love him. I knelt next to his bed, placed my head on his chest, and for the first time hugged him tight. After a moment Kazu spoke again but in a stronger voice than before: he said he would ask his mother to ask Liao's permission for us to become engaged. He told me that he would marry me in Japan.

I felt a rare and elating sense of security. Yet I was too scared to tell Wai. If he was opposed, what would I do? Better to mention nothing. In China people didn't normally marry before they were twenty-six, it was said, though Liao himself had said that was too old for a woman. I didn't tell Liao. It never occurred to me to tell Zhou, either. Hadn't I learned it was best to keep some things to oneself?

Several days later, Kazu had made a full recovery. He spoke of my going back to Japan with him and learning Japanese. He also intimated that his father would strongly oppose any marriage to someone who was not Japanese. His mother, he said, would soon be talking with Liao.

Sure enough, on a Sunday afternoon in that spring of 1964, Liao's wife called to say that someone was waiting for me. This, I realized, must be the day.

Liao was sitting in his study when I arrived. I walked in apprehensively, and for once I did not look Liao in the eye. With him were Kazu and his mother. Liao reached out to pat me as he always did, then drew me closer to him.

"How come your hands are so cold?" he asked cheerfully.

Liao seemed completely relaxed. When I finally looked up into his eyes, I saw their usual warmth, and, reassured, I began to look quietly around. Kazu's mother had started to speak in Japanese. Liao interpreted and summarized.

"She would like you as her daughter-in-law," he said. "She says she will be very proud to have you."

I blushed when Liao spoke the word daughter-in-law. Liao seemed quite joyful about developments. He joked with Kazu and Madame Saionji in Japanese and then, smiling, turned to me. It was evidently Liao who had negotiated the formula: if I agreed, we were to be engaged. I would have to learn Japanese. Every Saturday and Sunday and during vacations, I would study with Kazu's mother, learning both the language and the customs of Japanese ladies.

Overwhelmed, I heard Madame Saionji ask if I wanted a ring. But in China, Liao was saying, that would not be appropriate. And since I was so very young, the engagement should be kept a secret. I had learned nothing about rings in China; it was unclear to me what they were discussing. To me an engagement meant that I could be with Kazu and not much more. That was what I wanted. The idea of living in Japan hardly registered. But everything seemed to have been fixed for me. Liao was so pleased with the match that he warmed up some Japanese sake and toasted our happiness.

For the next few months I visited Kazu's mother each weekend. Sometimes she came to my dormitory as well. The language was difficult, but I began to pick some of it up. The ceremonial aspects of proper Japanese behavior were stricter than the Thai, which had a sensuous quality I had only partly mastered. My years in China had not helped me develop its subtle ways. In China, women could talk slow or fast, and they tended to walk briskly; by Thai standards, I talked too fast and moved my head and feet too fast. Wai, having always thought I lacked enough of the appropriate Thai manner, liked my learning the Japanese customs. He did not, however, know of the engagement.

When Kazu's father, learned what was up, he was bitterly opposed. Married to a foreigner, his son could not play the role he envisioned for him. It would be too difficult for me to make a life in Japan. The union would not last.

When I met Kazu's father, he was polite. He bowed and shook my hand but gave no indication that he was treating me any differently than he would treat any other young woman he might meet.

AS THE WINTER OF 1965 APPROACHED, the public political rehetoric took on a chilling tone. At first it all seemed remote to me. Liao did not seem particularly concerned about it, nor did Zhou. The papers had been talking about "revisionism" for years, and the ever-escalating inflammatory language seemed to have little to do with my immediate world—except for Kazu. He and I had spoken of politics from the beginning: it was as much a part of his life as of mine. I never spoke very specifically, though, of my background, especially of my father, and knowing that I was under Zhou's organization, he also knew not to ask. In some ways, like Wai, he kept his relations with the Chinese correct and friendly, but he was in no way "family."

Kazu's elegance and grace tended to mask his strong political determination and convictions. In this too he reminded me of Zhou: dedicated, convinced that the world needed to be changed, but flexible and thoughtful. In late 1965 the latter qualities were becoming harder and harder for people to retain.

As a prince Kazu was coming under attack from Japanese students, who, like most other foreigners, were heavily influenced by Chinese ideological and propaganda lines. Unwillingly, he was subjected to the rising din of struggle meetings, his progressive leanings having made him vulnerable to charges of being a revisionist. Historically, of course, his family had actually been quite left-wing; the world of his detractors was his as well, and he did not wish to turn away from it. Increasingly, therefore, into our daily life and our relationship came the harsh language of betrayal, class origins, revolution.

Although he was an exile, Kazu maintained strong ties to Japan. And his attachments to the Japanese in China reflected his obligations not only to his father but to the world to which he would one day return. He had joined a Japanese youth group that studied Japanese newspapers and discussed Japanese political and economic issues, and he spoke Japanese with his family and others. He moved in a far more propagandized milieu than I ever did. Zhou had not brought me up that way; he and Liao had not wanted me to be directly influenced by that world.

The unrelenting propaganda barrages of various campaigns had been carefully screened out of the elite world in which I moved, and its intrusion now was disconcerting. I'd shuttled between both worlds and kept the two apart. But Kazu had not. The reigning slogans of the day spoke of going back to make revolution in one's own country; to those who envisioned such a role for Kazu, I hardly fit into the picture. And he, by the same token, was assumed to be ruining the plans of China's leaders for my own future revolutionary role in Thailand. To some, however aloof I might seem, my high connection could only mean I was being prepared for that role. Kazu, it was said, was threatening to undermine my future task.

As a consequence, the struggle meetings he attended, increasingly focused on our relationship. At the weekly sessions he was told that if he cared about his commitment the relationship would have to end. Kazu was careful never to say we were engaged; nor did he ever mention Liao. And about Zhou he himself never really knew much.

One night in early 1966, Wai asked Kazu to take me home from the university. The evening bus stopped at the Friendship Hotel, where many of the struggle meetings were held, and one of the people who had been attacking Kazu got on and came up to us. Kazu stiffened when he saw him and left me to go sit with him. By then Kazu may have promised to stop seeing me, and here he was caught with me. I didn't know the details; probably he was not supposed to tell me. But a few days after that chance encounter, Kazu told me I was to start coming to the meetings with him. That was their demand.

I was not involved in his groups and their politics, and I protested. I began to wonder if ours was to be one of the many stories I knew of personal relations forced to yield to the demands of political alliances. The unhappy tale of Liu Shaoqi's son was only one of the most prominent.

"Should I go to those meetings?" I asked Liao.

"That's nonsense," Liao said. "Whether the two of you are going to get married has nothing to do with going to meetings!"

I didn't go. Nor, it seemed, did Liao directly raise the issue of Kazu and me with his Japanese friends. That would not have been appropriate. Indirectly, he sent the clearest possible signal. "Kazu's girlfriend at the university is my adopted daughter," he told some of them.

It was not enough. Times were changing.

CHAPTER 11

"Principles Without Humanity"

"YOUR MOTHER WILL BE HERE SOON," Liao told me one weekend when I was visiting him. It was the middle of March 1966. "I'll let you know the details as soon as I can."

My sisters were delighted. Never having really been happy since they had come, they were homesick. Moreover, since Wai and I were seldom at home, they saw us only occasionally. Now they hoped to go home: life in Thailand had begun to change.

Sarit's death in July 1965 had eased the political climate somewhat, so that after being jailed for seven years, Father was finally summoned before a military tribunal on September 9, 1965. His became the first of many trials fo the intellectuals, writers, journalists, lawyers, and university professors who had been arrested without any formal charges and sent to jail under Sarit's military dictatorship. There they had stayed, vaguely accused of being Communists or Communist sympathizers. The trial, open to the public, was widely covered in Thailand. Wai followed events closely, and Liao's office provided us with daily summaries.

Sarit's regime had never made any pretense of even the feeblest trappings of a legal system. And even now, Father's case, which clearly should have been heard in a civilian court, was being tried in a military setting. Never before in Thai history had so many people been held so long without any formal charges. When the charges were announced after so many years, they essentially amounted to the accusation that Father was a Communist, that he shared the views of all the contributors to his daily paper, *Satienraparb*, and that he had books in his extensive library on Marxism, capitalism, China, and Soviet Russia.

Specifically, he was accused of publishing subversive and seditious articles on China from October 3, 1956, to September 21, 1958. His article about the Buddhist monks' visit to China in 1956 and his account of the Chinese attitude toward Buddhism were particularly attacked as Communist propaganda. Also attacked were articles seen as sympathetic to socialism, as well as ones critical of U.S. policy toward Taiwan in particular and Southeast Asia generally.

Father was allowed to conduct his own defense. We read how he argued that he was being tried for violating martial laws that had not existed when his alleged crimes were committed. He stressed how the Thai constitution itself provided for procedures whereby the government was impelled to warn a publisher whose publications were viewed as violating national security or undermining public morals. The government, he showed, had never invoked this authority against him.

The real reason for his arrest, he argued, was that he was opposed to the rule of Marshal Sarit Thanarat and, more important, that he had been a close aide of Marshal Pibul Songkram. As for harming the national interest or the country's morals, his articles, he insisted, were factual, designed to broaden Thai understanding of the world and particularly to show how people lived under different political systems. As for Marxism, he had treated it objectively, as a subject to be studied.

Witnesses for the prosecution insisted that an examination of Father's works showed his Communist proclivities. But under Father's cross-examination they all admitted to never having studied Marxism-Leninism or even read Marx and Lenin. Nothing was said about Father's role in Pibul's government, and nothing at all about Wai and me or any aspect of his secret dealings with China.

The military judges quickly dismissed all charges. Father's writings were not a threat to national morals or the national security, they concluded. The prosecution witnesses had failed to make their case.

Father was free, and Mother was coming to see us. The joy I felt was not unalloyed—there were still the growing attacks on Kazu. I had asked him to meet my mother when she came and he had agreed. But by late March the meetings involving him escalated yet again and in the newspapers the attacks against revisionism became louder and louder.

LIAO DID NOT ANNOUNCE Mother's arrival. He did what he so often did—simply called and asked me to come right over. Old Lai, still our driver, was not around, so Liao sent his car to get me. Not finding him in his study, I walked over to his mother's compound. There he was, leaning over one of her paintings, adding a few finishing touches. She was looking on.

The old lady kissed me as Liao finished; she was much amused by his comical additions. Amah insisted on seeing how my calligraphy was coming, and as I showed her my less-than-brilliant efforts, she suggested ways to position myself better.

As soon as Liao and I were in his study, he told me that Mother was already in Macao.

"You and Wai and your sisters can all go down to meet her at the border," he said. "Please greet her on Premier Zhou's behalf and mine. Qiu Ji will make all the necessary arrangements."

Within two days Wai, my sisters, and I were in Guangzhou. The flight was now much shorter, a three-and-a-half-hour flight on a Trident instead of on one of the old propeller planes. We were met by Dr. Pridi's wife and daughter and the Chinese functionary assigned to look after us. We spent the night talking with Pridi and his wife, all of us curious about the news Mother would bring from Thailand.

When we saw her in Macao, she was aglow with happiness and relief. Father was out of jail: her eight long years of trial were over. Each day of the proceedings she had squeezed into the small room to watch while crowds gathered outside in hopes of finding out what was happening.

Father, she said, was taking things well. After he was released, he had asked first to visit his hometown in Samut Prakarn to see his aging mother. When he arrived and looked out over the sea he had known so well as a boy, he grew frightened. Now it all seemed too vast to him. He was unable to sleep in his old bed after all those years in jail because he had gotten used to sleeping on the floor. Those, however, seemed to be the only effects of his confinement. In political circles he was as active as ever.

Father still lived under some restrictions. He had no passport, and he could not travel. But he could write again and meet people, and he listened to the radio—Radio Beijing, Radio Vietnam, the Voice of America, and the BBC. He had been isolated from so much for so long.

Mother's reunion with Pridi was an emotional one. They discussed Pibul's death and how their personal histories had been interwoven with his. When Pridi learned that Mother had often cooked for Pibul, he asked her to prepare a meal of Pibul's favorites dishes. In return, he cooked a French dish for us. It seemed that when he and Pibul lived together, he had done the cooking and Pibul had cleaned up. The meal was a touching celebration of their friendship and long history together.

Our discussions about China were not as hopeful. Mother was anxious about what Father had been hearing of the escalating political conflicts in China. Another campaign was coming, he felt certain. I assured her that I had seen many come and go, but Pridi shared her concern. He was disturbed at the bitter attacks on the leaders he knew in Guangdung province, but he thought that foreigners would be safe. "This is an internal struggle, hard for outsiders to understand," he said, "but not one that will involve us."

Jing Puchun, Liao's wife, and Qiu Ji greeted us at the airport when we returned to Beijing. Mother wanted to settle in as quickly as possible, and she spent the next few days immersed in daily details: cooking Thai dishes, learning some Chinese dishes, and shopping in the nearby Chao Yang food market. She seemed happy just to be with the four of us. For the first time in years, the political storms that buffeted our family had subsided.

I said nothing of my inner agonies. Kazu was still away in meetings, and I had heard little for weeks. I left phone messages for him, but he did not reply. I was sure he was not getting them. The voice at the other end was abrupt, hostile, cold. One often heard that cold voice at the worst political moments in China, when all was being subsumed by some proclaimed political principle. I had once asked Zhou about that attitude. He was quiet for a moment, and then he said: "Principles without humanity are a mere formality."

In the beginning of April, Liao's secretary called and asked us to join Zhou and Liao for a "family lunch" at the premier's residence at Zhongnanhai. Our arrival was as it always was, the car gradually slowing to a halt at the bottom of the steps, the protocol person rushing down the steps and then escorting us to the meeting room, where Liao was waiting. Zhou and his wife came soon after. All of our caretakers were there this one time, including Qiu Ji and Shanan. It was an informal, and affectionate, reunion for us, and the first time Mother had seen Zhou in nine years.

Zhou broke protocol and hugged Mother. "How could any of us have anticipated what misfortunes fate had in store for your family?" Zhou began with Shanan interpreting. "I have the greatest admiration for the heroism and fortitude of Sang and other Thai friends of China. They have been through so many trials and tribulations."

Mother's tears flowed as she thanked Zhou and his wife, Liao, and the Chinese government for their kindness and help. She described Father's great joy when Zhou's man had been able to contact him in prison. "Your assistance in those years helped to keep all the families together and rally our spirits. Behind bars they no longer felt so isolated. You have raised Wai and Sirin these many years, and in the hour of our direst need, you brought my two younger daughters here as well."

She dried her eyes. "They are as much your children as mine," she said. "You have all gone to such great trouble in bringing them up. We owe you an inexpressible debt of gratitude.""You have suffered greatly all these years," Deng Mama said to her. "You have fought on and endured, and we appreciate all that you have had to overcome."

At dinner Zhou told Mother that he had read the account of Father's trial. Shanan had translated it for him. "It is a valuable historical record of a struggle in which truth triumphed over falsehood.

Sang's defense of himself against a brutal dictatorship in a military court was a brave and memorable feat."

"How long have I been in contact with Sang?" Zhou asked at one point, turning to his wife and Liao. "Since they were that high," he laughed, looking at Wai and me and lowering his hand toward the floor. "But Sang and I have never met. Sang has been a devoted friend of China for more than a decade. Please tell him that he is welcome at any time he is able to come as our guest."

Zhou asked after many of the people who had been a part of the formative stage of Thai-Chinese relations. How was Madame Pibul? And Prince Warnwai, Mr. Aree, and the others who had been jailed with Father? Zhou's remarkable memory never seemed to fail him. Neither did his gift for conveying deep concern for those he was talking with—on occasions such as this one he never talked about himself or what he had been through, only about the others.

Then the conversation turned lighter.

"I felt so bad for Chang Yuan when she told me she couldn't find a proper doll for herself when she arrived in China," Zhou said. More than nine years later he still remembered such details. "And now you are too big for one," he added affectionately.

Noticing that Shanan was strictly observing the cardinal rule of his job—never eat while interpreting—Zhou urged him to have something. "Chang Yuan can help.

He asked after Liao's mother, referring to her as He Lao Ren, the respectful term he always used for her. "Has she got over her cold?"

Liao smiled. "She hates taking her pills. She vows to paint them instead of taking them."

To Mother, Zhou said, "You have met his remarkable mother. She reports to me that every time she does a painting Liao sneaks figures into it!"

For a moment Liao looked like the "little Liao" he was with his mother.

"The beautiful names of your children were given by her," Zhou continued.

As we left later that evening, Zhou, pointing to Liao, laughed and said, "If you want to discuss the recent history of China in which Sang is so interested, well, we have an embodiment of Chinese history here, a most reliable living source of half a century of Chinese history. He is my close comrade and has been the father to your children."

Zhou then leaned down to me and said, "Take good care of your mother for me, will you? Don't hesitate to get in touch with me or Liao if she needs anything."

EARLY ONE JULY MORNING IN 1966, I stopped by to see Liao for a few minutes. He had been about to ask me to come over, he said. And what, by the way, was the delicious-smelling parcel I was carrying?

It was one of Liao's favorite dishes, Thai curried chicken, which, Mother had made for him. On the spot Liao decided it would make a fine breakfast, and I went off to the kitchen to reheat it. When he was done, he led me by the hand to his study and closed the door as he did whenever he had something to discuss.

"An emergency Congress of Afro-Asian writers will be held here in Beijing in a few days," Liao said. "Do you think Thailand can send a delegation?"

"What about Kularb Saipradit?" I suggested. He was a famous Thai writer long supportive of progressive trends in Thai politics. He had led a Thai writers' delegation to China in 1957 and had gone into exile with his family in China after the coup later that year.

The suggestion did not come as a surprise to Liao.

"The aim of the conference," Liao continued, "is to rally as many progressive writers as possible in the two-front fight against Soviet revisionists and U.S. imperialists. Perhaps you would like to join Mr. Kularb at the conference as part of his working team."

I was taken aback; I had never publicly associated myself with any such causes in all the years I had been in China.

Liao sensed my hesitation. "There has to be a first time for everything. I know you can do it. Help Mr. Kularb and his wife. You understand certain things about China very well now; you can explain it to them so that it will make sense to them. In that way some of our Thai friends might understand our policies better."

Though I was still reluctant, Liao did not often ask me to do things. And I felt the conference might be a diversion from my anxious preoccupation with Kazu, who was now entirely out of touch with me.

The conference began several days later at the Jing Xi Hotel. The Thai delegation consisted of the Kularbs, one other Thai writer, and myself. I used my Thai name publicly for the first time, though only Kularb's name was to be published on the roster of participants.

The list of Chinese writers in attendance was a compendium of my favorite novelists. Mao Dun came over, bowing graciously to us. He was a fragile, tiny man whose glasses and walking stick made him look every bit the quintessential Chinese scholar. His thin hands and long fingers suggested a life of refinement, and when he spoke he reminded me of a willow tree, his words gently and slowly moving like the breeze through its branches.

I was in an elegant Thai dress that Liao had wanted me to wear. "The Thai nation has the most harmonious mixture of colors," Mao Dun said with a smile. "It is always a treat for the eyes." Every day of the conference he complimented me on my colors. Never before had a Chinese commented upon such a thing.

Lao She was quite a contrast. He was younger and taller than Mao Dun and far less the picture of a refined scholar. He could have been one of the humble Beijing characters in the teahouse made so famous by his play. He spoke little, though, and he appeared to be cautious and tense, as though he was playing a part assigned to him as a duty.

Ba Jin was plump, short, and rather rough. He seemed quite at ease; he'd come to our table, he said, because he loved the sharpness and hotness of Thai food. Did we really mix it all up with chili sauce? he asked. "Every meal," I told him. He deflected any comments about his work. "I'm here to be reeducated by the new, younger writers of the world," he said with a smile.

The youngest writer was Cao Yu. He had written the most widely read novel in China in recent years, *Storm*, a disturbing and powerful account of the decadence of Chinese society in the 1930s. He was a charming merrymaker with a lively sense of humor, moving from table to table during the lunches, fan in hand to cool himself.

Yet the exterior cheerfulness of some of these writers did not fool me, nor could the growing storm outside be completely concealed from others. One look and anyone would know something was drastically askew. Directly outside the hotel, youngsters with red armbands shouted that they would "drag out" Ba Jin, Cao Yu, and the others, and not until troops of the People's Liberation Army intervened were they driven away. Although the troops remained, stationed at all the entrances to ensure order, Ba Jin and Cao Yu acted as though they had seen nothing. I was uneasy, but like them, I acted as though nothing were amiss.

 Brilliant red banners draped the hall proclaiming "Long Life for Chairman Mao," "Be Concerned with Matters of State!," "Long Live the Three Red Banners." The theme of the conference was heralded by the biggest banner of all, praising Mao's "Talks on Literature and Art" at the Yan'an Forum, the speech he had given in 1942 arguing that art and writers must serve a political purpose.

As soon as the conference was called to order, there was a surprise announcement: the first speaker was to be Guo Moro, a famous scholar and poet. The man who had first deciphered the Shang oracle bones from Anyang, Guo was a prolific master of a wide variety of literary genres and one of the most dynamic figures on the Chinese political scene for the last forty years. A hush fell over the audience as he strode to the platform.

Guo was enormously charming. When I was eleven, he had accompanied Wai and me down the Yangtze River, telling us one story after another about the Three Kingdoms. He'd see a cliff or a jutting stone, and off he'd go with its historical associations and poems from this great epoch.

Zhou and Liao both spoke to me at various times about China's intellectuals, a sensitive subject in a culture in which so many political debates reverberated through cultural allusions. Zhou felt China's intellectuals were weak; they were not a threat. They had briefly played great brief at historical moments but then lapsed back into their accustomed weakness, swept along by political currents, surviving as best they could. In later years I learned how he and Mao had disagreed on this point: Mao feared China's intellectuals; Zhou felt comfortable in their presence.

I watched Guo carefully as he began to speak with his usual deliberation, as though he were reciting a liturgical text. I listened with growing disquiet as he got to his point. He solemnly declared that China was entering the great historical era of the Cultural Revolution, a revolution that was touching the soul of every member of society. Then in front of all these writers, many of whom respected his work, he burst forth in an emotional confession.

"My books are of no value. Please burn them in the searing fires of the Cultural Revolution."

To suggest burning books, whether as metaphor or not (and I realized this was no metaphor), was a stunning way to ask writers to unite in a cause. Father had dedicated his life to words, and big words had shaped mine. Burning them had not yet been a part of things.

While part of the audience would have clapped at anything, many were quiet and deeply upset. Some thought—or hoped—that this was Guo's modest and traditional Chinese way of expressing his support for the recently launched Cultural Revolution. Others thought he was inexplicably indulging in hyperbole. The presence of soldiers outside suggested that the truth was neither of these.

When the conference came to a close a week later, our Chinese hosts invited all the delegates to travel around China. Our first stop was the triple city of Wuhan, so called because before 1950 it had been three separate cities. I had been there before, and I knew its role in contemporary Chinese history. It had been the cradle of the 1911 revolution and Generalissimo Jiang Jieshi's temporary capital after the fall of Nanjing to the Japanese in December 1937. Here Zhou had begun his work as the Communist foreign minister and the ambassador to the Guomindang in everything but name.

Wuhan lived up to its reputation as one of the notorious "ovens" on the Yangtze. We arrived on a scorching day in mid-August, and with relief the Kularbs and I accepted an invitation to take a boat ride the next afternoon to watch a major swimming event.

The spectacle that afternoon had all the flair, color, and fantastic detail the Chinese could be such masters of. In the blazing sun some ten thousand young people holding red banners aloft swam across a river well over a kilometer wide. Some of the swimmers fighting the powerful current were no more than children. Everywhere slogans were shouted. Those in the front of the pack seemed particularly emotional, caught up in a frenzy of chanting.

Then, coming up against the current, we saw a boat approaching. Ours sounded its horn in a succession of quick bleats to salute it, and as it drew nearer there were louder and louder cheers. "Chairman Mao! Chairman Mao!"

At last I saw. Sitting on the deck, wrapped in a white robe and waving to us, was Mao himself. He had, I soon learned, just completed his "historic" crossing of the Yangtze, swimming in front of those red banners with thousands following behind. Everyone on our boat was jumping up and down, straining to see, shouting "Chairman Mao! Chairman Mao! I saw Chairman Mao!" Pandemonium reigned as people pushed for position, craning to see him and wave back.

That evening in the great city hall we were received by Mao. With his suntanned face, he looked radiant; I had rarely seen him looking so well. He shook hands with all the various delegates. When the Thai delegation's turn came, he recognized me, greeting me as I shook his hand. After all the handshaking there was a group photograph with him, and then he departed.

When I returned to Beijing a few days later, it was a city transformed. The Red Guards with their armbands were everywhere. I walked down to Tiananmen Square, where a huge demonstration was scheduled to take place. I wondered what Mao was up to.

Almost a million people could fit into Tiananmen Square, and on this day it was packed as I had never seen it before. Everywhere there were chanting, marching, and near-hysterical acclamations of "Chairman Mao, Chairman Mao!" And at the center of the rostrum stood Chairman Mao in an olive-green People's Liberation Army uniform. As he waved to the crowds, they began to cry and scream for him even harder. They think he's a god, I thought. "We will die for Chairman Mao!" they shouted again and again.

Around me the sounds echoed like the chanting of a prayer. I was confused and drew back into myself. I couildn't belong to this, nor could I fathom it. Neither of my guardians had wanted to talk about what was happening in recent weeks. In public there was a "glorious cultural revolution," in private a guarded silence.

"Old Man Mao," I thought. "Something is wrong."

I shuddered, remembering how the Red Guards had threatened to burst into our quiet courtyard several weeks earlier. Houses were being ransacked, I'd heard. Why some people were picked out and not others was not yet clear to me. But apparently our house was a target because the Red Guards, seeing the lions, wanted to smash them as symbols of the old ways. Old Lai and Old Feng managed to hold off a group of about fifteen of them that were particularly threatening, as others milled around. Finally Old Lai informed them that the house was under the protection of Premier Zhou. They looked disconcerted at this news, unsure what to do next, and gradually their fervor wilted and they left. In those days, they didn't know for certain what they could and couldn't do. The rules had not yet been clearly defined.

Shortly before, I had watched in horror as Red Guards humiliated and cursed an old couple on our lane. And one old man had been paraded down the street in a dunce cap, the Red Guards chanting the glories of Mao and the vices of this revisionist. Again I had felt the shame I'd experienced on seeing my teachers spat upon in 1957.

A few days later, Mother went shopping with an interpreter in the Chao Yang market. "I saw a long row of open trucks pass by," she told me shakily when she returned. "They kept coming. In each of them there were a few men and women standing, their heads shaved, their hands tied together. They each had a black placard on their backs with their names upside down." She had asked the interpreter who they were, but the woman seemed frightened, saying only that they were old capitalists and that the Red Guards had swept them up.

Mother had just returned from a pleasant trip to Yan'an, Hangzhou, and Wu Xi with Wai and my sisters. The acute humiliation of these people upset her deeply. And now another Red Guard attack on our house seemed all too likely. She began to think it was time to leave, and quickly.

Wai was worried. He had already gotten several horrifying accounts from his Chinese girlfriend and her family. He knew the gossip and the stories of the Beijing streets. "This movement is far more dangerous than any we have known," he said to me one night. "It's like what we read about in Chairman Mao's stories about the countryside—the landlords being humiliated. Now those methods are coming back." He spoke of the fear in the city, saying, "The party is crazy to do all this to its own people." We all sensed that a major political crisis was coming. Although she rarely said how worried she was, Mother no longer deflected my sisters' entreaties to leave with her. Perhaps they could go to Paris to study, an idea my sisters loved.

Because our passports had long since expired, Wai and I could not simply leave, even if we had wanted to. No Thai embassy would issue new ones for Thais who had been in China. Nor was it clear where we could go. I had no thoughts of going back: amid all the turbulence, my world, the world of Zhou and Liao, still seemed secure. Wai himself was quite involved with his girlfriend; for the time being he could wait. Besides, we both understood the dictates of political reality.

Wai asked Mother to give Father his diary of our official meetings with Zhou. He wanted Father to see for himself his detailed accounts of all our discussions with Zhou and how seriously he had fulfilled his assignment all these years. I sensed his pride as he handed his papers over but also an uneasiness about what was to come, a sense that his notes should be in safer hands.

Mother asked me to inform Liao of her decision to go back home and to have my sisters leave as well. Liao popped in for dinner that night, calm and very much his jovial self. He talked at length about the many ups and downs of the Chinese Communist party and expressed full confidence in China's future. He made no objection to my sisters' departure once Mother told him of the arrangements for them in France. Father was now free; the family's situation was no longer desperate. Liao promised to convey to Zhou Mother's thanks for all the premier had done. She did not want to disturb him, she said, knowing how busy he was now. But she did ask cautiously about how safe it was for Wai and me amid the apparent "disorder."

"As long as Premier Zhou and I are here, no one would dare touch them," he said firmly.

The next day, she and my sisters left. At the airport she fought to keep her tears back, but Tukta and Pongsri felt under no such compulsion. When, I wondered, would these partings stop?

Wai and I were driven home. Our own quietness was now matched by the quiet of our house. Only Old Lai was still there; increasingly the cook and the rest of the staff were away in meetings. Ji and Shanan, we heard, were involved in them as well.

When the first wall posters had gone up at Beijing University, I had found them hard to read. Their tone had repelled me. That spring I had felt sickened on reading the later famous wall poster by Nie Yuanzi, the Party cadre who was secretary of the Faculty of Philosophy. She had bitterly assailed the president of the university, Lu

Ping, who had been helpful to me. He and others, she declared, were "actually smashing the Cultural Revolution." Zhou had gone secretly the night the poster was put up to look at it. He had immediately known how serious the situation was, had known perhaps far better than did many of the people under attack. Years later he told me how angry he had been over its posting.

All important posters that attacked such high leaders were connected somewhere, somehow, to struggles within the leadership. Chairman Mao had seized on Nie's wall poster, proclaiming that its content should be broadcast throughout the country. When I heard that, I remembered seeing Cao Yiwu, the wife of Kang Sheng, an ominous figure in matters of security, in the crowd milling around the Faculty of Philosophy building. She had been dressed very plainly. Our eyes briefly met, and I understood her wordless message: Do not recognize me!

I knew little of her husband except that he was consulted on the highest-level questions. I had met him only on official occasions like National Day or at the Chinese New Year's party in the Great Hall of the People. Mao, I knew, held him in high regard, but I found something alarming about him. I didn't trust him at all. His face had a cold, cruel look to it. Whenever there had been rectification movements in the Party, he had been behind the most chilling investigations into key Party people. In public I never saw him talk. He was not a part of Liao's circle, and Zhou spoke of him carefully. An exceptionally cultured man, he said.

He also had a special relationship with Mao's wife, Jiang Qing. They came from the same county in Shandong, and Kang was known as the person who had introduced her to Mao in the 1930s, when she was a Shanghai film star who had gone to Yan'an. Years later I learned that Kang Sheng had sent his wife to lead an underground "theoretical investigation group" at the university that operated apart from the Central Committee to mobilize student political groups and attack key targets. At the time, though, I barely sensed how bitter the struggle might become. I told Liao where I had seen Kang's wife, adding that I felt there was something sinister about him. He didn't criticize me for being so blunt.

"We all swim in the big sea," he said after hearing me out. "Whoever gets to the shore will have the last word."

Liao looked somewhat worn. He still came out in public to recieve guests, but he was subdued, less lively. When I recounted various incidents that had shocked me, he only said, "Be patient. Things will work out in the end."

I was not so sure.

Yet for Wai and me things continued much as they always had. Our privileges remained intact; the house was guarded and safe. No more Red Guards threatened to burst into the courtyard. Zhou's writ still held, at least for us.

Regular university classes had ended in June 1966. Special classes had been arranged for the three hundred or so foreign students by the university's Foreign Liaison Department, but classes for the Chinese students had been suspended. By October almost all foreign students had been advised to leave China. Wai and I started living exclusively in our house again, forsaking the dormitory for the time being.

I was no longer able to spend weekends with Liao. His house was often surrounded by Red Guards. Once, to comfort myself, I went to the Beijing Zoo, where Liao, fearing what would become of his favorite dogs at the hands of the Red Guards, had discreetly placed them. I stood there watching all the dogs in their pen. Suddenly Mo Gu, "mushroom," saw me and ran toward me, barking. As she jumped up and down excitedly, I reached out my hand to stroke her. Then I fled before anyone could notice.

If, in our house, life seemed largely unchanged, outside, the world I had known and thought stable was dying fast. Lu Dingyi, the father of my first Chinese friend and one of the chief organizers of the antirightist campaign of 1957, was under bitter attack; the newspaper carried a prominent picture of him, humiliated, his eyes cast down. Then it was Peng Zhen pictured with his hair cut off and a big placard hung around his neck. Although I knew him only slightly, it seemed he met all the Thai delegations, and his charm and sense of humor had always appealed to me. Zhou, too, had spoken well of him over the years. Now the people I knew were suddenly called evil. It was impossible to know what to believe: no one said these people were innocent, and I myself couldn't say it either. I became more and more confused.

Occasionally I visited my old dorm, still technically open to me.

There, on one of my visits, several of my old Chinese classmates urged me to attend an extraordinary meeting in the Great Hall of the People. Jiang Qing was to address it.

The assembly room, though cavernous, was packed. Slogans hung everywhere, and Mao's *Little Red Book* bobbed in front of people's faces. When I entered, Jiang Qing was already onstage, leaping up and down as she shouted slogans in her unpleasant high-pitched voice. "Learn from the Red Guards" was the principal one on this occasion.

"Learn from Auntie Jiang Qing" came back the chorus.

We read Mao's quotations out loud. We sang songs. We waved the *Little Red Book*.

Then she spoke. She told in minute detail how Chairman Mao had had to fight off the wicked persecution and hostility of Liu Shaoqi's revisionist coup d'état attempt. The audience roared its support. She began to talk about Mao himself. She spoke of how his younger son had been damaged mentally by his suffering in the old society. I looked around; everyone was listening raptly. Never before in public had I heard Mao's family history mentioned. Jiang Qing wept as she recounted Mao's personal pain, drawing the audience in. Many appeared deeply moved, and then angry as she ended with a fierce denunciation of people I knew Zhou greatly respected: Peng Zhen, Ye Jianying, Chen Yi, Deng Xiaoping. As I left I heard rumors that Zhou himself was suspect.

With less and less to hold on to, I clung now, although only inwardly, to Kazu. Bewildered as I was by his disappearance, I still had hope. In early January 1967 I finally heard from him. A brief note was all. "I have to go. I love you very much. Wait for me. I will try to find a way once I get to Japan."

Despite all the months of uncertainty, I was utterly unprepared for the blow. I had not mentioned to Liao how I was waiting for Kazu in anguish each day. I had hidden the truth from Wai, too, and from Mother, blithely explaining away her not meeting him with excuses.

How long would he be gone? It didn't really matter. It was over. But why had he not at least come back to tell me? I felt my pride stiffen. He had not wanted me—so be it. There was just the note, and now he was gone.

CHAPTER 12

Father's Mission

IT WAS A BITTERLY COLD DAY IN EARLY 1967, only weeks after Kazu left, when Zhou's office called with the news that my father was coming. Wai and I were to go to Macao to meet him and then fly back to Beijing with him. We had not seen him since 1956.

Wai and I had no clear idea why he was coming. We doubted it was to take us home. When I tried to remember what he was like, I wasn't sure. I couldn't clearly separate my memories of him from the stories I knew so well. "We'll be able to get to know him better," Wai said, although not without a certain diffidence. Perhaps it was too late to get to know a father we had lived without for so long.

There was other cause for trepidation, too. Father had sent us to understand China, but the China we had grown up in was crumbling. We knew he would ask us to explain it, but that would not be easy. The Cultural Revolution seemed more than just another power struggle with one group toppling another. Its scenes of humiliation, its shrill and dogmatic slogans, its marching Red Guards had deeply shaken my sense of how things worked. And Father would undoubtedly wish to see Zhou as well. It was hardly an auspicious time.

As Old Lai drove me to Liao's house to discuss my father's trip, I tried to focus on what I needed to talk about. Driving through the tumultuous streets of Beijing only served to make me more and more uneasy. The Red Guards' chanting never stopped; mobs surged everywhere, waving the *Little Red Book*. When we approached Liao's compound, I saw a crowd of at least a thousand people milling about in the street, banners flying, armbands emblazoned with the sign of the Red Guards. They swarmed around the car, banging on the roof and shouting at us with growing fury as we inched forward.

Old Lai stiffened. He, too, had never witnessed anything like this. He said nothing, but I sensed that he was afraid. To my relief, Liao's guards came out quickly and waved us on. We pulled through the gates and into the empty driveway.

I got out and walked into the courtyard. There was no one around. I entered the house; here, too, no one, nothing—only echoes of the ominous sounds from the street.

The house was a shambles. Liao's beautiful books had been torn to shreds, his precious Japanese dolls dismembered and scattered all along the hallway. His beloved statue, the Michelangelo nude he had brought from Italy, had been smashed. I glanced toward the study where Kazu and I had so recently become engaged. Still there was no one, only the shards.

I went inside the study. Liao sat there waiting for me, impassive. His seriousness frightened me. I felt as if a mountain was about to fall.

"Who did this? What is this all about?" I cried.

"It is a severe test for me," Liao said. "The stuggles in the Party have been very complicated and involve tremendous sacrifices. We all have to stand up to this new test."

"What is going to happen to you? How could anyone do this to you"

I had never seen him like this, spiritless, dressed in plain cotton clothes, shabby. Something else was different as well.

"Your photos," I said, "where are they?" All the photographs that had covered the walls and tabletops, the snapshots he had taken of all the country's leaders, were gone.

"Burned."

"Who did it?"

"I did."

I started crying. Liao touched my shoulder gently and said, "You must be strong. Have patience. Politics can be very cruel."

I tried to calm myself.

"You have been under Premier Zhou's care for many years. You should be able now to recognize what is right and wrong. It's a good test for you, too."

"But why is this happening?"

"I don't understand it myself. But I have lived my life believing that a revolutionary, a Communist, should be able to face truth and even suffer humiliation, abuse, and injustice for the cause."

I detected no bitterness in his voice.

"A Communist must follow the Party when he is riding high with it and no less when he is being rightly or wrongly attacked."

Becoming quiet for a moment, he looked intently at me and then continued; "You know, when I joined the revolution in my youth, some people in the revolutionary army didn't trust me. During the Long March, Zhang Guotao thought I was an enemy agent. I was kept handcuffed the whole way, and I nearly had my head chopped off. I was only saved at the last moment by Zhou, who knew my father and me."

He sighed deeply. "There are some destructive elements in this movement, but they are not the masses. We must keep out faith in Chairman Mao. Have courage."

We discussed my father's visit. What would he be able to do in a city under siege? Whom could he meet?

"Don't worry; Zhou and I will still be able to meet with him. The struggle meetings against me will in no way affect my carrying on with my daily work."

"How can you live here? Where is everyone?"

"Zhou has asked me to move into Zhongnanhai. It will be best there. Mother will remain here. Zhou is protecting her."

"How is Amah taking all this?" She was deaf now and could walk only a few steps without her wheelchair.

"She's well. She's still in her wing of the house. It was left untouched. She has not seen the damage, and the Red Guards were moved out onto the street after Zhou intervened."

"May I go say hello to her"

"No; you've been crying. Seeing you like this will only upset her. We're not telling her what has happened. She knows only that Zhou needs me with him in Zhongnanhai."

I had seen the paper banner with its official markings that had been put up to protect her part of the house. So at least there was still sufficient government authority to stop the rampaging Red Guards. With what little power Zhou had left, he could protect Amah. But he could no longer protect her son in his own house. And I realized he might not be able to protect me much longer.

Liao was sad when we said good-bye, but he told me, "Don't be afraid of the future."

Old Lai and I drove back through the jeering crowd. "Cut off your hair, you bourgeois bitch!" they screamed, pounding on the roof, leering into the windows of the car. "Come on out!" they yelled. "We'll drag you out and do it for you!" I stared straight ahead, feeling my world slip away.

As WAI AND I PREPARED FOR OUR TRIP, all the news we heard was bad. Marshal He Lung's house was ransacked by the Red Guards. An attack on He Lung could not help but undermine Zhou: they were the closest of friends. When I thought how proud he was to have been one of the creators of the new China, I was pained by the idea of his humiliation.

On the streets I began to see wall posters accusing Zhou, along with Liu Shaoqi, Peng Zhen, and Lo Ruiqing, of plotting a coup back in February 1966. Suddenly there was a new slogan: "Down with Zhou Enlai." The only thing that seemed constant and inviolable now was the ubiquitous presence of Mao—his face, his books, his calligraphy.

Early in February 1967, Wai and I, accompanied by protocol people from the Foreign Ministry, flew to Guangzhou. We received the usual privileged treatment, even though none of Zhou's people was with us. Late the night of our arrival, we dropped in to see Pridi to tell him of Father's impending visit. We could speak only briefly, but he made it clear he was considering leaving China. He had seen pictures of Liu Shaoqi with a black "X" across his face. "What kind of country is it that is treating its leaders this way? This is no way to run a country. This will not come to a good end."

We drove to the Macao border early the next morning and spent the night in the remote frontier town, where Father was expected the following day. Even there the tumult of "power seizures" was evident everywhere. Gongs and drums reverberated through the streets; speakers blared throughout the night, announcing the victorious revolutionary developments in the local organizations. The porters, too, had risen to "seize power."

At dawn the next day Wai and I were up, both of us tired from a night of disturbed sleep and, though excited, also nervous and confused about what was to come. We waited outside the customs house for some time, not talking. Our Chinese hosts stood off by themselves.

Suddenly, there was my father. He was smaller than I had remembered—Wai stood a head taller. But as soon as he embraced us and began to talk, he was the same—voluble, effusive and earnest.

"I told you we would meet again someday if we lived long enough!" He gave each of us another big hug.

Then, turning to the officials from the Guangzhou Foreign Affairs Department, he launched into one of his beautiful flowery speeches. He spoke of how he had longed to see his daughter and son, how after all these years in prison it was at last possible, and how appropriate it was to reunite with them on Chinese soil. By the time he finished, even the cautious Chinese officials were moved.

Finally, the official ceremony was over, and we were driven to Guangzhou. Father left us to go see Pridi, and for the next two days and nights they talked, disagreeing, arguing, happily exchanging their views of the last half century of Thai history, on China, on Thai literature. I saw them bending over books, talking excitedly as they looked up what seemed to me arcane political and philosophical points. I'd never seen Pridi so animated or vigorous. They had been on opposing political sides for thirty years, but they showed only the deepest respect for each other. Sometimes I listened, but often they discussed areas I knew little about, and I went off with Madame Poonsuk and her daughter.

Unexpectedly, Colonel Phayom Chulanon, the chairman of the Thai Patriotic Front, called on Father. I had met him at the writers' conference. There had been a cold, supercilious air about him, something more frighteningly "revolutionary" even than the attitudes sweeping China.

Colonel Phayom was one of those Father had saved from execution after an unsuccessful military coup against Pibul. General Pao had arrested him, and while the other coup leaders were shot, he was spared because of Father's intervention. "I knew Phayom as a promising and progressive young officer," Father told me. "I asked Pao to show mercy, and I guaranteed that he would henceforth stay out of politics if his life were spared." Soon after, Phayom had disappeared, joining the Communist forces in the jungle. Father had not seen him since.

Phayom told Father that the headquarters of his united front organization was in Beijing and that, as he was only in Guangzhou for medical treatment for a nervous ailment, he did not think it appropriate that they discuss politics. He was merely calling to express his gratitude for Father's generosity to him. I was suspicious. Phayom did not know what our connections were, yet Father was clearly visiting under the auspices of some highly powerful leader or he would not have been there at all.

Finally, on the last night before we left for Beijing, Father said he'd like to talk to Wai and me privately. We still did not know how long he meant to stay or where he wished to go. So far, he had only said that he wished to spend his time with us. "How can anyone have the heart to go sightseeing with the country in such a state?" he asked. "People seem so cold and hostile."

He began by telling us how much he had longed to see us all those years in prison, how much he respected what we had done. Now, he said, he would be able to rely on our good advice.

"I want to discuss a most important political matter with you," he said. "You have grown up here, you know the people and their feelings better than I do. I am carrying with me on this trip an extraordinary message from President Lyndon Johnson of the United States. I am one of the very few people in the world who know of his intention to open up direct talks with China on Sino-U.S. relations and the situation in Southeast Asia. Johnson appears to be willing to reconsider the Taiwan problem and the question of whether to recognize the People's Republic of China."

I was stunned. I had hoped for a pleasant family reunion, some rest from politics. But now this. The last time around, I thought, gazing at him in disbelief, you collaborated with the Japanese. Now you're lined up with the Americans. What next?

"So how do you feel about this?" Father asked calmly.

Wai was furious. "Say nothing about it at all," he said. "Just let it go and leave the country. Stay with us a month, two months, then leave. Don't mention it to anyone. Don't mention meeting with the Americans at all. The Chinese will take it very badly if you do."

I agreed. God only knew what was happening to Zhou and Liao. I wasn't sure if I'd even be able to reach them now. At this point, I realized, a message from the Americans might only add to their troubles. What would the Red Guards think—or the radicals in the Foreign Ministry? What more lethal ammunition could we give Zhou's or Liao's enemies than this?

Father listened silently to our objections. Looking at each of us in turn, then, he spoke just as I remembered him speaking in the past: "People in politics should treat major international issues involving peace and war and affecting hundreds of millions of people with full gravity and with due consideration for the long-term interest involved. Certain political views might be wholly correct, and yet it might take a long time for them to be implemented. In the interval their proponents will be subject to slander, persecution, and suffering."

At such moments Father's sincerity was overwhelming. There seemed not a trace of self-interest in what he said.

"Many political figures," he went on, "many statesmen, have suffered such hardships. Years of negotiating on the heavy seas of Thai international relations and of brooding in jail have accustomed me to taking a dispassionate long view."

Father was justifying himself to Wai and me, explaining why he had acted with us, as on other issues, the way he had.

"Politicians must dare to express their views on major issues in unfavorable and even perilous circumstances. Otherwise they are opportunists and adventurers more than politicians."

"Tactics were also crucial, I thought. Zhou had often said that a good principle without a good method was not of much use.

"Don't speculate about the outcome of the message I'm carrying to the Chinese," Father concluded. "Concentrate on just two questions. First, should President Johnson's message be relayed to the Chinese or not? Second, would it do the Chinese government any harm to learn about this new development?"

"I don't see how it can hurt the Chinese authorities," he added, answering his own questions for us. "They are entirely free to respond either positively or negatively."

It was hard to say no to Father on what he presented as a matter of principle. Mother had never been able to. I was not convinced, though; the dangers seemed enormous. I reluctantly conceded that perhaps he might talk things over with the Chinese, but tactfully, very tactfully.

"The outcome is sure to be negative," Wai added. He knew that I was the logical one to reach Zhou or Liao, but that would not be easy given all that was happening. "But if you think your sense of duty and self-respect require it, I will not stand in the way."

He waited for a moment before asking, "What will we do if the Chinese are furious and drive us out?"

"I'll have to see the Chinese response first," Father replied, "and if it is totally negative, I'll have to find a way to get you back to Thailand after my return. I still have some old friends and followers in the army and the government who might help. As long as you are safe and are not forced into doing anything anti-Chinese by the Thai government, there is no reason why you can't return if you have to. But first I must talk to my friends in positions of authority."

I found that a disquieting response. What, I wanted to ask, would happen to us in the meantime? The conversation returned to the logistics of transmitting the message. Talking with Liao and Zhou was a problem. Was there any way to get a message directly to them? Not now, I knew. Father would first have to explain his intentions to the Chinese officials we would met in Beijing, and I was uneasy about who that would be and whether we could trust them. Yet perhaps Father was right; perhaps something in this would help end the war in Vietnam. What would Zhou do if he were in this situation? I asked myself.

"I decided to come here when your mother relayed Premier Zhou's invitation," Father said. "I heard from overseas Chinese friends of the turmoil in this country, so I am not totally shocked by what I see, however saddened I am by it. Pridi had advised me to go ahead, but he is not at all optimistic about the outcome."

He then explained how it was that he had come to be carrying his message. He had wanted to come see us and find out what was going on, but he had had no passport, and the new regime of Thanom Kittikachorn and Prapass Charusatian had turned down all his requests. He had applied to Thanom himself for a passport. Again nothing had happened. Finally he had recieved a phone call from an American, Norman Hannah.

"Do you remember him?" Father asked. "He remembers you."

Hannah, I knew, had been the person Father talked with most in the American embassy in Bangkok in the 1950s. Hannah had been the labor attaché, though his contacts had seemed to carry him to the higher level of the U.S. government. Now he had returned as second in comand at the embassy in Bangkok.

Hannah had asked Father to meet with him at the American embassy, greeting him as an old acquaintance. He made it clear that he knew of Wai's and my stay in China, asking after us and how we were doing.

"I told Hannah that our personal friendship could not stand in the way of my frankly criticizing America's aggressive policies in Vietnam, Thailand, and the rest of Southeast Asia.

"I asked him, 'What makes the U.S. government think it can win the war in Vietnam?' And Hannah replied, 'To tell you the truth, we no longer believe that. Our men in Vietnam want to get out. They don't want to fight there.'"

Then why didn't the United States get out? Father had asked.

Hannah had said they couldn't simply pull out. The Vietcong, he maintained, had rejected any kind of negotiations or peace talks, and that made it harder for the United States to leave. The government and the army didn't want to stay a day longer, though, given the serious losses and the growth of anti–Vietnam War sentiment at home.

"I didn't hide from Norman that I was a friend of China. I asked him frankly; 'Does your government still dream of invading China?' Norman appeared shocked by the question. 'No! No! Definitely not. What we would like to do in Vietnam now is to try to stop the war. We certainly don't want to expand it. After we have stopped the fighting, our troops will have to get out and go home.' A number of senators, including Mike Mansfield and William Fulbright, he told me, shared my point of view and had voiced their opposition to U.S. official policy of Vietnam and Thailand."

Father explained how the discussion had then turned to China. Hannah had told him that the Sino-U.S. ambassadorial talks in Warsaw were not going well. There had been no new developments even though the United States was changing its thinking, moving toward a new policy.

At that point Hannah had asked about Wai and me. Were we safe amid all the unrest? Father had told him the government would not issue him a passport. Hannah had seemed to think that not much of a problem. Then, evidently, he had got to the real point of the meeting.

"President Johnson," he had said, "wishes to hold discussions with the Chinese govenment of Sino-U.S. relations and the general situation in Southeast Asia and to do so on reasonable and mutually acceptable terms through any channel at any time at any place. The U.S. government considers you, Sang, a possible intermediary in view of your close relationship with Zhou Enlai. We know he is the guardian of your children."

Father was not shocked by Hannah's knowledge about Wai and me. The secrecy in which we had left Bangkok and lived in China had never meant that absolutely no one knew of our whereabouts or what Father was up to. It only meant that such knowledge was kept in the tiniest of circles, stored away for times such as this.

"I saw no need to be anything but frank with him," Father told us. "I told him that unless the U.S. government was willing to display some flexibility on the issue of Taiwan, the situation was insoluble."

The days had passed, Father said. Then Hannah had asked for another meeting. It seemed President Johnson was willing to give his assurance on the issue. With that, Father had agreed to be an intermediary.

"Then Norman said that if my children had problems in China because of this mission, they would be welcome to go to the United States and continue their studies there."

I felt a chill when Father said this. To go there would be to destroy my association with China entirely; the people who mattered to me in my world would never tolerate such an act, such a desertion. Fortunately, Father had recognized that as well. "I know that is a political impossibility," he quickly added.

A few days later, Father had his passport for "Hong Kong and Japan, valid for six months only."

"We have been friends of China for years. You have been raised by them. Johnson's message is not sinister, and in time American and China will have to develop a new relationship," he said.

I thought Father was mad. He had to be. He had been in a Thai prison for too many years: what did he know of China? He had sent us here to learn about China, and now he simply ignored our advice about what was sure to happen. On the surface his remark sounded plausible; his lofty ideas often did. Again and again I asked myself what Zhou or Liao would say. But all I saw was Liao's ransacked house.

In the end Father got his way. A couple days later we returned to Beijing with him. As we walked off the plane, I looked around nervously to see who was there to greet us; that would be the first signal of what was to come. Father, it turned out, was received by leading members of the Revolutionary Committee of the Foreign Ministry. None of the people who had worked on relations with Thailand under Zhou and who were familiar with our situation were there. Qiu Ji was absent, Shanan gone. The rebels in the foreign section of the premier's office, I thought, had evidently joined forces with the rebels in the Foreign Ministry.

Then I recognized the woman interpreter from the Foreign Ministry staff. At first, the sight of someone I knew was welcome. But I quickly saw how taut her face was. When she greeted us, her voice became harsh. Then she mentioned Chen Yi and Liao: "They'd better be serious about their wrongdoing and accept the criticism of the masses. If they try to evade their responsibility, it will be the end of them, no matter who they are. We are all equal before Chairman Mao's revolutionary line."

I felt sick. I had known this woman for years, calling her "Auntie Lin." At the same time, she had always praised Liao in a fawning tone that made me uneasy. "We are so lucky and proud to work under him" she had told me repeatedly. How could people change so fast and behave so shamelessly? Now she was a threat to us.

After brief formalities we were driven to the Beijing Hotel. Our house staff was no longer able to accommodate even one guest. Father had a suite, and we had rooms on either side of him. It seemd ironic to be back in the very hotel where we had come as children to start the new lives Father had chosen for us.

On our way from the airport, we had passed the entrance to Zhongnanhai. Thousands of rebels were sitting out in the cold, red banners flying, loudspeakers blaring messages and revolutionary music twenty-four hours a day. Even though the noise was blocks away from the hotel, Father said the next morning he could hardly sleep for all the drums and gongs sounding all night. How, I wondered, could the leaders I knew bear up under that continual assault of noise?

Father was shaken; the nerve-racking atmosphere was rapidly wearing on him. He was unable to follow his daily routine of writing and making notes. Instead he stood for hours by the window, listening to the clamorous city, looking at the bare streets, and feeling the wind piercing the loose casement.

"This is not the Beijing of my hopes and expectations," he said. "The cold winter outside and the chilly political situation inside bode no good."

Our host had arranged for daily political discussions with us. No Foreign Ministry official came to talk to us, only people with red armbands. There were usually three or four of them. The leader of the group was in his early thirties; he didn't say what he had been doing before the Cultural Revolution. He much preferred telling Father emphatically how the whole nation was responding to Chairman Mao's call to carry the great Cultural Revolution to the end.

"China will never change color," he said with absolute assurance. "We have now understood Chairman Mao's repeated warnings against the danger of revisionism, especially inside the Party. We shall never forget class struggle. Chairman Mao's insights have taken Marxism-Leninism to new heights."

Others spoke of how valuable it was to read Chairman Mao. Perhaps Father would like to do so as well. Reading the *Little Red Book* had been a particularly helpful experience for them, bringing them ever closer to Chairman Mao.

"Every word of Chairman Mao's is worth ten thousand words, as Vice Chairman Lin Biao said," another of them avowed.

The leader said, "We wear Chairman Mao's badge close to our hearts to show our infinite loyalty to the reddest red sun. We are happy to give you this English translation of the *Little Red Book* and a Chairman Mao badge."

Though we stayed in the Beijing Hotel, the meetings were held in our house. Sometimes when the leader paused for me to translate, his eyes would dart about, examining the house. At those moments, a scowl appeared, a menacing hostility provoked by the luxury and privilege he saw all around him.

Father found it hard to be very animated as the talking at him continued. "They are becoming very arrogant, aren't they?" he said after yet another session. "What is one to make of this Mao cult?"

The next day, in the midst of their praise of Mao and further explanations of the Cultural Revolution, Father asked after Qiu Ji.

"It's time for Qiu Ji to touch his innermost soul. If he follows the masses, no harm will befall him, the masses will pardon him. But if he resists, he will only destroy himself and his reputation. We don't know whether or not he is a traitor. He was in jail under the Guomindang and then released. Why? How could the ruthless Guomindang have spared him? We are setting up an investigation group to go into his mysterious past. You see, our Party and our country have been ruled by dubious people like him."

Father sat listening grimly, but he did not reply. To his occasional venturing of his own opinions, they seemed completely indifferent. Everything was upside down. Usually the Chinese practice was to listen to one's guests before offering any opinions of one's own. Now it seemed these people's lecturing would never cease.

That, I decided, was all for the best. After several days of such treatment, even Father might see that this was not the time to relay his message. Everything we had told him had proved true. But early one morning he told us that it was time to move the talks to his message. Regardless of the outcome, that was his task. Its merits were great regardless of the risks to himself or us, he said. So that morning he told his official hosts that he had an important political matter to discuss and that he would appreciate their sparing some time for it. He began by expressing his gratitude to the Chinese government for having brought up his children so well and for helping his family through a trying period. He prized this intimate relationship with China more highly than anything else in his political life. He did not mention his relationship, or ours, with Zhou. He merely stressed that as a friend of China he felt it was his obligation to relay an important message on a vital international issue. Then, with great tact and eloquence, he presented his message, ending with a request to see Zhou.

Their hostility was palpable. How, they demanded, had he received the message?

He told them about Norman Hannah.

As he did, I sensed their cold rage. They concluded the discussion abruptly by saying that Zhou was much too preoccupied with domestic affairs to receive foreigners and that part of his duties with respect to foreign affairs had been transferred to them anyway. No one said a word bearing on Father's report.

All through the meeting a man had been taking down everything Father said, while the interpreter, Mrs. Lin, had continually used pejorative words and phrases in her translation. Wai and I had interrupted her repeatedly to correct her inaccuracies. This had not pleased her.

As we left Father asked how I thought it had gone.

"Badly," I said. "Very badly."

But I did not tell him how badly. When we returned to Beijing, I used all the numbers I knew to reach Zhou and Liao. Finally I reached one only a special aide ever answered, but the voice was different. I knew instinctively from tis tone that something was wrong. My last direct link with Zhou had been cut.

FATHER, WAI, AND I were taken to a pleasant hostel on Fragrant Mountain in the Western Hills a few miles outside Beijing for a rest. I knew we would stay there until some response to Father's extraordinary message was worked out. How this would be done I no longer knew. Father bemoaned the disorder that was wrecking China. He feared for Zhou, Liao, and Chen Yi, the people whom he knew most about and for whom he had great respect. I feared what was to come.

A few days later we were informed that a senior official would receive my father. For a moment I had a flicker of hope. The official was someone who had known of the initial negotiations between

Zhou and Father in Rangoon. He had met Wai and me when we had come to China eleven years before. Even then, when we couldn't speak the same language, I had thought him kind because his face was so expressive and so quick to smile.

Now it was a different face. I sensed his reluctance when Father embraced him. Never had I seen him so cold, so serious, as when he sat down surrounded by the leaders of the Foreign Ministry rebels. In our years in China he'd invited us to dinner with his family several times. He lived in a lovely Foreign Ministry compound on the eastern side of Beijing. The house was modest but stylish, with books lining the walls and decorated with beautiful art from the countries where he had served. Once he had taken us to the Chrysanthemum Festival in Beijing, buying us two plants that over the years had grown and blossomed in our courtyard. Other times, he had come to visit Wai and me in our house, and whenever he did, I served him Thai style, kneeling on the carpet to pour his tea while he sat on the sofa. Zhou had always insisted on our observing certain Thai manners, and no Thai custom was more important than this way of showing respect to older people, serving them without standing above them. Then he had accepted the practice with good grace. But now, as I bent forward to kneel down, he winced and commanded, "Get up! It's time to break with these old feudal customs."

I turned red with embarrassment. Father chose to ignore the rudeness. He had gotten used to it the last few days.

"You have been a friend of the Chinese government and people for many years, so you should readily understand that the Chinese government categorically rejects any so-called peace talks concerning Vietnam as an outright sellout," the official said sharply.

"For the Chinese government to try to persuade the heroic Vietnamese people to lay down their arms when confronting a ferocious imperialist power would be a betrayal of the people of the world as well as of the people of Vietnam and China," he went on. Even to act as an intermediary for such plots, he said, was "to stab China in the back." Father, he snapped, had turned himself into "a lackey of the imperialists."

For once Father was speechless. But he rallied himself, fervently denying the accusations.

"How have I harmed China?" he asked. "When I was in jail all those years, I was called a Chinese lackey. But I was not then nor am I now anybody's lackey. I am an independent Thai. I am not about to change my feelings and positions now. You know full well that I am not a representative of the U.S. government—certainly not a lackey on its behalf. I am merely transmitting a message which I think might be of use to China and to world peace. In my opinion it is a strategic error for China to remain in 'a war on two fronts.' it is only a matter of time before China and the United States come to some understanding. The United States cannot persist much longer in recognizing the Taiwan regime as 'China' and ignore the real China. That is the trend of world events as I see it."

Then, drawing on the full strength of his deep voice, he emphatically stressed that "If I have done anything to displease the Chinese government, I will apologize as a guest to a host, but I will not do so for the bearing of this message." With that, the official abruptly ended the meeting.

We talked little that night. There was nothing to do now but wait, and we did not have to do so for long: the next morning, we were summoned to meet with the same official and the rebels. The official was clearly the spokesman, but did he believe in what he was saying? It would not be the first time the Chinese had chosen someone to deliver a message precisely because he did not agree with it.

The official spoke almost at the top of his voice. "China regards U.S. imperialism as her number one enemy. It has built military bases in a half moon surrounding China, which it is planning to invade." Growing ever more angry, he warned that no matter how many troops the United States deployed against China, "they will receive a deadly welcome. While the Chinese navy and air force lag far behind America's, China's army, militia, and armed people are powerful enough to repel and crush any U.S. invaders."

I knew this was just the windup for the real message. I watched his face tighten; he was acting under duress, I thought. He had not, I realized, mentioned anything about our relations with Zhou Enlai, even though he knew about them. He had not raised any questions about the way we had lived, nor had he mentioned Liao at all.

"As you have acted on behalf of U.S. imperialism, no matter how heroic and meritorious your previous record, the people of Thailand and the world will throw you into the garbage can of history. You have betrayed the people of Thailand, of China, and of the world."

Pausing only briefly, he looked directly at Father and said between clenched teeth, as if he were swearing, "You are welcome here no longer. The Chinese government orders that you leave immediately."

None of us was surprised. Father was quite calm as he said his farewell. "I have been and remain a true friend of China. As far as you yourself are concerned, Your Excellency, I shall never forget what you have done for me and my children. Although I am departing with a profound misunderstanding between us, I shall never do anything unfavorable to China."

The official agreed to let us accompany Father back to Macao. There was little left to say now, and as someone was with us almost every minute, it would have been hard to speak in any event. Father promised to do all he could to help us. It's too late now, I thought. You leave, and my world here is destroyed. Now you are an enemy of China. Once we could live here as friends; now that is gone.

We saw Pridi, and Father told him the story. I no longer listened. I saw more banners denoucning more people I knew; Pridi talked more about the leaders now under attack. He was soon to leave for France—he had had enough of China and its Cultural Revolution.

But Wai and I had no way out. Father felt it was not an appropriate moment for us to leave anyway; we might be at risk, but the bond of friendship was still a fragile one. To turn away now would be misunderstood. And it was true that I still felt a part of China, at least as long Zhou and Liao were there. Perhaps, Father suggested, this abnormal situation would change. Hasty decisions should be avoided. He begged me to understand him and be patient.

"Get in touch with Premier Zhou when you can," he said. "Explain to him what has happened. I have complete confidence in him."

The words that might once have comforted me had long since lost their attraction.

As Father left Wai and me at the border station where he had entered, he could only say, "Well, I've done my duty. I've caused you trouble, true. But I will not be irresponsible; I will do something for you."

What he would do, though, he didn't say. "I believe in you and believe you are strong enough to come through the storm. Life is struggle. Keep in touch!"

CHAPTER 13

The Denunciation

KEEP IN TOUCH! I pushed the words away—they were too painful to think about.

When Old Lai met us at the airport in Beijing, he told us Mrs. Lin was coming to see us that night. He was very worried, but he said nothing else. It could only be bad news.

She arrived shortly after we returned to our house. Stiff and cold, she quickly came to the point: "There is a meeting being held tomorrow that you must go to."

"About what?" Wai asked.

"Go and listen and find out," she said and then left.

Shortly afterward, one of Wai's Thai friends called. Did Wai know what had been happening the last two days? They had been called into a big, organized meeting condemning our father. The leader was Colonel Phayom. He had shamelessly gone from fawner to denouncer within just a few days.

Wai insisted on going out that night. Father was being denounced everywhere. He wanted to find out what was going to happen, to prepare for our defense. I thought of Liao burning his photos.

"Perhaps we should burn some of our papers," I suggested. So that evening before he left, we burned many of Wai's letters from Father and memorabilia of our time in China. If Mother had not taken Wai's diaries and notes of our meetings with Zhou, we would have burned them as well.

Early the next morning Old Lai drove us to the meeting. Wai told me that the meetings against Father had been organized by Colonel Phayom in combination with the Chinese rebels in the Foreign Affairs Office. I knew this script well. It would be unprincipled for the Chinese Foreign Ministry to act directly against us. They would be there only for the opening, to signal their backing, then would withdraw to the sidelines. It would be the Thai "masses" who would speak out through the Thai Patriotic Front.

"We are not alone," Wai said as we drove on. "Vatcharachai Chaiyasithivet and Amphorn Suwarnabon are with us." And Pisit Sripen, who had accompanied us to China, remained a friend.

Vatcharachai was Pridi's former secretary and, like Pridi, a political exile. He admired Father and had long been a good friend of Wai's in Beijing. Amphorn had been one of the two Thai parliament members to undertake the first secret mission to China in 1955. China had granted him political asylum after the Thai military junta's coup in 1958.

The other Thais who lived in China, working as teachers, broadcasters in Thai-language radio, or translators at *China Reconstructs*, did not know much about us or our background. Many of them, supporters of Pridi, had fled when the persecutions had intensified against alleged communist sympathizers. They were employed by the Chinese as "foreign experts." We did not mix with them; our worlds were separate.

Old Lai dropped us off, saying he would wait outside. We went into a room where a platform in front was draped with a red banner inscribed with a Mao quotation. Only about twenty or so people were there. Most stared at us as we entered—no greetings, just grimly appraising eyes.

Someone began by reading from Mao: "Who is your enemy? Who is your friend?" Then another person joined in and another. I found it harder and harder to focus on what was happening, mumbling my way through what had become a joint reading.

I looked at Wai as I read, and for a brief moment our eyes locked. We had long lived in a society that picked out its targets of attack. Now it was our turn.

Then Colonel Phayom rose and began to speak. "Do you have any idea what has been happening in these last few days?" he all but screamed. "A shame has been visited upon all Thai people residing in Beijing! Sang Phathanothai was a traitor in the Japanese war. Now he is a running dog of the American imperialists."

Phayom worked himself up to an impassioned denunciation. "At the time I joined the anti-Japanese resistance with its thousands of patriotic fighters, Sang was collaborating with the invaders and cold-bloodedly selling out the Thai people."

I bowed my head. The words pounded at me. I had no doubt about what else was coming. "Running dog . . . imperialist . . . American lackey . . . spy."

A shrill voice made me look up. "Smash the American lackey Sang's dog's head!" shouted one of the other Thai leaders.

This harangue went on for some time. I was startled to hear a firm, insistent voice saying, "Please, be concrete, be specific." It was Wai. No longer was he my quiet, reticent brother. For years he had studied and thought about who our father was—studied Thai history and World War II, asking Zhou for materials on Chinese history as well. This was the moment when, for him, the elements of his role in China came together.

"You make these accusations freely, but you must be specific," he went on calmly. "And you, Colonel Phayom, who only a few days ago was thanking my father in Guangzhou for saving your life, why have you forgotten to mention this now? I thought you said you were grateful. It was my father who gave you a second life."

Phayom turned crimson all the way down his neck, and momentarily he looked dumbfounded. People did not talk back at struggle meetings, let alone say such things.

"You are a diehard," Phayom finally responded. "Up to this very minute you are still on the side of your father. He was a collaborator then, and he is a collaborator now. The masses condemn him, and they will condemn you, too, if you persist in your die-hard ways."

I looked around at the "masses." I never knew what the word really meant in China. Who were they? The people? Mao was always speaking of the masses deciding the future, deciding destiny—go with the masses, be with the masses. But was this roomful of people the masses? Zhou had never used the word with me, only "people."

"Be specific, please," I heard Wai say again. He was writing down everything that was said. "You have not analyzed the Japanese occupation. Please do so."

"Sang sold out Thailand to Japan!" Phayom screamed. "How can you deny it?"

"No," Wai responded. "There is another interpretation of history involved here. You will be proven wrong."

Wai was cut off. They did not wish to hear the intricacies of Thailand's actual history.

"All through Thai history," Wai went on, undeterred, "it was important for Thailand to learn to . . . "

"Stop, you diehard! Stop this! We will not listen to such rubbish!"

I said nothing. Wai's world was not disintegrating; mine was. As the hours went on, I sank into a paralysis. But not Wai; he could not be broken. That night he would go out with his Thai friends to plan the next day's strategy.

When we returned home, Old Lai said very little, but quietly, in ways he could, he tried to help. "There is food here," he said. He had put water in the iccbox so there would be something to drink. I couldn't focus enough to do anything: I cut mayself badly trying to fix some food. "I'll be in my room," he said. "If you need anything, come to me." His was the only friendly Chinese voice I had heard in days.

The next morning, the attack focused on Wai and his Thai friends.

"You opposed the Great Leap Forward and Chairman Mao's policies," Phayom began.

This was by now a standard way to attack Party leaders who had not been totally enthusiastic about the Great Leap Forward or who had pursued policies in its aftermath that Mao opposed. Wai had indeed questioned the proclaimed successes of the Great Leap Forward: he had known of some of its failures. But he had hardly been involved in any internal Chinese politics. No matter—a correct stance now was a litmus test for revolutionary loyalty to China.

As the hours went on, I found it hard to listen to Wai or any of the acrimonious debate. This spectacle was running its course, and that course would not last much longer. Would they put us in a labor camp? I wondered. If not that, what? Anything could happen now.

One of Wai's Thai friends dismissed the idea when I broached it after the second day of meetings. "It violates all their rules of dealing with foreigners, of what is internal and what is for another country to deal with."

"Who is observing any rules here?" Wai replied. He too expected the worst soon.

The third night back in Beijing, Mrs. Lin called. "Are you alone?" she asked me, knowing full well Wai was not home. It was all part of the script. She would be over shortly.

She arrived with Colonel Phayom and Miss Nitaya, whose reputation I knew of from her long years as a Thai Communist Youth delegate to the Moscow conference in the mid-1950s. The fates had not been smiling when they picked such a cruel and bitter person to attack me, I thought as I saw her. Old Lai withdrew into the background when they entered. They were clearly very tense.

"Wai is a diehard," they said. "There is no way to win him over. It is astonishing you both grew up here and this is the attitude he expresses. Wai's thinking is deeply reactionary and bourgeois. He will not change."

I looked up, wondering what next.

"Wai will be expelled from China along with his Thai friends," they said.

I recoiled. "When?"

"Tomorrow."

After all these years he was simply to be thrown out.

"In the name of revolutionary fraternity we have asked the Chinese public security to cooperate, and they have said they will do so. It's a shame that China has wasted so much on an ungrateful bastard like Wai, who had eaten Chinese rice and then spat on the heads of the Chinese people."

I looked up at the woman who had pronouced these lines with such hatred.

"You have said nothing so far," they went on. Did that mean, they asked, that I supported my brother or disagreed with him? "We will wait and see."

I said nothing.

"You have been sympathetic to China in the past. The Communist party stresses the differences between individuals even if they come from the same mud like you and your brother. You are an independent person, and there is no need for you to run after your brother all the time. But you yourself have to choose your own destiny."

In all the years I was in China, no one had ever talked to me in the name of the Communist party.

"There are two roads open to you. One is to follow the reactionary footsteps of your father and your brother and the other dregs of society with a hopeless future before you. The other is to take the bright and glorious road of revolution."

Their rhetoric seemed to lift their spirits.

"He is leaving. Are you ready to draw a sharp line of demarcation from your brother? From now on he is your enemy. You have to denouce him. He is to be deported tomorrow."

"Must Wai really leave?" I whispered.

"It is an absolute order from the masses." My accusers were becoming impatient. I was given ten minutes to decide whether I wanted to go with Wai.

I couldn't think. I sat very still. My heart, far from pounding in agitation, seemed to be pumping more and more slowly. Any moment, I felt, it might stop.

In traditional China to be deported was considered the next worst punishment to execution. I'd be labeled an "enemy of China." Perhaps I also felt—though I would not have been able to put it into words—that Father had abandoned Wai and me once again. And I would not abandon the people who had taken me in. If they had said to me, "Zhou and Liao want you to get out; you have lived a rotten privileged life and have become a bourgeois," then I would have gone.

"I'll stay," I murmured.

They were pleased. "In that case you must denounce your brother tomorrow. You must denounce him along our line without playing any of your little tricks. The masses will know if your feelings are genuine or not."

Their faces were aglow with triumph. "Blood relations are not the true relations," Miss Nitaya was saying. "Only the relation with the Party is the true one."

I'd seen a film of a wife denouncing her husband, a son his father, but that had not been my world until now.

I stared blankly at "Auntie" Lin.

"You will need to denounce Wai for his anti–Mao Zedong views of the Great Leap Forward and the Cultural Revolution and as a die-hard follower of your father," she concluded, glaring at me.

"I just wish to be able to stay and live among the ordinary Chinese people," I said. I knew then that my one hope was to remain some-how under Chinese, not Thai Communist, supervision.

"Don't tell your brother," they said as they prepared to leave. They were adamant on that point. "Don't discuss it with him. We will know if you do. You burned your papers. We know."

I wept for hours while Wai was out. I tried to see mayself as one of the revolutionary heros I'd read about courageously denouncing their own family. But this revolution was not like the one I'd once enjoyed imagining. It was cruel and brutal, filled with big words about the masses and Chairman Mao. What had happened to all those words about being a bridge between Thailand and China? Why did Chairman Mao need the Red Guards to protect him? What had gone wrong?

Wai returned late that night. He had met with his Thai friends to plan their course of action the next day and then had stopped by to say good-bye to his girlfriend in case the worst happened. He was shaken and on the verge of tears. His girlfriend's house had been ransacked and her parents labeled "ghosts" and "monsters" and pa-raded through the streets. The news of what was happening to him had not yet reached the "masses," but it could not be long in coming. With Father and now Wai regarded as anti-China elements, there was no future for their relationship. Her family would have to pro-tect themselves if they possibly could, but he no longer knew how that would be possible. His own world had once served to protect them; now it was likely to lead to even greater trials for them. His girlfriend had collapsed, Wai said, when they parted. It had been over five years since they had met at the conservatory, and Zhou and Liao, approving of their relationship, had arranged for her to go to the Foreign Language Institute and study Thai so that she would feel at home in Thailand. Wai had told me of his plans to marry her. "I doubt I will ever see her again," he said in despair.

I burst into tears when he spoke of their separation. Of ours I said nothing. The cook, or someone, was likely to be listening to our conversations now. To avoid thinking about what he had just been through, Wai talked of his plans for the next morning.

"How much time will he have to say any of this?" I thought to myself.

The next morning, I felt very, very cold and, still saying nothing to Wai, went off to the meeting with him. As soon as it began, the rebels asked if anyone wanted to speak. They looked straight at me.

Hands folded, I sat with my head down, barely able to talk. "Wai is a diehard protecting my father," I said. "For years he has been saying negative things about China. I am talking on his behalf." I expressed "regret" for what he had done and said. I dared not look at Wai.

It was all choreographed down to the last humiliating, insulting detail. Before Wai could respond or come toward me, People's Liberation Army troops burst into the room, seizing him and his Thai friends. Never had I expected the PLA to be involved. They acted quickly, decisively, restraining Wai and two others, Vatcharachai and Pisit.

Then I saw Shanan. I had not seen him for months. He looked ghastly. He stood at the front of the room, emotionless. But as he looked at me a flash of pain crossed his eyes. Then he spoke.

Wai had committed "criminal acts," he said, reading from a text I knew he had not written. "He has never shown any sign of repentance these last days, though the revolutionary masses have tried very hard to win him over. He refuses to be transformed. Therefore, the People's Revolutionary Committee has decided to deport him."

I heard Wai and the others being dragged away, but I couldn't look up. What must Wai think of me? How could I have denounced him? I couldn't explain—and there was no time. I was not to be allowed even to say good-bye to my brother. I had no family anymore, no brother, no honor; only shame. I sat perfectly still.

The room grew quiet for a moment after Wai and the others were taken out. Then Phayom and a few others came over to me. Beneath their serious demeanor, they were laughing at me, I felt certain.

"You see, we warned you. . . . We have been trying to help your brother. . . . He didn't take help. Now it's your turn. You have to speak now." They told me I was very sick—ideologically sick. "We are your ideological doctors." They could cure me if I cooperated, they said. But that would depend on how I behaved.

Hadn't I lived a life of luxury? I said I was sorry.

"Not good enough," was their reply. "You must change your soul."

I could not stand up. I shook with cold chills and felt nauseated. It was impossible to think. I said whatever they wanted to hear.

"Why didn't you demand to live among the Chinese masses when you came to China?"

I said I had.

"That is not true."

Okay, it was not true.

"You demanded a car."

"No, I didn't."

"That's not true."

Okay, it was not true.

"Who authorized your house? Who brought you to China?"

"The authorities," I said. "I have no idea who." I did not mention Zhou.

And then questions and insinuations about Liao. How did I know him? Were we close? How close? But they could not probe too far yet; Liao's case was not yet publicly decided. They still had to be cautious. If they could get me to talk, fine; but they could not make accusations. They knew the rules.

No, I said, I knew Liao only officially. That was all.

I started vomiting in the afternoon and pleaded to go home. But it seemed I no longer had that "black den," as they now referred to it. Well, perhaps I could have some clean clothes and some personal things? Never mind, they said, you can do without such fancy clothes.

Very well, then, I could do without.

The house was sealed so they could make a careful search of everything and uncover the counterrevolutionary plots of my brother. I thought sadly of my paintings and photos from my ten years in China and the piano from Zhou, now condemned as a bour-

geois instrument. Whyever had I stayed? My bewilderment grew
and grew as the denunciations came hurling at me.

At last they put me into a dark, stuffy room in the Beijing Hotel.
At key moments in my life in China I always seemed to end up there.
This time it was my cell. There was no phone, and I was not to leave
the room for any reason. They left me that first afternoon and the
next day as well. I was clearly too sick. I no longer felt pain or sor-
row. I could only weep.

Soon, though, they were back, "Auntie" Lin and her Thai companion, Miss Nitaya. I was to write my self-criticism, they said. I was
to go into every detail of my corrupt, decadent ways.

"You must tell everything if your soul is to be saved. You are the
offspring of a capitalist American spy and traitor. You have associated with Chinese leaders who led the capitalist road. Your luxurious
life testifies to how they have sought to propagate an elite living on
the hard work of the masses."

My "capitalist roader" friends were China's sworn enemies, they
concluded. "You took to the capitalist lifestyle like a duck to water.
Perhaps you will need to go down among the masses to learn from
the masses you have so long despised."

I remained silent.

They left me so that I could write the story of my ten years in
China. I was to reflect well on my father, too; he had always been a
decadent bourgeois reactionary. And I was to tell them in exact detail of my relations with Chinese leaders. I looked at my pen for a
long time. I knew I had to write something. Doing nothing would
bring even worse abuse. I wrote how spoiled I was, how my privileges had corrupted me and given me a bad attitude. I thought of all
the examples I could. I began to fill the pages. But no word of Liao
or Zhou. Their sudden disappearance from my life meant they were
in difficulty; it was dangerous even to refer to them. I criticized myself for not having anything to say about the Chinese leaders. I had
only seen them officially, I didn't understand. And I was too ideologically backward to figure it out. I should have studied Chairman
Mao's works more.

Colonel Phayom returned with the others the next day. They
hated my self-criticism. Phayom paced back and forth, stroking his
little mustache. I hated that mustache; to me it seemed a symbol of

his deep self-love and self-importance, his vanity hiding under his revolutionary rhetoric.

I had been told to write in Thai, but I was far less fluent in it than in Chinese. Worse, I had never learned to write in the clichés they wanted. Most of all, I had failed miserably to supply them with any material useful against their other targets.

"Where is the story of your connections with China's 'black gang'?" Phayom shouted at one point. "You are sick, sick. You must confess!"

I said nothing.

"You are hiding the truth. You will surely be punished if you do not change your ways."

As he screeched on, I turned to "Auntie" Lin and spoke to her for the first time during those sessions.

"Auntie, every time Liao came to our house you were present. You should be able to convey what happened better than I can. He trusted you a lot, I know. I was only a child, what can I say?"

Her face twisted into a furious grimace, and she exploded in anger. "You bourgeois scum, tell us the truth! Don't evade the facts!"

To speak, I now understood, was to open myself up to even further attack. Thereafter I said as little as possible. Finally, Phayom picked up my self-criticism and threw it at me. I was to write it again. I was to do it over and over until I had bared my soul. They would be back the next day. And the next day it was much the same. They hated my new draft even more. As I became more and more worn down and incoherent, they couldn't quite decide if my confusion was real or not.

"Your front and back don't touch," one said in exasperation. "You are lying."

"You are no longer to run away from your past," Phayom admonished, shaking his finger at me.

"Okay, I will not do that."

"You must promise to examine yourself more deeply now."

"Okay, I will."

"You must examine the history of your father from the standpoint of the masses. Who were his contacts over the years? Detail them!"

"Okay, I will."

"And tell us who the Chinese black gang was who supported you in such extravagant style all these years."

"Okay, I will tell all."

Once again I was left with a blank piece of paper. I could no longer remember what I had written the last time, and by now my hand seemed barely able to shape the letters of the wooden words I was expected to use. Even the details of my own life were somehow vague and uncertain to me. That night I hardly wrote anything.

They were utterly exasperated the next morning and did not stay long. My sessions stopped. For two days no one came.

Then "Auntie" Lin returned with a woman from the Foreign Ministry. A decision had been reached.

"You are to condemn your father on Radio Beijing. You are to solemnly declare that you are severing all relations with your father and your family and turning to the road of the revolution."

They went through all the points on which I was to condemn my father. Then they left; I had one night to write it.

"No good, no good at all," they said the next day. Neither they nor I was surprised. It no longer mattered—they had arrived with a text for me to read. I was to say Father was a lackey of the American imperialists and the reactionary Thai government. That he was engaged in a sinister mission to collect information about the Great Proletarian Cultural Revolution and to feel the Chinese government's pulse on the possibility of a cease-fire in Vietnam, and thereby to facilitate the destruction of the Vietnamese people's armed struggle for independence and national unification. I dimly sensed, however, an even more sinister objective—to publicly discredit Father was to indirectly go after Zhou himself.

My vision blurred as I read, and Miss Nitaya, impatient, had to help me again and again. I barely recognized some of the Chinese clichés in Thai. I stumbled over the words; I couldn't figure out where to pause. I stopped trying to make sense of it or of what was happening. I just wanted the ordeal to end.

Then they were gone. I didn't know for how long: days and nights were indistinguishable except for a little light that occasionally came in through one of the windows. Then one day they returned. A car was coming to take me to the radio station. As we stepped out of the hotel, I recoiled at the sun's bright light. It was the first time I'd been outside my room in a month.

"Don't make mistakes in reading your statement," they said.

I practiced when I arrived, but I stuttered badly and often mumbled. They were angry, but they stopped attacking me long enough for me to read the statement through once more. The rebels at the radio station were impatient to get it over with. They had other revolutionary things to do.

In a haze, almost persuaded I was watching and hearing someone else, I sat in front of a microphone and began to read aloud. I stumbled at spots. As I came to the end, arriving at the point where I was to announce that I was cutting off all ties with my family, I choked up. Tears streamed down my face, my voice broke, and I barely mumbled out the last words. They were furious. But they accepted my performance as adequate—minimally. It demonstrated that I had not really made a start on my inner revolution.

And yet I was utterly transformed inside. I was alone. I had denounced my family, my brother was gone, Zhou and Liao could not be reached, Kazu had left me. It was unbearable to think of them, any of them. I pushed them away. My family wouldn't want to know me now anyway. I, who had once felt cast out, now felt that I was the one doing the casting.

THREE WEEKS PASSED. No one came except the hotel staff to clean and to provide food. They did not speak. Nor did I. I sensed the fear—and the coldness.

With nothing to listen to, nothing to read, I lay in bed, too tired to dress. What would become of me now? What were they going to do? I dreaded being handed over to the Thai radicals living in China. Perhaps they would send me into the jungle in northern Thailand as a hostage guerrilla.

At night I dreamed painfully about Kazu. By day I worried about Wai. Had he gotten out? I told myself I had no control over my fate—why worry? They would come when they were ready. And they did, the same three—Phayom, Mrs. Lin, Miss Nitaya. I found it hard to concentrate on what they were saying. Something about how much they had to pay to keep me in such a hotel. Vaguely I sensed they were not sure what to do with me. I was not of much use to them at the moment.

Timidly, feebly, so as not to suggest the idea was anyone's but their own, I said, "I could go back to my dormitory at Beida so I could learn from the Chinese masses."

They exchanged quick glances. "Very well. Get ready. You have fifteen minutes."

I was driven back to my dorm and left there. My worldly possessions now consisted of two pairs of pants and three shirts. I had no money. In the three months I had been gone, the university had changed. The dormitory was largely deserted; I was the only foreign student. Soon I was entirely alone there, too—my Chinese roommate abruptly moved out, having heard my family were class enemies. She said nothing, just left.

When I looked out the window, I thought of Kazu walking toward my door. I rarely left my room, fearing I would be attacked. I turned the light off early each evening and scarcely moved about in the dark. For some reason the canteen was still operating, through few used it. Weak from hunger, I went one morning. The cook recognized me. I waited for the blow. But instead he gave a slight smile. "What are you eating?" he asked. After that I knew I could come. If I forgot to turn up, he would inquire about me. "Why didn't you come for lunch?" We never spoke of anything else but the weather. He and the other cook were humane. They were the only ones.

The university itself had become a battle zone. Verbal fights had given way to pitched battles. The campus was divided into two warring states, the conservative faction and the rebel faction. Both had loudspeakers with which to blare vehement denunciations at each other twenty-four hours a day. Both pledged undying allegiance to Chairman Mao. Both were his most loyal followers; their opposites were evil incarnate. Each faction had its own armband for identification. Anyone who entered the wrong zone was sure to be pelted with stones and accused of spying. Laboratories were turning into miniature arms factories to produce tear gas and hand grenades.

My dormitory was in the conservative zone, protected by a newly erected steel gate. I got up one day to look around and decided I had better try to learn what was going on. I thought I'd join the faction I was living among. That would be better than total isolation. I knew that the conservative group was not attacking Chen Yi or any of my old friends, while the other was. I asked one of the members if I could join. I made out an application and went to a meeting.

A few days later some of the leaders of the organization came to my dormitory. I immediately knew they had come not to praise but to denounce. I was right: they returned my application. "You are the daughter of a traitor, and our organization can only have members who are pure Red." They continued to read their pronouncement, but I was no longer listening.

For days afterward I kept to my room, eating only occasionally. The loudspeakers blared away incessantly, but I rarely heard them. Once, though, I was startled into listening to a story that was being broadcast. In great detail it compared the kinds of speeches Khrushchev had made when Stalin was alive and what he did after. Khrushchev, the article said, was always saying that everyone should study Comrade Stalin's great works of genius. But weeks after his death he was already plotting to destroy Stalin's reputation. Stalin was so pleased with all the praise, it had gone to his head. And then Khrushchev had denounced him.

The message was not covert: it fit Mao and Vice Chairman Lin Biao all too well. There was not a word about Lin, of course, but the language about the genius of Comrade Stalin, about the whole nation's studying his works, that was Lin's false flattery—the unctuous praise that made one of Mao's words worth ten thousand of a mere mortal's. Liao, I knew, had never like Lin: he had no pictures of him, for one. Zhou had spoken of his brilliance as a general but not about his role as defense minister after 1958.

For the first time I felt there might be hope. Perhaps not everyone in my world has gone made, I thought. I must try to find out what is happening. I will not survive if I stay here. The only step, though, seemed a dangerous one. I had to contact Zhou. In desperation I decided to phone. But I only vaguely remembered the number now. What if it was the wrong one? I dialed and immediately recognized the voice of the aide who answered; its tone was normal.

"This is Little Yuan, Uncle. What shall I do? There is *wudou*—physcial struggle—here."

"Where are you?" the voice asked.

"At Beijing University."

"Go and contact Comrade Lu at the headquarters of the workers' team stationed there."

That was all. For a moment I was heartened. Then I became afraid—whom could I trust? Perhaps even one of Zhou's closest aides could no longer be counted on. He would report me to the university's Revolutioinary Committee, which had already sentenced some of my old professors to jail and sent others to physical labor in the countryside.

I went back to my room, locked the door, and waited. After several days there was a loud knock. I did not stir. The knock came again.

"Chang Yuan, open the door." The man had a thick voice; I didn't recognize it or his accent.

"I am Old Lu. Open the door."

Although I still hesitated, I knew I had nothing to lose—anyone could break the door in anyway.

Lu walked in quickly. He glanced at me, then around the room. "How can you live like this?" he asked.

I knew instantly that he was a friend. I knew it from his eyes. For so long I'd seen only cold, piercing, resentful eyes. His were gentle. He was a member of the university's Revolutionary Committee, but I quickly understood that he was a part of Zhou's old network.

He asked how long I had lived "like this" and why no one had told him I was there. He had only heard that day, when the premier's office had called and asked him to look after me. I started to cry, for once with relief.

Old Lu took me away with him and placed me in a guest house on the far side of the lake. It was tranquil and beautiful and out of reach of the never-ending noise of the loudspeakers and battles. I was to rest and eat, Old Lu said. He would stop by whenever he could. He was kind and talkative, but for both of us reserve about anything important was now second nature. He took me out one day to buy some new clothes, since I had none, and he gave me a hundred yuan.

After several weeks I told him I was afraid the rebels in Zhou's office would come hunting for me again. We agreed that I had to get away. Zhou could sometimes act to help in an emergency but these days no one was safe for long. If I were caught again by the Thai rebels or by the rebels in the Foreign Ministry, it would be difficult for anyone to protect me.

Was it possible, I asked Old Lu, having spent those weeks considering various alternatives, for me to go live in the countryside? I could change my name and hope no one but him would be able to find me.

He sounded doubtful. Could I stand life deep in the countryside?

"It would be safer than here."

"That is true," he said reluctantly. "Perhaps we have no other choice."

I had had pleasant visits to the rural areas in my travels around China over the years, but I was under few illusions about living there. Zhou had told me repeatedly how hard it was, and Liao had never wanted me to work there even for a short time. Now it seemed my only recourse.

Two days later, Old Lu was back. We agreed that I should change my name to Pan Hong. I was to stay with a People's Liberation Army work team in a large model commune in Hebei. Together, the two of us traveled by bus deep into the rural areas. It was the start of a very different life for me, in a China I had never known.

CHAPTER 14

In Hiding

"WRITE TO NO ONE," Old Lu said as the bus wound and bumped along the dirt roads. No one else was to know where I was. My torment was only beginning, I thought. The few people who knew my destination might disappear and, with them, my slim hold on the worlds from which I had come.

Old Lu explained to me as we got off the bus that there was still a way to go—we would walk. We started down a small road, Lu carrying my few belongings. After a while a tractor sent by the army found us. The bumps of the bus drive had made me slightly nauseated; the tractor was far worse.

The land seemed so vast and dusty. There was dust everywhere, covering me. My hair was caked with it, and it felt somehow, oddly, as though the inside of my stomach were lined with it. I glanced at the crops along the road: soon I would be tending them. Only my Thai and Chinese tormenters could make this seem like a momentary refuge.

For a moment I remembered a child in a film I'd seen, a daughter of a faithful mandarin lord persecuted and banished to a faraway place like this. Hadn't she resolutely faced her destiny and gone on? Wasn't this now my role? I dismissed the thought—a futile fantasy—as Old Lu left me.

Helping to sweep it aside, perhaps, was the overwhelming stench of manure everywhere. It was the village's only fertilizer. My stomach clenched at the first whiff, and I fought desperately to calm the waves of nausea. In the future, long after I had forgotten precisely what the houses looked like or the names of the people, I could still conure up that smell.

The People's Liberation Army was stationed in two of the village courtyards, in a large compound housing approximately a hundred and fifty soldiers. immediately sensed their discipline and their high priority on order and cleanliness. The mud floors were swept clean, the wash hung neatly on the lines, everything seemed perfectly organized. A young woman led me to one of the rooms, explaining that four people lived in each one. Under each of the four beds a basin stood in precisely the same spot as the others. The blankets were rolled up exactly the same way and neatly placed at the head of the beds.

"The horn wakes us at four forty-five A.M., and drill starts at five," she said. "We march to the dining hall, and exactly thirty minutes later we are on our way to the fields to work."

She was briskly efficient but friendly as well. She must have thought I looked horrible, two dark eyes staring out of a gaunt face. She, after all, was just the opposite, her square, full, red face exuding cheerful energy and goodwill. A more suitable model of PLA purposefulness and vigor could scarcely have been found.

First she had me clean up. I washed as best I could with the bucket of earth-colored water, though I actually felt stickier afterward. I unpacked my few clothes. I had brought a small mirror with me, but I put it away without looking at myself.

Within the day all formalities were complete. Having set me up in the army barracks, my guide cut my hair and shepherded me through the daily PLA activities.

A great revolution in production was being heralded in the village when I arrived. Every PLA soldier had his or her own *Little Red Book* and searched through it each day to find quotations to help the peasants with the problems that came up. I was assigned to help write materials for the local radio and for the public meetings. The big red banners, the Mao books, the gongs were soon so habitual as to be something I scarcely noticed. After a week or so, I was strong enough to join the other members of the PLA who worked in the fields, the officers as well as the ordinary soldiers. They had a warm camaraderie, and they worked as hard as the peasants.

They also ate like the peasants. But I could barely eat any of the food. Some of the PLA soldiers saved the fatty parts of the meat for me; I couldn't keep that down. Finally, they gave up and let me eat just vegetables in the summer. When winter came, I lived largely on salty tofu.

After years in China, I had learned to bathe only once a day. Now it was to be once a year, with dry baths the rest of the time. I'd have willingly washed my clothes daily, but the others would have laughed at such an exercise, so I washed them once a week. When there was soap available, it was so coarse that it bruised my skin, and the smell of the lavatory always overpowered me. I'd start to gag whenever I used it—the smell was equaled only by the thorough lack of hygiene.

I was determined to push on. Hadn't Zhou and Liao often spoken of having to pass through many hardships and sufferings to become a person? There was nothing heroic about this, though. It was merely survival.

Although my mind urged me on, my body started to rebel. I broke out in a severe rash, and my face swelled up. I was given antihistamines and, when my condition became too servere, sedatives to induce long periods of sleep. At night, though, I couldn't breathe. I had developed asthma that struck whenever I'd start to think about what was happening to me. When I was alone and the lights were off, I'd begin a fierce internal lamentation. Why hadn't I left? Why had I clung to my pride in belonging to China? Was I being punished for it? For my condemnation of my family? Why had everything been taken away from me? Would there be no end to this? Worst of all were my thoughts of Kazu.

During the day it was easier: I was able to stop thinking. Tired from lack of sleep, I still greeted the first light with relief. I threw myself into whatever activity I could.

The work was arduous, especially in the fall, when we harvested from dawn until ten at night. Once we'd cut the wheat, it could not be left as it was, or it would get soggy and spoil. So in the evening the cut wheat had to be gathered, the chaff separated, the bundles bound and stacked. The peasants were very kind, making only the gentlest jokes about my awkwardness. Often I would cut my fingers using the scythe, and they would come to my aid and urge me to rest. But for me the hours of physical labor were the only times I didn't have to think. It was the only time I felt safe.

The PLA leader was a tall, thin, good-looking officer. Perhaps sensing my loneliness, he told me that he was there if I needed help; both of us knew that little more could be said in those days. About the physical hardships he could do nothing: the village was desperately poor. I did my best never to complain. I had learned to adapt to very different worlds, and in this one, the harshest of them physically, I intended to do so again.

One day the young woman who had taken charge of me the first day watched me washing my clothes and began to laugh, no doubt at my clumsiness and inefficiency. Evidently she told the others, because one day shortly thereafter the PLA commander took me aside. We could do the washing together in the future, he said. What he really meant was that he would wash my things for me. He did so quietly, drawing no attention to what he was doing. And he found other discreet ways to cheer me up.

"I was a follower of Peng Dehuai," he confided. "But don't tell anybody. I served under him." This he said with great pride. "He was much loved and respected by all of us. Have courage."

These words astonished me—they were not only support but support of an especially brave kind. Peng was still being condemned as one of Chairman's Mao's worst opponents, his first critic during the Great Leap Forward. Lin Biao, who had replaced him as defense minister in 1958, hated him. Zhu De, on the other hand, loved him enormously, and what I remembered in him was precisely the type of sincerity and strength that Zhu De himself embodied. Like Zhu, he had changed little after going to live in the cities in 1949. The first time I saw him at Tiananmen Square he was saluting Mao, but I felt it was as an equal. Despite the accusations against Peng, I never heard a critical world from Zhou about him.

I knew of Mao's meeting with Peng in the fall of 1965, a reunion that had seemed to go well, only to be followed by the most vitriolic attacks ever on Peng and practically everyone connected with him. I no longer thought, though, about what Mao might be thinking. I could barely think about Zhou either. I knew he was still in power: I saw his picture in the papers posted in the village. But his world was now enormously far away; almost as though I too were a peasant, I shared the sense of an almost cosmic distance between me and the people of influence at the top. Imagining them was like looking up at the stars in the sky—they were that far off and that unlikely to look back down. The world of my daily life was the only one I now felt existed, and though the mention of Peng Dehuai briefly hinted at another reality, I could no longer bear to hope.

I was not unjustified. The good-spirited, generous comaraderie of my PLA cohorts was infected by the bitterness and humiliations I thought I had left behind. Mao's call for struggle had been translated into yet a new need to attack the old landlords. As in the books and films of old China that I had read and seen when I had first come to Beijing, the bad were to be separated out from the good and struggle engaged in by all to triumph over the bad. I was to help organize the struggle meeting of a local landlord who had already been picked out. Perhaps Mao was right, I thought, perhaps such rooting out of the old was necessary. Certainly the old ways were wicked, the old class privileges unjust. And certainly the peasants were kind and humane; Mao seemed to know much about their strengths and weaknesses. Zhou had thought so. Mao, he had said, constantly fought to root himself in their experience.

This was what I tried to persuade myself of. But as soon as we approached the meeting room, I felt a familiar dread. Up front was the old landlord, looking utterly helpless, bent over, a placard already wrapped around him, a hat—that tall, tall hat with the black name splashed on it. His head was shaved, his clothes were dirty, his dignity stripped away.

His humiliation was total. There was nothing he could do but sit and cringe as the accusations rained down on him, blow after blow, day after day. The gongs sounded, the drums beat, and the PLA led cheery-sounding songs of victory. Laughing, the peasants joined in.

I tried to put myself into the position of the peasants. Surely they had valid grounds for their grievances. The old society had been brutally hard and vicious; it had to be destroyed. And yet it was with this old man, with this person reduced to wretchedness, that I identified. I was determined to go through with the meeting nevertheless. I wanted to be able to go along, to proclaim, however mildly, my willingness to belong. I couldn't assume that I was right and the others wrong. I couldn't simply reject what everyone was saying: He took the land from the masses. . . . He did this awful deed, then that one. . . . The record over the years added up and up. . . . The punishment will never be adequate to the deeds.

I'd stay for a few minutes until nausea overcame me. He looks the way I feel, I thought. I would hurry to the toilet, a ten-minute walk away, and by going frequently enough, I was able to miss most of the struggle meetings over the course of the following days. Afterward I couldn't get the old man out of my mind. Perhaps he had been a terrible brute in the past. I thought that was likely. But between the moments of high drama, the peasants were laughing at him. They did not seem consumed by fury.

Something is wrong with me, I thought. Something inside me isn't quite right. Where was the redeeming logic in all that was happening? Could it all be wrong? And Mao too? Was he mad? "Politics is cruel," I heard Liao say. "Some attacks are unjust," he had said, but the masses ultimately were not. Were these the masses? They seemed good natured and expansive in their narrow, constricted world. What was it, then, that allowed such ghastly spectacles to go on? And why did no one else seem repelled?

AFTER ABOUT SIX MONTHS my unit was ordered to move to another location. I was to remain behind. The commander seemed very worried about what was to happen to me.

"Life with the peasants will be somewhat harder," he said. "But try to take it in stride. I've picked out a family I think is the most reliable of all. I'd never feel at ease leaving you alone with just anyone."

The next day he helped me move into my home, politely introducing me to an elderly-looking woman he called Lao Da Ma. I was to stay until Old Lu returned with other arrangements; the commander had no idea when that would be. When he got ready to leave, I tried to thank him. He had been my lifeline, but any expression of real feelings was now too hard. After he left, I couldn't even remember his name.

Lao Da Ma's son was the leader of the Revolutionary Committee in the village, a hardworking young man of nineteen. The family had suffered bitterly under the old landlords, but now they were proud of their new ways and hopeful about the future. They took me in as part of their social duty.

They had built their three-room house themselves, and in it lived the son and his new bride, Lao Da Ma, and another son. One room had been taken over by the newlyweds, one was used as the kitchen, and one was for the reigning matriarch. A *kang* was spread in the kitchen at night for sleeping and rolled up every morning. The front yard was a vegetable garden.

These desperately poor people took pride in being hospitable and insisted on giving me the newlyweds' room. I was the honored guest. They never asked questions about me or my world. Like other peasants, they had learned over generations that questions could be dangerous.

I tried to eat what they ate, but once again I could not. One day, having failed to find anything else for me, the old lady killed one of their special prized chickens for soup. I looked at it, knowing that if I refused she would be deeply hurt. I took a few sips and immediately rushed outside, feeling as though my insides themselves would surely pour forth. After that she wearily asked what I could eat. "Potatoes" I said. For the rest of the winter, along with tofu, that was all I could stomach.

By now I had learned to wash my clothes more efficiently. But my hands were blistered all over. A rash was beginning to spread all over me.

The old lady, of course, knew I was from some kind of soft background. "You never learned how to cook," she said matter-of-factly one morning.

"No, not yet," I answered, making up my stories as I went along. "My mother had only one girl, and she spoiled me."

But I got along well with the family, especially the old lady. Soft as I was, she viewed me as a treasure, useful for teaching her the quotations of Chairman Mao, which she wanted to learn by heart. After several months of my reciting them with her each evening, she could recite them by herself even without being able to read all the characters. That evidently gave her greater stature in the neighborhood. She was not, therefore, about to have me take my efforts elsewhere. I was one way the family endured their very harsh world.

"Don't be too friendly," she warned. "You don't know all their backgrounds, so be careful! Anyway, you're with us, the leaders of the village. You know everybody already."

Each day the old lady rose eagerly, gathering all of us in front of the large portrait of Chairman Mao hanging in the place of honor on the wall facing the front door. Each of us held the *Little Red Book* in our hands, and she or her son led the group in bowing three times and reciting a few quotations. The old lady mumbled her lines; she now knew them by rote, but the particulars were clearly of no interest to her. For the first time in my years in China, I bowed to a Mao portrait; my hosts would never have understood if I had not. The ceremony was repeated before lunch and dinner and before retiring for the night. For added protection, a poster with a big *zhong* character, loyalty, inscribed inside a heart, was prominent in every room. The family venerated Mao; they felt they owed their new life to him.

To the old lady, such veneration fit snugly with her traditional beliefs. One spring morning, I was sitting quietly in the kitchen when hail began to pound on the roof. The old lady, swearing about damage to the crops, seized a huge chopper and dashed outside. She stood in the storm mumbling incantations, and when she finished she carefully placed the chopper on the windowsill. She came back inside soaked but heaving a huge sign of relief. "That will take care of the hail," she said, smiling.

When visitors came to see her son, as they often did, he preached to them of the new society, thus reinforcing his role as chairman of the Revolutionary Committee. But she lived like the mothers-in-law of old. Her daughter-in-law came back from the field every day to prepare tea at four; she did the laundry and prepared dinner. The old lady dominated her in countless ways, and there was little the daughter-in-law could do: the weight of tradition held her down. She could visit her own family only once every two years. Cut off from them, she had little relief from her daily misery.

In the months I was with Lao Da Ma's family, the ceremonies venerating Mao the emperor continued unabated, but the struggle sessions lost much of their force. The peasants had become bored with them even before the PLA had pulled out. They wanted to spend less time in meetings and more time working or staying at home talking with their friends, the men drinking tea or liquor.

The great excitement was not the Cultural Revolution or the struggle meetings. My arrival at Lao Da Ma's coincided with a sensational murder endlessly gossiped about even after it had been solved.

Everybody talked about it, but sometimes they did so rather quietly; it all depended on what they were saying. Powerful people were involved. The dead man was the prospective brother-in-law of the man in charge of village security, whose wife was the elder sister of the dead man's fiancée. Moreover, the county security head, Old Zeng, was the father of the village security man.

At first everyone, including Old Zeng, was puzzled as to the motive for the crime. The young man was popular. No one seemed to dislike him; he had no obvious enemies. It was not clear whom his death would benefit.

The ax was found buried in a field. It was new, and Old Zeng, who was clearly the hero in the constant retelling of the stories, traced it back to where it had been bought. It belonged to an ex-landlord in the village whose house had been occupied since 1952 by relatives of the murdered man. Zeng Min or "Little Zeng," Old Zeng's son, loudly proclaimed the ex-landlord guilty. The motive was class revenge. The Great Proletarian Cultural Revolution had proclaimed the true depravity of the landlord class; the struggles against it had to go on. So Little Zeng ordered the ex-landlord's arrest, and the conviction of the accused seemed certain.

Old Zeng was not fully persuaded. He was a stolid, careful examiner of the facts. He was doing his duty. While his son's ideological conclusions came fast and easy, he insisted on further investigation, looking through the files again and again. After repeated efforts, he discovered a small, faint fingerprint on the ax and an identical one on the body. They were not the landlord's. He was puzzled.

He pondered this for days. One night, as he was out trying to think through everything he knew, he decided to stop at his son's house. A bitter quarrel was going on inside; he hesitated to enter until the quarrel subsided. His daughter-in-law raged on, attacking her husband at the top of her voice, complaining how he had carelessly ruined her most prized gloves. "You tore one of the fingers," she sobbed repeatedly. In response he heard Zeng Min demanding the gloves, threatening her with divorce unless she gave them to him.

Old Zeng's heart sank. Summoning all his fortitude, he walked into the house without knocking and told his daughter-in-law to give him the gloves. Zeng Min turned pale.

"Min Min," Old Zeng cried, "confess everything now. What have you done?"

Little Zeng fell on his knees and begged for pardon. But Old Zeng was firm. Zeng Min had risen fast and far in the village in the cultural Revolution, and I detected a satisfaction among the residents that he had been brought low. The peasants were uneasy with the uppityness and shallowness of those who were rising so rapidly over the older people who had worked long years earning their trust. Their ways had sometimes been plodding, but they had often proved themselves. I never tired of hearing the story of Old Zeng. Perhaps this was what the real revolutionary heroes were about.

I ENDURED, but I did not become stronger. My place of honor was a place of terror: each night, as I tried for hours to sleep, the mice appeared. Or sometimes rats—I couldn't always tell. They climbed down from the rafters, slowly making their way to the ground. To the peasants they were a welcome diversion, a source of amusement. But I couldn't stand them. I'd close my eyes to try to ignore them, but, there was no way to shut out their constant squeaking. Worse, closed eyes brought images of familiar faces: Kazu, Liao.

I tried not to think of Wai or our life in Beijing, or of my family and our house in Thailand, or of Kazu. When I finally did doze off, I'd scream in my sleep. I did this so often, and it proved so upsetting to the family, that they decided it might be better if others were in the room with me so I would feel protected. Often I'd dream of having to walk through a horribly long, dark tunnel. There was no air to breathe, but mice were everywhere, and sometimes a cat would leap on me. I'd scream and scream until one of the peasants shook me awake. Sometimes an armed person would chase me; I'd run until finally, exhausted, I'd falter and he'd grasp me by the throat in a grip so tight I couldn't call for help or breathe. I'd wake up struggling in my bed, relieved to be in relative safety. Sometimes, though I dreamed of the house I had grown up in in Thailand, and when I awoke, the contrast was agonizing. The grueling physical work during the day still took my mind off my torments, but each night they awaited me. That never changed. Any day in which I could not work was agonizing. I could pass through the daily rigors, the formalities, and the riturals easily, but my thoughts were elsewhere. I tried to ensure that they stayed there. I lost track of time.

Many months after the PLA left, Old Lu reappeared. He had come once before, while the PLA was still there, bringing food and kind words. This time he said he was worried by how I looked. I had not improved as he had hoped.

"You're thin as a rake," he said. "You'll disappear."

When he said I must leave with him, I was afraid. I'd be attacked again. I couldn't bear hearing those voices again. My internal demons were enough. I knew I could not survive long if my tormentors returned.

Old Lu knew my fears. "We'll go back to Beijing together," he said. "I'll protect you at the university. Just take a few days' rest there, and then we can talk about what to do next."

Old Lu told the old lady and the family that I had to go to Beijing for medical treatment for my asthma.

"Does this mean she's leaving forever?" the old lady asked, forlorn. Before I could answer she turned away and went to pick some tomatoes and corn from her small vegetable garden. After I had packed my bag, I found her sitting outside the house, weeping.

"Have we mistreated you in any way?" she asked, weeping.

As I stood numb and mute, Old Lu took great pains to explain my sorry physical condition to her. When he finished, I hugged her tightly and thanked her again and again. As we left, she thrust the bag of tomatoes and corn into my hand. The whole family stood there in tears. On the bus I thought of my arrival in the dust. Somehow I'd survived on my own. I thought not just about the loneliness and the taxing chores but about how I'd learned to sew, spending long hours with the country women as they stitched their clothes and shoes; mending was a big social occasion. Into their dresses the peasant women patched the brightests greens and red. As our bus passed the fields, I remembered the plentiful watermelons. Those, I thought, must have been what inspired them.

I RETURNED TO BEIJING with Old Lu in the spring of 1969, more than a year and a half after I had fled. I almost cried when we passed a fruit store. I asked Old Lu to stop and buy some for me before going on to the university. He laughed, and we bought an assortment of apricots and pears.

Beijing looked more crowded than I'd remembered. The city was still draped in red banners, Mao's portrait still hung everywhere, but the Red Guards were no longer everywhere. The PLA appeared to have encamped. Something was changing.

Old Lu put me up in the university faculty compound. It was a pure luxury—a room to myself, a bathroom. and a reception area with big sofas and settees facing Kunming Lake. A few days later he checked me into Capital Hospital. The doctor who examined me was astonished by my condition. Who had treated me like this? I told her that I had, that I had been able to eat little in the countryside, mainly potatoes and heavily salted vegetables. She put me on glucose, and for the first time in a year and half I slept soundly. I seem to have slept for days, and when I awoke I felt somewhat rested. Old Lu was much relieved when he took me back to the faculty compound.

I wandered around the university every day, reading the new wall posters. The attacks continued, and the list of my friends who were under attack had grown. Now there was an emphasis on deepening revolutionary order. Calls for sending educated youth to the countryside were everywhere. I was suspicious of anyone who looked at me. My tormentors might come again at any time. I didn't know what had happened to them, but I feared they were still riding high.

I was standing reading one of the posters one day when I saw a young foreigner on a bicycle stopping nearby. I thought I recognized him as a student from England named David Horn. I had seen him in the middle school but had never spoken to him, and I thought he might have been at Beijing University as well. His Chinese, I knew, was fluent, and he wore the same type of clothes as the Chinese students. Only his European looks gave him away.

His father, Joshua, was an orthopedic surgeon who had been working in China for nearly fifteen years. During the Cultural Revolution Dr. Horn had become well known for his revolutionary commitment and his support of "barefoot doctors," paramedical personnel who took medical knowledge to the countryside. I had read articles lauding him and his dedication to China, and I was familiar with his writings as well.

David became my first companion in a long time. Learning how fond I was of fruit, he often brought me some, including the dried apricots I particularly liked. After weekends spent with his family, he'd bring marmalade his mother had made. I knew his father was very "Red." He was often quoted among the foreigners extolling the Cultural Revolution and Chairman Mao. I said little about what I had been through or where I had come from. But David remembered my brother.

"I didn't much like him when I first met him," he said. "He was the one who told Zhou Enlai about being called an 'American imperialist' by one of my classmates."

I said nothing about Wai, nothing about his expulsion. I was not just being secretive: I didn't want to think of where he might be—or what he felt about what I had done.

"Your brother always finished first in the races at school. I'd be up early every morning, practicing in the cold, in the heat, at night. But he didn't. And he always won the first prize."

Like his father, David was strong-headed about politics. He was an active member of Jinggangshan, the very leftist rebel group at the university. His enthusiasms didn't move me, but they didn't offend or frighten me either. How, I wondered, had a young Western man, someone of my own age, developed such a profoundly different view of life from mine? I learned how he had come to China at the age of ten with is sister and his parents. His father's surgical career in England had been cut short by the onset of multiple sclerosis, which had profoundly affected his hand and leg muscles. He had come to Beijing at the urging of his doctor, who correctly predicted that the climate would be helpful. He was now a prominent physician at Jhi Shui Tan Hospital, which was renowned for its treatment of orthopedic problems.

David had grown up among Chinese, and now as a university student he lived in the Chinese dormitory and ate in their canteen. Our paths had thus seldom crossed. He avoided mixing with the foreign students, despising their Western luxuries and privileges. Unlike Wai and me, he had passed his national examinations for the university. The product of the best Communist education and dedication, he lived frugally and seemed to ejoy doing so, and he believed, word for word, what the propaganda told him.

David did not ask why I was alone. In those years people were alone for various reasons, though he did not seem perturbed by the possibility that I might be in any political trouble. Within a few weeks he was inviting me to his family's home in Beijing. I accepted, grateful for both the distraction and the protection, for the chance to put behind—or at least aside—the terror of the Thais and their Chinese counterparts.

The Horns lived in a very small house whose courtyard they shared with a senior Chinese doctor. A great deal of effort had gone into making the house look unimpressive, and it was clear that utility alone had dictated the decor and setup. A few simple bricks made up the bookshelves, the dining-room table was a plain wood plank, and the kitchen was tiny and, like the rest of the house, in urgent need of repair. There was, of course, no central heating; only the bath was nice and big. David's parents' room and the sitting room were neat; the rest of the house was in disarray.

I respected this type of proletarian Western style, though it was far from anything I felt I could adopt myself. But I felt sheltered at the Horns'. And David was very kind. In those days, that meant a great deal.

Old Lu could not assure me that my troubles were over. The Thais who had persecuted me were still very influential, their Chinese sympathizers still powerful. Though Old Lu had placed me in safe quarters, there was no safety. He could help, but there were limits he knew only too well. So when he came and asked if I would like to go work and live at a factory, I readily agreed.

A few days later I arrived for work at Beijing Textile Factory Number 3, a nationally famous model of productivity and revolutionary spirit. As far as I could tell, no one at the plant knew who I was. But the national leaders often had links with the model factories and communes. Old Lu clearly had his.

I was determined to do my share of the work, and survival was far easier than in the countryside. I could eat more of the food; the rooms were clean. The rats were gone. I shared a room with three others, and I slept better.

I spent a year in the facotry, working the night shift and sleeping part of the day. Before the Cultural Revolution, the factory club had been a center of social, cultural, and athletic activity. Now there was little to do. There were few movies and no plays, amateur opera, or music. Games were largely forbidden, and books had largely disappeared. People were friendly but cautious: the most popular—and safest—subject was courting; the second best was matchmaking. All the young women seemed to want to marry PLA men, while the male technicians and the other better-educated men in the factory lived under a stigma that made it hard for them to find girlfriends.

At first I felt apart from everyone around me. I have no other place now, I thought; no place in the world. I couldn't envision a life here, but I couldn't envision leaving either. I learned how to weave, how to watch the loom and the loops and how to stop the machine and rejoin the thread when the loops broke. The mechanical repetition distracted me, and for months I moved in a state where that distraction was the only relief.

The days of struggle in the factory were over by the time I came. The rebels had won. The old Party leadership was disgraced, its senior members branded "targets" in the class struggle and held under strict surveillance. I shuddered when I thought of them confined to separate quarters, pounded away at day after day, forced to write self-criticism. Would my own tormentors return?

My roommates were about my age, but they were active in the leading revolutionary body of the factory and largely left me alone. When they were not working, they were in meetings. The ex–Party leaders at the workshop level had been allowed to become rank-and-file workers again. Perhaps because they were shunned, I instinctively sympathized with them—and somehow, they with me.

My first friend in the factory was just such an old Party member. Zhao Shifu came from a working-class background and had been in the factory since 1949. But she had been set aside because of her "old thinking" during the Cultural Revolution—and worse, because of her presumed loyalty to archenemy Liu Shaoqi, whom she had once

met at a national textile conference. Most of the younger workers
had been helped by her over the years, and they still liked her, but no
one was close to her.

Often during my night shift, I would become terribly sleepy at
about 2 A.M. I had noticed her observing me, but because she did
not seem critical of me, I paid little attention to her. One night, seeing me begin to wobble, she rushed over with a cold towel to help me
stay awake. Thereafter, she urged me to doze off for a few minutes
each night while she kept an eye on my two looms as well as her own
four.

We began to talk after that. She bore her troubles amazingly well,
I thought. Regularly attacked for her ideology and entrusted with
the care of her father-in-law, who had Parkinson's disease, she talked
about the details of life without sounding defeated or even cynical
about the political atmosphere. She didn't ask about me—knowing
too much could only be difficult—but she opened up to me fear-
lessly. I lived in daily dread; she, under attack, did not. She seemed
to have a calm that I lacked: my inner torments returned whenever I
was alone.

One day I asked her how she took all the criticism. Why didn't she
feel bitter? Zhao smiled.

"Let me tell you one of my favorite stories," she said. "During the
period of the Three Kingdoms, there was a very powerful general
called Zou Ji in the Kingdome of Qi."

I nodded; like so many others, Zhou had loved telling stories from
that era.

"He felt he was very handsome indeed," she continued. "Each day
he stood in front of the mirror, admiring himself. One day as he did
so, a really handsome man, named Xu, passed by. Zou Ji immediately turned to his wife and asked who was more handsome, he or
Xu.

" 'You, of course,' his wife replied. 'You are much more handsome.'

"Zou was pleased but not quite convinced. So he turned to his servant next, only to receive the same answer. Now he was even less
convinced. Perhaps I should find out for myself, he thought, and he
walked over to Xu's house to get a better look. Xu was standing
there, and Zou Ji got a good look. A very, very handsome man, a rare

specimen, he said to himself. He returned home very unhappy. Clearly Xu was more handsome. But no one had told Zou so. Why had they all felt it advisable to say he was more handsome when clearly he wasn't?

"He thought for many days but decided he needed help to answer his question. So he went and asked the emperor who was more handsome.

" 'There is no comparison; of course, Xu is much more handsome!' the emperor said.

"Zou Ji became serious and said, "You are right. My wife said the opposite because she loves me, the servant because she is scared of me, and my friends because they flatter me to get something out of me. So nobody told me the truth. Just like the people around you, who rarely tell you the truth. They only tell you what they think will please you.'

"The emperor thought about what Zou Ji had said. 'There is great truth in what you say,' the emperor said. Thereupon he issued an edict that officials and ordinary citizens who could point out any of his faults directly to him would receive rewards of the first order, while those who did so indirectly would receive rewards of the second order."

Zhao paused in her telling, then grinned. "It was only by this and other such measures that the emperor could maintain prosperity throughout his reign. If the Communist party wants to lead the country and the people successfully, Party members must learn to listen to criticism of their faults and mistakes and not only to praise."

She shared with some of the other old Party members a conviction that they had been committed to something of great value and that, whatever the hardships they now encountered, there was some redeeming aspect to it all. Her world had come apart, it was true, but even amid the criticisms she felt the world was better than the one into which she had been born.

Zhao introduced me to Big Sister Liu, the former factory Party secretary. She, too, had come from the hardship of the old society. Her father had been a garbage collector; only three of her parents' seven children had survived. At age twelve she had been deemed strong enough to work in the textile factory. She worked nineteen hours a day.

After 1949 her father had worked with Shi Chuanxiang, whose devotion as a garbage collector had earned the praise of Liu Shaoqi. The family status had risen; her father had got a job with the municipal administration, and the family had moved into a small but new apartment. Big Sister Liu had become literate and joined the Party. Although she had married late, she had two children, and she devoted herself to her job and her family, including a querulous old mother-in-law.

Big Sister Liu worshiped Chairman Mao, but she didn't have a inkling of what the Cultural Revolution was about. It made no sense to her, and when the subject came up, she was always confused. At first she had thought it was a movement like all the rest. When the young rebels had shouted at her that "Rebellion is justified," she had condemned them just as so many of the Party leaders she respected did. But in the great revolutionary storm of January 1967, the rebels in the factory were proclaimed the winners, and she made a long self-criticism, stringing together various high-sounding words whose meaning eluded her.

"When big animals fight, the grass gets crushed," she said to me and sighed. But still she rallied herself: We must have faith in our chairman! It is all for the good of China."

These old Party people still believed in Old Man Mao. I hardly knew if I did, but I felt at home with them. They had endured and remained human, and even in my blackest moments I did not forget that.

One day, though, I made a careless mistake. I received a letter from David Horn, read it, and casually threw the envelope away. A few hours later, I was summoned to the headquarters of the Revolutionary Committee. There was no reason not to expect the worst. Had I been discovered? Were attacks against me about to begin again?

A stern-faced woman, the vice president of the committee, greeted me coldly.

"We the Chinese people and revolutionary people all over the world love Chairman Mao. He is the red sun in our hearts. Whoever goes against Chairman Mao will come to a bad end. We will trample him to death."

What had they found out about me? Was I to be taken away? I watched as she picked up a crumpled piece of paper; it was the envelope I had discarded in my room. My roommate had turned it in, saying nothing to me.

I knew at a glance what I had done. The stamp was of Chairman Mao; in those days all the stamps were. But one never threw away his picture, not if it was on a stamp, not if it was in the newspaper. It was to be cut out and neatly put away. Not only had I forgotten, but in opening the envelope I had torn the stamp in two, separating the chairman's neck from his head. Then I had thoughtlessly tossed the envelope with my name on it into the basket near the toilet.

I was accused of wanting to chop off Mao's head. "You hate Chairman Mao. You are an enemy of the people."

"I am very sorry indeed," I mumbled. I knew more was required than that.

She peered at me, furious. "Down with whoever is against Chairman Mao and his thought. We will smash his dog's head in a stream of blood!" she said. "The masses must decide. We will deal with this tomorrow." I was dismissed.

I fled back to my room, shivering. These were the same words that had been thrown at the landlords in earlier days; the slogan had been resurrected to reassert the danger of opposing Mao in any way. I had long ago set myself a rule for survival: never challenge the great proletarian line, never say anything against Chairman Mao. Now I found myself accused of a heinous crime. Even if I reached Old Lu, could he help? Would he understand?

I dreaded another meeting with the masses—the denunciations, the cold eyes, the shrill voice. All night at work I sturggled with the machines, tangling the threads, unable to focus. Zhao Shifu came over to help, keeping her own looms going as her expert fingers quickly set mine to rights. She came to my rescue again and again that night, patting me on the back each time. She could do nothing more; nothing else was possible.

I felt too beaten down even to think about whom I could reach out to—it didn't occur to me to try. They would begin with the stamp, but what if they asked about my past? I had been placed in the factory by Old Lu. Would they know that? Would it help, or would that be used against me—and him?

When the night shift ended I walked back to the dormitory room in a daze. As I passed the canteen I smelled smoke and, looking up, saw huge black clouds billowing out the door and flickers of flame starting to shoot up. The workers around me threw down their belongings and dashed into the building. I heard screams from inside, and suddenly it seemed that the fire was leaping from place to place with incredible speed. As though fear had finally been lifted from me, I dashed in with the others. Amid the pandemonium, we searched to see who was trapped, what of the equipment could be saved. I came on two small children, scooped them up, and staggered outside with them. I scarcely felt the relief of the air before I ran back in. The fire was everywhere, but I didn't seem to care. I ran further and further into the inferno, though wood beams were crashing down and parts of the ceiling begining to fall. I saw another worker up ahead, immobilized and badly burned. As I moved toward him, I saw something falling my way. I was too late.

I remember nothing of being carried from the wreckage by the other workers. When I regained consciousness, I was in the hospital. Bewildered as I was, I saw I was in a nice room; there was something special about it. I focused on the man sitting attentively in the chair by my bed. He smiled broadly. It was Old Lu.

I should have known that he would have kept close tabs on me. And that in this China his watchfulness had to be cautious, always from a distance. But I had not been abandoned.

"A heroine," he said. "Don't worry about the rest."

I relaxed. We didn't talk about my leaving the factory; I told him I was managing. He would keep in touch, he said; I knew he was doing what he could.

The two children I had helped came by to visit with their parents. They thanked me and solemnly swore that they would learn from me how I had applied Chairman's Mao's thought to guide my herioc deeds. I did not point out how far Chairman Mao's thoughts had been from my own, nor did I say much when the Party secretary appeared with a huge red flower to proclaim me "protector of Mao Zedong Thought."

In two days I was released from the hospital and escorted back to the factory and to a grand reception. There to greet me as though I were her long-lost favorite daughter was the woman who days before had castigated me as an enemy, a threat to Chairman Mao.

I listened vaguely as she spoke to the gathered factory workers, praising me as a model of proletarian dedication. My spirit of self-sacrifice, she was saying, was inspired by Chairman Mao's teachings. "Serve the masses," "willing to risk one's life"—it was no more real to me than the attacks against me had been. As I watched her I thought of the contrasting black and white faces of Beijing Opera. "No middle," Zhou had said. "No middle."

Nothing more was said about my severing of the chairman's head. The stamp seemed to have been forgotten even by my offended roommate, who welcomed me back politely.

CHAPTER 15

The Dowager Empress

DAVID HORN AND I often arranged to meet on my weekend day off. After so much coldness and contempt, his presence was comforting, and I looked forward to our long walks and the easy friendliness of our conversations. To him, though, I sensed there was something more; I thought he might be falling in love.

His ardent Maoist politics never wavered. He wore his Mao badges with great pride, and he echoed the prevailing line on people and events without any doubts that I could detect. Yet he did not seem put off when I remained quiet; nor did he criticize me for my lack of Mao buttons and badges. I still never talked of my past. Although like his classmates in the middle school he had known of Wai's and my connection with Premier Zhou's organization, even now he was not inclined to ask about it. His family, too, while always welcoming, kept whatever questions they might have had to themselves. Like so many foreign friends of China, they were more Maoist than Mao: his sisters embroidered portraits of the chairman, and his father, perhaps the most fervent admirer in the family, insinuated Mao into even the most private moments. I rarely spoke when I was with them, though their beliefs made me no more uncomfortable than I felt in other religious settings—as long as I did not have to join in.

In the spring of 1969 David told me he was returning to England with his family. He asked me to join him as soon as I could. My reply was a murmur; whether that was assent, I wasn't sure. I had come to care for him, for this person who had reached out to me. He was the first to have done so for years. But to leave China? I had no passport, no way to make direct contact with my friends. I stumbled through the days one at a time.

One day as I was bicycling down a small alley off Wangfuging Street, I saw Wan Li's daughter coming the other way. We had known each other for years; she and Du Du and I used to spend long nights gossiping about who was seeing whom and matchmaking for our brothers. She lived right down the street from Liao, but until now I had not known if she had survived the bitter attacks on her father as a member of the "black clique" of Peng Zhen. We locked eyes for only a second; it was too dangerous to speak or signal each other. But as we silently passed by each other, I sensed a flicker of renewed determination. We had survived.

Shortly before David left, I went with him to meet two friends of his parents, Sol and Pat Adler, through whom he intended to send his letters to me. I, in turn, was to send mine through them, for it was far too dangerous for me to receive letters from abroad at the factory. I said little during the first visit, or when I came to pick up David's letters later.

But with Sol I sensed that there was no dogma, no Party line. One afternoon, Sol stood looking out his window at the hotel attendants lining up in military formation for drill. Their shouted slogans echoed around us as we watched. "This cannot last long," Sol said, shaking his head. "You cannot go on indefinitely governing a country as though it were an army."

As the months passed, Sol let me learn more about himself. That he knew Zhou was the first surprise; he had first met him in the 1940s when he was the Treasury attaché for the U.S. embassy in Chongqing, China's wartime capital. An even greater surprise was that he knew Liao, who had been a guest at his and Pat's small wedding in the mid-1960s. Sol's cosmopolitan Western world—he'd quote Shakespeare, the Old Testament, Joyce's Ulysses, and Groucho Marx—was not one I'd known before, yet he made me feel at ease within it.

Even as I came to trust Sol and Pat, I still said nothing about myself.

ONE SUNDAY AT NOONTIME, as I walked down the busy lane outside the Adlers' hotel, I saw a familiar face, though much distorted by age and anguish. There was a fresh-looking scar across the woman's forehead that was only partly covered by her hair and a big scarf. Our eyes met, and for a brief moment we must both have looked astonished. It was Jing Puchun, Papa Liao's wife. I had not seen her for nearly four years.

We didn't hug. We didn't want any attention drawn to us. But I whispered, "How is Papa"

Jing nodded and in a barely audible voice answered, "Next Sunday at the same time in Dong Dan Park."

We went our separate ways with no show of emotion. But when I rushed into the hotel, I was full of excitement. I knew they had survived.

A week later, when I took the bus to Dong Dan Park, a brief, careful letter to Papa Liao was stuffed in my pocket along with a note from Sol, whom I had finally told about my relationship with Liao. As I entered the park, I didn't see Jing at first. Perhaps she couldn't come; perhaps I'd have to wait for another Sunday. I looked around cautiously, then began to wander about, trying not to appear as though I were looking for anyone in particular. There she was at last, sitting motionless on a bench, a large bush partly concealing her from view.

Jing smiled when I approached, and I couldn't hide my tears as we embraced. We both knew that even here the meeting had to be brief.

"Three years," she said, "for three years Papa Liao has been in prison. They put him in solitary confinement in a small room in the old Foreign Service office building opposite Zhongnanhai. Oh, they know how to be cruel. They made sure he knew its previous occupant was a friend of his, the wife of Wang Bingnan. She killed herself by banging her head against the wall the day before he was placed there. Her blood was left smeared over the walls to remind him."

I was remembering Liao the last time we had met, so serious and sad, speaking of his trust in Chairman Mao.

"At first Papa Liao took the injunction to examine his soul seriously, making self-criticism every day."

I could hear Liao's voice as she talked. Yes, I come from a bourgeois family. Yes, I have a lot of bad habits. Yes, it was time something should be done about me. I am ready to give myself to the masses.

"But that's not what they wanted. All those drafts of all those self-criticisms, one after another. Papa Liao knew soon enough that's not what she wanted."

"What she wanted?" I asked.

"The *chou yao po*, the stinking witch," Jing replied in a voice filled with hate.

I instantly knew she meant Jiang Qing. Liao had never said much about Mao's wife, but I was aware that she had a particular dislike of him, as she did for other people who knew of her early background in Shanghai. I remembered her late night call to Liao shortly before the storm had broken against him. Jiang Qing's daughter had been at a reception Liao had hosted for a visiting delegation. Evidently, he had not lavished enough attention on her.

"Your treatment of my daughter is the way you think of me," Jiang Qing had told him. "You beware."

We did not talk much longer that day. As we parted I asked whether there was anything I could do for Liao. Her eyes flickered, and for a moment she looked stricken.

"He desperately needs a Japanese heart medicine—and sleeping pills. You know how he has always had trouble sleeping. And you know the games they play in the hospital, reporting to that witch and her henchman."

"Give me the names of the medicines," I said, not knowing what I could do. But I promised to have some word for her when we met again, in a different place, the next week.

That Jiang Qing was behind Liao's problems did not surprise or shock me. But Liao's wife's vehement attack on her and on the Cultural Revolution were the harshest I had heard spoken yet. ' "The stinking witch," ' I thought. Around me, on the posters, in the press, even among those I found most humane, no one criticized the Cultural Revolution or disputed the slogan "Learn from Comrade Jiang Qing." To doubt, to go against such a great movement, where did that leave one? In Jing's words I found confirmation of my own misgivings. Someone was breaking through the ideological fa;alcade.

"Stinking witch," I repeated over and over again, and as I did I felt a rare sense of confidence and hope.

Sol gave me his stock of sleeping pills and contacted his brother, a doctor, in England. Western medicines were difficult to get in China, so arrangements were made for his brother to send them through friends who had occasion to travel to China on business. He also reached a friend who visited China via Hong Kong, where the heart medicine could be procured without a prescription.

Over the next month, I met Liao's wife once a week. Liao, she said, had been even more relieved to hear about the Adlers taking care of me than about getting the medicine. My fate had weighed on him for years. He had had no idea what had become of me.

Jing told me more and more about the bitter conflicts that had torn apart the elite world I had grown up in. Yet as she did, I detected underneath the fear and suffering an inner serenity—obviously shared with Liao—based on a faith in the future. "Let them fly ever so high," she quoted an old saying at one point, "one day they will fall and be broken to bits."

Somehow, she seemed to be saying, the worst was over. I wondered how her assurance could be so strong: everywhere one heard Jiang Qing's name and that of Chen Boda, another key aide who I knew hated Liao. But having found that one of my most important links had somehow held, I was prepared to believe that Liao's and her faith could not be misguided.

"How is Uncle Zhou?" I asked nervously. Zhou was seemingly as present as ever, rarely far from Mao. One was always hearing of him; whenever a serious incident occurred, Zhou was there. Yet for years I had feared he, too, would be pulled down. After all, so many of his "hands" and "feet" had been chopped off. I had only Old Lu.

"Without him," she replied, "your papa would have been dead already."

She told me how, a few months earlier, when she had gone to see

Liao on one of the weekly visits she was allowed, she had entered his room, finding him shaking and pale, barely able to speak. The guards, claiming he had faked a heart attack shortly before, had refused to give him any medication. He had been put into the hospital for two days in a common room where he wasn't even watched over. The investigation team sent around to see him had concluded that he was malingering in the hope of being released.

In desperation, Jing called Zhou. Without hesitating, Zhou said that he himself would go to Liao's cell. And he did, bringing a heart specialist and an ambulance. He issued a personal order on the spot for Liao to be released to an outside hospital. He would brook no defiance. But he surely knew how carefully he was being watched.

Jing looked around nervously to make sure no one was listening. "Zhou took him to the hospital and stayed until he made sure Liao had a private room. 'You are now accountable to me,' he told the staff. But the doctors are scared; they watch over their shoulders about the medicine, wondering what will happen. That witch is everywhere. That witch and her clique are worse than the Guomindang!" she spat out. "Liao was thrown in their prison several times, but never like this."

"But why does Chairman Mao let her do it?" I asked.

"He's senile now," she said, pointing to her head. The old man could no longer control his wife.

I had given Jing only the sketchiest account of what had happened to me, but I asked her now if I should try to leave China. I told her about the possibility of going to England—David was still insisting on my coming—but my feelings were not at all clear to me. I had chosen to stay in China once, and even with all the consequences I was not desperate, even now, to leave. I lived in dread, it was true, but I couldn't imagine a place where I would fit in. England, perhaps, was a refuge, but going to England and David was not something that seemed real. I would be getting out—but to what? Marriage was no more than a vague thought in all this. When David had urged me to come, it was my family and Kazu I had seen—and I had pushed them away.

Liao's wife bent close to me. "I asked Papa what you should do," she whispered. "If you have a way, he told me, by all means leave."

Perhaps I felt I was being given permission. He understood, and he was not saying good-bye. He was telling me to look to myself, to take care of myself. Separation was a way of caring, not of setting me adrift: there was no more he could do.

His advice could not have been more prophetic. A new group of workers arrived one day shortly thereafter at the factory, and there among them was the daughter of our old cook. I showed no sign of recognizing her, praying that she would not give me away. She said nothing, but undoubtedly her path still crossed Mrs. Lin's.

A few days later, as I returned from my night shift, I blanched when I saw who was waiting for me. I had not seen the Thai ultra-leftists who had tortured me since I had denounced my father on Radio Beijing. Now here were Colonel Phayom and some of the other Thais.

"A new task awaits you," the colonel said. I was so frightened I could barely focus on his words. I wouldn't go back to those terrible times, I could not. "You are to return to the university, and we will contact you there. You are now under our responsibility and authority."

I was silent.

"If you don't come willingly, we will expose your background to the masses in the factory. You concealed your identity and even changed your name to Pan Hong to deceive the masses and to infiltrate the Cultural Revolutionary movement."

I returned to my room when they left, my tiny room where there now seemed to be too little air. I knew I had to leave the factory, at least for a while. I didn't say good-bye to any of my workmates. I thought I would return. I never did.

For days I waited in my dormitory, hearing nothing from Phayom. But Old Lu, never out of touch, came for me. He had arranged for me to be admitted to a hospital. I had developed pneumonia, and for a few days I was given a respite. The same doctor who had treated me after the fire, a friend of Lu's, took charge of my care.

I phoned the Adlers, whose hotel was just around the corner, and they arrived, bringing me fruits. But they could only stay for a brief time—the less attention we attracted, the better. Sol whispered to me that his foreign friend had brought the medicine for Liao.

The next day Colonel Phayom visited. He paced around the bed, delivering his pronouncements. Gradually, he came closer and began touching my hair. The day after, it was much the same, but now he started to stroke my breast. I felt nauseated and pushed his hand away in disgust. Later, when Sol and Pat advised me to leave the hospital, I returned to the guest house Old Lu had put me up in.

Colonel Phayom found me there a few days afterward. He'd arrived in the private car assigned him as president of the Thai Political Front. He was famous in those days, honored in the *People's Daily*, a revolutionary hero in a time of ultrarevolutionary rhetoric.

I heard him walking up the stairs, telling his bodyguard to wait outside for me. This was worse than the hospital; I was more alone and vulnerable. The guest house attendants, who might have protected me, were thrilled by the presence of a famous revolutionary; the head of the staff went running out to greet him.

Phayom strode quickly to my room; bringing fruit. The next day, he came with a fancy radio. He came every day, and each time I heard him coming. I would run down the stairs so as to meet him in a public area. He would take me for a stroll around the lake, flattering me, admiring me as I pretended not to know what he was up to. I feigned illness; I played stupid; I tried anything to fend him off.

"You have a beautiful face," he said to me one day, staring at me. I backed off.

"How could anyone want to harm you when I am here to protect you?" he said. "You think about it. I'm not old yet." His chest swelled. "I am very determined and will pursue you to the topmost peak of the highest rock until you agree."

He moved toward me. "You could enjoy a very comfortable life if you lived with me. You would be safe. No one would dare to lift a finger to touch you."

He reached for my arm. I pulled away. Fury swept over me, all the unexpressed anger that had lain buried. I looked at his ugliness and screamed—as loud as I could, louder than I ever remember doing in my life. "I already have a boyfriend!" I raged. "Soon I will join him. Go away."

I ran to my room, but he was right behind me. "Are you mad?"

"I hate you, I hate you! I'm not mad." I screamed. No one in the guest house could possibly have missed what was happening.

He pushed me down on the bed and tried to kiss me. With all the strength I could muster, I slapped him in the face and kicked him fiercely, screaming at the top of my lungs.

Humiliated, he stormed out of the room, white with rage. I heard him stop in the hallway, perhaps to calm himself before he faced the others. Then the car door slammed and his car sped off.

In all of China, it seemed, there was only one place I could go. As Pat Adler opened the door, her face radiated a strength and kindness that promised unquestioning support. When I told her and Sol what had happened, they both insisted that I stay. I warned them that I might soon come under public attack again, but Sol cut me off. No arguments; I was to stay.

For almost two months their apartment was my haven. Yet I knew, as did Sol and Pat, that someday I would be found; the Thais would locate me. And indeed, at the end of the second month, a Chinese official called on Sol to give him notice that his "guest" could not remain with them indefinitely. The local hotel administration was complaining, the official said. Sol had no doubt as to the real source of the complaint.

I had hidden in the bedroom, the place I always retreated to when unexpected Chinese or foreign visitors arrived. After the official left, I could see Sol's anger even though he tried to break the news matter-of-factly. The rules of the game were utterly clear: no one, from the top leaders on down, owned his own house. All houses belonged to the organization, and the organization could issue directives about their use. Its decisions were final: I had to leave.

Now there was no safety. I went back to the university guest house to wait, but this time there was to be no waiting. The minute I entered my room I was informed there was a phone call for me. A voice told me curtly that a meeting was to begin in my room the next morning to discuss my "situation."

They were all there first thing, Colonel Phayom scowling fiercely in the background. My fate was to be settled, they said.

With great solemnity they began reading, in Thai, quotations from Chairman Mao about class struggle and how hard it was to change one's class nature. For five days, fourteen hours at a stretch, the meetings went on and on. This time there was little discussion of saving my soul—the goal seemed to be annihilation plain and simple

"You are a bourgeois diehard reared first in a bourgeois Thai family and then by Chinese capitalist roaders. And now you are shamelessly pursuing foreign boyfriends," they said.

"You are a loyal lackey of the Chinese 'black line.' Tell us who is behind all this! Tell us now who let you live like this! Who is the evil black hand behind it all?"

If ever I had been in doubt in 1967 as to whom they were after, now I was clear. Some sixth sense for survival had prevented my mentioning anything about Zhou then and nothing about Liao beyond my official relationship. I knew with the utmost certainty that what had then been sheer instinct was now common sense.

I did not respond. No one, of course, would say Zhou's name unless I did.

They cursed me for deciding to marry without consulting them or revealing my boyfriend's political background. When they found out it was Joshua Horn's son, they blustered angrily.

"Some foreigners shout loud slogans of Chairman Mao, but they never have to touch their own souls. Look at this family. If they were really so loyal to China, would they have left? Their deed speaks for itself!"

Unlike my first time under their fire, I said nothing and confessed nothing. I just sat and listened. That made them even more furious. They continued the attack on me and on the Horns. Still, I detected the tiniest amount of caution on their part; it was dangerous to attack a very Red person like Joshua Horn. You never knew who was supporting him.

"Why don't you say something?" the younger Thai woman yelled at me. "Are you deaf and dumb? Open your dog's mouth!"

That only made me more stubborn. I said nothing.

"Admit your relation to Liao Chengzhi. Tell us of your life with this capitalist roader. Confess!"

Silence.

"Just what were you and Liao doing?" The undertone was decidedly unpleasant.

I stared down at the floor, I looked around, I counted the feet of the people in front of me. What, I wondered, would they decide? What would they come up with now? Would I share Liao's fate?

"After you repudiated your father," one of them was saying, "you began to relax. You never really tried to join the revolution."

I continued looking at their feet. They were all wearing simple cotton shoes; no leather here, I thought. I turned my thoughts to their socks.

"You refused to draw a sharp line of demarcation between yourself and your bourgeois-reactionary patron and his associates."

I felt like a tire being blown up and up. Yet they, too, were getting tired. They began intoning Mao's admonition about the patient who didn't want to be cured by the doctor. I was to go study more Chariman Mao and live among the masses. I didn't have any idea what that meant; perhaps at that moment they didn't either.

As the meetings seemed to wind down, my guard slipped for a moment. Without being altogether conscious of what I was doing I opened my mouth.

"I am leaving China. I love China and will always be her friend," I said, stunned to hear the words coming out of me.

As though they themselves were stunned, there was a pause before the inevitable torrent. "You are an incurable patient and a renegade to China who is seeking to flee into the enemy's arms."

Having revealed my hopes yet still lacking a way to leave, I worried that they could now easily block anything I might try to do. "A loose mouth kills," Father had said. But it had not killed my determination. Somehow I would survive this.

Very early the next morning I sneaked away to talk with Sol and Pat.

"You must contact Old Lu immediately," Sol advised. "There is very little time. You must ask him if there is a way he can help arrange your escape from these lunatics. He must be told how extreme your situation is."

I reached Old Lu and told him I needed to see him. No explanation, just could he meet me at the Adlers'?

"I will be there this evening. I will meet you outside, by the gate," he said. He hung up.

When he came, I had barely pulled myself together. I felt that surely I was about to slip back into that ugly world all over again. Never, I vowed, would I go back to that.

Old Lu greeted me with unusual briskness. He had found a little spot in the courtyard where we could sit alone and undisturbed.

"Please help me for the last time," I asked as I explained what had happened. I was tired of it all, I told him. I wanted to get out of

China, and I had let my inquisitors know.

Old Lu stiffened visibly. He knew how extremely dangerous the situation had become with my announcement to them.

"You must help me. I have no papers, no travel documents, no passport. I need some papers for the British embassy in order to leave." Everything else had been arranged by David on the British side.

"I will do whatever I can," Old Lu said. "It may take a little time, but I will see what can be done. If we cannot get you out soon, the Thai Communists may well seize you, and that would be very serious. I would never forgive myself!" In the meantime, I was to stay with the Adlers. That, apparently, could now be arranged.

A week later Old Lu was back. Zhou had signed a special document authorizing me to go to England on Chinese travel papers. A letter was attached from the Ministry of Foreign Affairs asking the kindness and cooperation of the British government in allowing me to join my fiancé in England. I was of Thai nationality, it stated, but I had the permission of the Chinese government to leave for England, and Zhou had requested the British authorities to facilitate my trip. As Old Lu handed me the papers, I actually jumped up and down like a small child.

"Arrange things quickly," Old Lu said. When all was prepared, he would have something else to tell me.

A week later I had everything ready. With the British Home Office file complete, thanks to David, and with the letter and the pass, I received a visa on the spot.

I had met with Liao's wife for a last time and told her my plans. She nodded with relief. "It is the only way in such a dangerous situation. As Papa said, 'Get out. We will somehow find each other again.' "

We made arrangements for Liao to continue getting his medicine. It was awkward for Jing to meet with either Pat or Sol in public, and as neither Pat nor Sol could write Chinese and Liao's wife spoke no English, we worked out a way for Pat to regularly send Jing the date when she could come and pick up the medicine.

After all these years, there was no one else to whom it was possible to say good-bye.

• • •

"YOU WILL SEE PREMIER ZHOU SHORTLY," Old Lu said. He had mentioned nothing when he called to ask me to meet him outside.

"You will have only ten minutes. He will meet you in his car in the driveway between the Great Hall of the People and Qian Men."

We took the bus and got off in front of Tiananmen Square. He walked me to the southern gate of the hall, flashing his special pass so we could enter. As we did, a car drove up. I jumped into the backseat as Old Lu strolled away.

Zhou took my hand and then patted my shoulder wordlessly. He pressed the button to close the window between us and his driver. He had aged tremendously. His skin was no longer firm, and his eyes were sunk deep inside his face and circled with black. His hair was white. When he looked at me now, his eyes expressed only suffering and pain, as though they had taken in every horror of the preceding years.

"It has been so long," he said. "You have been badly treated. I have not taken care of you as I promised."

He took my hand again, and I burst into tears.

"I know you have suffered. So many have suffered. Aren't we all suffering now?"

"No matter," I said. "No matter."

"Are you all right?" he asked quietly.

"What can I do? What should I do now, Uncle?"

"Get out," Zhou replied. "You must get out of China as quickly as you can. Everything has been arranged. But you must leave. It is the only way I can protect you for now."

"I am ready to go," I told him.

"I will contact you. I don't know how or when, but you will hear from me."

"Uncle Zhou, what has happened? What has gone so wrong?" I tried to stop crying.

Zhou frowned and clenched his teeth, as he did whenever he was distressed. "There are so many things I couldn't do with my power," he said. "So many people I couldn't help."

"I don't know what I would have done if Sol Adler had not helped me," I said.

"He's a fine comrade," Zhou replied.

I looked up at him. "What will happen now, Uncle?"

"I can't answer you. I don't know. China is going through a very dangerous time. The outcome is uncertain."

"I don't understand, I don't like what is happening. Why, Uncle, why is it happening?" I asked again.

Zhou looked intently into my eyes and said softly, "We have a dowager empress on our hands."

I nodded.

"I should like to know what goes on behind her four eyes and those of her adviser," he continued.

"You must go now," Zhou said. "Don't worry. I think it will work out. But if not, we will go back to the hills and start all over again. If that is what we have to do, we will do it."

I got out of the car, and he drove off. I felt calm. The bewilderment I had lived with for so many years was gone. Never again would I confuse the line expressed in public with the assessment made in private. I realized just how badly awry things had gone and how savage the forces were that had shattered my world. But I knew, too, from Liao's wife and now from Zhou, how fiercely people were trying to fight back. I could leave China with the sense that the insight Zhou had given me—had always given me—remained intact.

I left Beijing the next day. Old Lu took me on a last trip around China—to the Yangtze River and to several places I had visited as a child. In Hangzhou I looked sadly at the boarded-up ruins of Yue Fei's tomb, the temple Zhou had told Wai and me to see our first summer in China. Of what had happened in the Cultural Revolution, Old Lu and I never spoke. I sensed only that he was deeply loyal to Zhou.

Finally, he took me to Guangzhou, where Pat met me. She would be accompanying me to England. He had given me the equivalent of two hundred dollars in English pounds for pocket money, and his relief that at last I would be safe was palpable.

I left China on July 23, 1970. As our flight to London took off, I picked up a piece of paper and thought of writing a letter to my father. I missed him. I put the paper down. Zhou, I knew, would somehow reach out again.

The Last Hostages of China

HOW STRANGE IT WAS to have the world I had been raised in suddenly gone. It took me years to regain my balance. As I did, I found I could never leave China completely behind. All those years ago, Father had sent Wai and me to be more than a symbol of a secret Thai-Chinese relationship. He had hoped that growing up under Zhou's auspices would make us intermediaries between China and Thailand for the rest of our lives. In caring for us all those years after Pibul and my father fell from power, Zhou had evidently hoped so, too. But when I first arrived in England, traumatized and shaken, such thoughts were far from my mind.

I married David a week after I arrived in England. I said little of my background to his family and little of my life in China. When David's relatives tried to find out about my past, I merely said I was an orphan. Whenever I thought of my family, my denunciation of my father rose up to paralyze and torment me. David, though, was good to me; I had some peace. For the moment that was enough.

Rarely did I open my mouth about Chinese politics. But because

Dr. Horn had published a widely noted book about his years as a doctor in China, we went to the National Day celebration at the Chinese embassy in London in October 1971. There I sought only to recede into the background of the many guests. My father's denunciation as an "American spy" had yet to be challenged and rectified. I knew the embassy itself was deeply factionalized, mirroring the conflicts in Beijing.

Yet that night I was approached by Yu Enguang, the chief of the Xinhua News Agency in London. If he could be helpful, he said, I was always welcome to come to him. Since he often worked at home late at night writing his dispatches, I was free to stop by there.

The gradual opening of relations between the United States and China—beginning in 1971 with the U.S. Ping-Pong team's traveling to Beijing and, later that year, the announcement of Henry Kissinger's secret visit to Beijing and Nixon's impending visit in February 1972—shocked the Horn household. But I saw Zhou's hand at work, and I sensed that sweeping political realignments both inside and outside China would come in the wake of these developments. When rumors of the fall and death of Mao's chosen successor, Defense Minister Lin Biao, spread in the summer of 1971, Dr. Horn dismissed them. That was the bourgeois press, he said. "Don't believe those lies about Lin. It couldn't happen to the number two person." In private I told David differently. "We are winning," I said. "You'll see. Zhou is winning." A few months later, I watched on television the historic vote in which China finally, after twenty-two years, won its lawful seat in the United Nations. Zhou was not going to have to go back to the hills to fight.

ONE AFTERNOON when I was home by myself, a tall blond man came to the door and announced, "I'm your sister Pongsri's fiancé." He fumbled in his coat pocket and handed me some pictures. In one he was standing with my sister, in another with my mother and father. "Your oldest brother, Man," he added, "made it a condition for his consent to Pongsri's marriage that I find you in London."

I said very little that day as he told me about my family. Of how Father had heard from friends in the British government that I was probably in England but had failed to find me when he flew to Lon-

don and spent weeks looking for me. Of Wai's life as a journalist and
of Man's plans to return to Bangkok after finishing his Ph.D. in the
United States.

Two days later Man called. I spoke haltingly, with little feeling.
Yes, it was good to be back in touch. Nothing about the past, nothing about China. Nothing about seeing them.

A few days after that a long letter arrived from Father. There was
no criticism in it, no reprimand. Indeed, only the faintest hint of
what had happened: "Even in the darkest days, I never lost faith in
you, never lost hope. I believed you could pass through your ordeals
with wisdom and courage."

I read on. It certainly sounded like Father.

"Two of the happiest moments of my life were the news of your
birth and the news that you had been found."

The letter quickly turned to politics. "We are working hard to
form a new party for the forthcoming elections. It is long past time
for Thailand to recognize China. So much has changed in the world
situation and in American policy toward China in particular. Our
family owes a great deal to China, and it is now time for us to show
our gratitude to China and to all those people who reared you. In all
this you will have much to do."

In the weeks that followed letters and packages came almost daily.
Still, I could not bring myself to reply in kind. I couldn't reconcile
the shame of denouncing them with the pain of having once been
sent away. A vengeful, angry feeling would well up only to be met
with guilt.

In Father's letters our family's political obligations, as always,
were central. "We need you to act as a link between Thailand and
China," he wrote. "Our goal of normalizing relations is not far off,
but there are difficulties with the Thai government. I am doing what
I can, but I am going to need your help."

My first steps toward reconciliation with my family opened up my
life with China all over again. In June 1972, mother came to London.
Though older and more worn since I had last seen her in 1966, she
was still spry and lively. Neither of us chose to say anything about
what I had been through.

During her stay we had dinner with Ambassador Song. I had
watched Mother act as my father's ambassador with Zhou Enlai. But

this time she spoke with an eloquent directness and confidence strengthened by her years of suffering. She spoke of how Premier Zhou had helped our family during Father's eight years in prison, and of her thanks to Zhou and Liao Chengzhi and his family for raising me. Then she turned to Father's activities: "You will be receiving some good news in the near future. We are confident that my husband's twenty years of effort will soon bear fruit."

That night, for the first time in many years, I spoke of "my family."

David Adler, Sol's brother, stopped over one evening a few days later. Sol, he said, had lung cancer and was to be operated on immediately. My mother urged me to go visit him. I could also help my father's work from Beijing, she said.

Armed with my new British passport, I was back in Beijing within a few days. It was August 1972. Lin Biao was dead. The Thai ultra-leftists were gone now, and for the first time in years I could move around Beijing without fear. But the atmosphere was extremely tense; revolutionary slogans were still emblazoned everywhere in the streets. Publicly, the Gang of Four appeared to be riding high.

Pat told me that Sol and Papa Liao were in the same hospital. Liao was still under guard and could not go out, though Zhou himself now came to see Amah and him. Zhou had told Mao that Liao must be restored to his position. He wanted Liao to work on Japan. There was no one else. In the meantime Zhou was protecting Liao from Jiang Qing by insisting that Liao stay in the hospital to take care of his ailing mother. Amah, now ninety-five, lived in the room next to his. She had broken her hip and could barely cope.

When I went to see Liao, he was waiting impatiently with his wife, Jing, and their son Ping Ping. Dressed in hospital pajamas, he was sitting in a big armchair, looking surprisingly well, cheerful as ever, but a lot thinner. I had expected worse. His face still had that spark; the humor was still there. But he was very gray now, and when he got up he moved slowly.

Jing tiptoed to the door and closed it, making a sign for us to be quiet. She trusted no one now; she wanted Liao and his freedom protected. Zhou's protection was not yet adequate. The room was probably bugged, so we communicated a lot with our eyes and hands. When Mao's wife's name was mentioned, it was spoken without rancor. There was nothing either in the words or in Liao's tone that could possibly be used against him. But as he innocuously mentioned her name, he drew a large picture of a witch, and then he stood up and slowly walked across the room, perfectly imitating her strutting manner. His hands dexterously imitated her way of taking her spectacles on and off. Then he leaned over, acting with horror as if her wig had fallen off, leaving her bald. He was wickedly funny; I had no idea whether she was bald or not. And Mao—the old reverence was gone. He screwed his finger into his temple to indicate that Mao was senile, then pointed up to heaven to suggest Mao was now God Himself.

It was a quiet celebration of our survival. As I left he said softly, "We are still living under their sky. This is a protracted war, and we need patience." I nodded.

Several days later, Liao phoned me at Pat and Sol's apartment. "Be ready in ten minutes," he said in English. "A car will get you." He needed to say nothing more.

On this drive to Zhou Enlai's residence, I noticed that the curtains in the car were faded, and as we wound through Zhongnanhai, the pots of flowers in front of each residence were fewer and less well tended. As I entered Zhou's house, however, I saw the same old carpets, and the same dining table and felt the same pervasive Spartan air.

Zhou and his wife were waiting. Just as when I had last seen him in his car days before I left, there were dark circles under his eyes.

Zhou smiled and hugged me warmly as he always did on unofficial occasions. "Are you doing all right?" he asked.

"I'm a British citizen now."

"I'm relieved," said Zhou. "It will stand you in good stead and protect you."

"And you, Uncle Zhou, how are you?"

"I'll have to go into the hospital. The doctors will pass the verdict on me soon. My time may be too short to finish my work, dear girl."

I flinched. "You've been working too hard, Uncle," I said, pushing away darker thoughts.

"The world will move on without me," he said, trying to make light of it.

I was relieved when the conversation turned to politics. I talked

about Father's new efforts toward normalizing Thai-Chinese relations. Zhou, of course, knew; he had heard the details from Ambassador Song of his meeting with my mother. Father's initiatives would
be well received by the Chinese government, Zhou said. If there
were anything urgent, I should contact him through Ambassador
Song in London. Zhou conveyed an impression of being very much
in command of the situation, unlike when I had seen him in 1970.

Zhou spoke of my father's disastrous visit in 1967. It was an awful
moment, he said. "The Red Guards ruined many of our old and ex-
cellent relations—at lesat temporarily. It is very distressing."

As we talked on, Zhou said fondly, "You have become the little
bridge we once spoke about. You are both a friend and a child of
China. There is much work to be done now. At last we may realize
your father's and my hope of normalized relations between China
and Thailand."

No sooner had I returned to England than my father called from
Bangkok. Wai, he said, was coming to see me, accompanied by Suchon Champoonut, a member of the Thai Parliament.

The Wai I met at the airport was not the lanky young man I'd last
seen being dragged away by PLA soldiers. He was well built and self-
assured. But his humor and warmth toward me were the same. He
didn't say anything about my denunciation except to joke that Father
had made a tape of it and used to listen to it with relief. "Sirin has
survived, she knows how to survive," he said each time he played it.

Wai recounted his expulsion from China. He had almost instantly
understood what my denunciation of Father and him involved. He
had pleaded with his captors to give me a letter and my expired passport, but they had refused. He had been handcuffed, taken back to
our house, and watched every minute until he was taken to a plane
the next day for the flight to the Macao border. He could take nothing with him. The violin Zhou had given him had been smashed.

"At the border I picked up a handful of earth," Wai said. "When
the PLA man asked what I was doing, I said, 'This beloved land
brought me up.' The PLA man knocked it out of my hand. 'Get off
our sacred soil.' "

An old friend of Father's in Macao had put him up for four months before Father arranged for his return to Thailand. Wai could make light of his experiences in a way I could not. The Chinese, he laughed, accused him of being a bourgeois, while the Thais feared he was a Communist spy.

Then he explained the reason for his visit. A Thai Ping-Pong team was going to China. Father had convinced the minister of commerce, Prasit Karnchanawat, the number three man in the government, to go along if China's leaders would agree ahead of time to receive him officially. The prime minister, Field Marshal Prapass, had secretly authorized the trip—and, at Wai's insistence, had put his consent in writing. I read in astonishment Prasit's letter, which General Prapass had countersigned. It authorized Prasit "to contact the leaders of China." And it spelled out exactly how this was to be done: "So that my mission may achieve in the best way the results which are expected, I would like to ask Mr. Warnwai Phathanothai to go to Beijing ahead of me, in order to have initial contacts, explain the nature of our mission and to arrange the necessary meetings with Chinese authorities." In the fluid political situation in Thailand, anything could still happen, and Wai did not wish to be labeled a Communist and thrown into jail, as Father had once been. This would be the first visit of a top-ranking official in more than fifteen years. The leaders of Thailand, so long one of the foremost anti-China nations and a base of U.S. operations in the war that still raged in Vietnam, were worried. Would Prapass be snubbed and lose face, endangering the government?

My task was to reach Zhou and make sure of the necessary arrangements. There were just ten days before the Thai Ping-Pong team left for Beijing. I explained the situation to Yu Enguang. "Perhaps Ambassador Song could be informed," I said.

The next night I met Ambassador Song at Yu's house. After I explained about Prasit's trip, he said he would convey my message to Zhou immediately. In the meantime one of his aides would talk with Wai and Suchon about further details.

The most difficult point, I well knew, was Taiwan. Pei Jianzhang, the Chinese embassy councillor, later explored the question with Wai, Suchon, and myself. "China has only one vital condition in establishing relations with foreign countries, namely, that they recognize the government of the People's Republic of China as the sole government of the one China. Taiwan is an inseparable part of China, and governments must be ready to sever any diplomatic relations they have with Taiwan." What was the Thai government's attitude towards this?

Wai knew how critical the issue was, but he had not been authorized to express any opinion. Prasit, he said, would be empowered to discuss details.

A couple of days later, Yu Enguang called. From his voice I knew the news was positive. "In the name of the government of the People's Republic of China, I wish to inform the royal government of Thailand that it warmly welcomes Mr. Prasit Karnchanawat and his advisers Warnwai and Sirin Phathanothai as special guests of the Chinese government."

In late September 1972, just two weeks from the time I left Beijing, I found myself back. Although now a guest of the government, I moved cautiously. A Mr. Cheng from the Foreign Ministry greeted me on my arrival and came the next morning to discuss the visit. I had first met him when Wai and I had passed through Rangoon on our way to China in 1956 and he was an aide to Ambassador Yao in Burma. But of this not a word.

When I called Papa Liao, Jing answered. Amah, she said, had just died. Liao looked pained when I entered his hospital room; he clearly had been crying. but he sensed I had returned for some significant reason. He turned up the music on the radio and led me by the hand out onto the balcony, speaking very softly.

"Strength through grief," I thought as I plunged into a quick description of my mission. "Papa, you must report to Uncle Zhou. First, we would like you to receive Prasit. Every Thai knows the Liao name—especially that of your father and mother. You might have problems in China, but in Thailand you are an image and symbol of your country. Prasit wants to meet you. After all, the relations with Thailand were started with your involvement years ago. So please ask permission of Uncle Zhou on my behalf."

I also asked Liao to see if Zhou himself would consider receiving Prasit. My requests were official. Asked personally, they would have been a different matter.

"I have been away for so long," Liao said. But he agreed to report to Zhou.

I told Mr. Cheng nothing of my meeting with Liao. I simply raised with him the question of having Prasit meet Liao as well as Zhou. My request startled him; Liao, after all, had not yet been publicly rehabilitated. Mr. Cheng responded that the premier was very busy. But I had done my part. In China it is never wise to neglect the front door even if you go in through the back.

Two days before Prasit's arrival, I was officially told that he would meet Liao in his capacity as director of the World Peace Committee. I felt relieved. When I saw Liao shortly thereafter, he again turned up the music on the radio, but he was different. Some of his old self-assurance was back. In years past, I had noticed how he and his mother altered their manner of talking whenever they shifted into their formal roles. Now Liao was speaking to me that way. "Premier Zhou attached considerable importance to this visit," Liao said. "We greatly appreciate your father's effort. Premier Zhou has asked that you be the interpreter in all official meetings." As for Zhou's receiving Prasit, I would have to wait to hear from Liao.

When Wai arrived the next day, he was jubilant. Liao's meeting would persuade Prasit that the Chinese government was serious. But Wai was worried about the uncertain meeting with Zhou. I tried to reassure him, but it was hard to put into convincing words what I already knew so clearly.

When Prasit arrived the next day, he was in good spirits, though concerned about how he would be received.

"Above all else," I said, "be frank and honest with the Chinese. They will be very frank and honest with you; don't be taken aback by it."

I had been with Liao on countless official occasions, including with Chairman Mao. But as I walked in with Prasit, it was the first time I'd been publicly with Liao in my new role. I'd never seen him so closely as he dealt with a representative of a foreign government. He was remarkably relaxed, conveying friendly affability but also sharpness, directness.

"There is an old Thai saying," Prasit said. " 'Chinese and Thais are not strangers to each other but brothers.' From this point of view, there should be no problem in our relations."

Prasit paused. He was not as comfortable as Liao. The circumstances for Thailand were complicated, he said. "It has sometimes been necessary for Thailand to link itself with other countries, especially with the United States and Taiwan after World War Two. Perhaps it is best not to discuss that so as not to arouse antagonisms."

Even as I translated, I thought of how my father had sought so hard to avoid just such circumstances. Liao, as I expected, did not simply sweep the past away; the problems were indeed difficult. "It is not quite correct to say that Thailand had no relation with China for twenty-three years," Liao said. Pointing to Wai and me, he said, "Once, with Prime Minister Pibul, we had good people-to-people relations. They came to China when they were children in the fifties, they studied, and they grew up here."

Prasit said that Thailand was perhaps not yet ready to normalize relations. First, U.S. pressure made it difficult, and second, Thailand was still afraid of Chinese ideology. The Thais were a peace-loving Buddhist people with a monarchy. The gap between the two nations might still be too great.

Liao listened intently as I translated. That was an internal problem for Thailand, Liao replied. But it was not quite true that Thailand was peace-loving. The Thai people were, but what of the Thai soldiers in Laos and Vietnam? Why was Thailand so afraid of China? In its long history, had China ever sent troops to Thailand? Tell the Thai people, he said, that we wish to be friendly with them. Let them come to China and see our country for themselves.

Prasit agreed with Liao's suggestion that the two countries could take economic, commercial, and cultural steps. The thorny issue of Taiwan might wait for a later stage, but Liao was clear: the terms of the Shanghai Communiqué were to be honored strictly.

In the days that followed Prasit had similar conversations with China's leaders. Han Nianlong, the deputy foreign minister, bluntly said that Thailand should withdraw her troops from Indochina.

But Prasit saw that such bluntness did not indicate China's unwillingness to reach agreement. He was learning how the Chinese negotiate. That night, Prasit, Wai, and I attended the Ping-Pong matches. Don't worry, I told Prasit when the Thais lost; your match is going well.

At midnight the phone woke me. It was Liao. Zhou would receive Prasit at 2 A.M. in the Sichuan Province Reception Room of the Great Hall of the People. He wanted Wai and me there first, at 1:30.

It was to be Wai's first meeting with Zhou since 1966.

Zhou broke into a glowing smile as we entered the reception room. "I am so pleased to see you both, to see you doing this. It is a great pleasure," Zhou said.

This was Zhou the diplomat now, wishing to convey certain messages officially, in his capacity as premier. "I want to apologize to your father on my government's and my own behalf for his unpleasant experience in China during the Cultural Revolution." And he invited Father to come any time "as my government's and my own guest."

Zhou paused, teeth clenched. "I apologize to you both for your suffering in the same period." Then he smiled and relaxed. "It is good to see two of my children undertaking this great task with ease and grace. Nothing makes me happier."

One of Zhou's aides signaled that Prasit was arriving. Zhou complimented Prasit on getting off to a good start, then carefully reviewed the history of Sino-Thai relations. As I was translating, Zhou interrupted: "They are part of the evidence for the existence of good relations between our two countries. They are now a sturdy bridge linking us together. Listen to her Chinese—she speaks Chinese with a better accent than mine."

I was embarrassed translating about myself, so Wai stepped in for a moment to help.

"China understands," Zhou said, "that at the present moment it is hard for you to establish diplomatic relations with us. We are always patient, so we can wait. But in the meantime our two peoples can start relations in trade, culture, and sports. So I hope that on your return you will inform your government that we understand its difficulty. And you know that in Indochina there must be peace. That war must end."

How often I had listened to such political discussions in China over the years. The directness in the official worlds remained; I knew, as I had learned from Zhou and Liao, how important the articulation of basic principles was to the Chinese and how integral they were to the way they presented their positions.

Zhou spoke of his regret at not having met my father and then asked Prasit about what had happened to various other friends of China in Thailand. I thought of all those people who had, in so many diverse ways, been part of Wai's and my own journey to this moment and of the price they had paid.

If Zhou was tired, he did not show it during the meeting. His face radiated the same spirit I remembered from our first meeting; his body still seemed animated. But as we left, after Prasit had already turned to go, I briefly glanced back at Zhou and understood how much such moments now cost him.

Father CALLED ONE DAY to say he would be coming to London. The last time I had seen him was that bitter February day in 1967 when he had crossed back to Macao, leaving Wai and me to our fates. When Father and Wai got off the plane, I felt embarrassed and a little withdrawn. But Father's joy was so great and he spoke so warmly that I was quickly coaxed out of my misgivings. For a moment he spoke of my mother's suffering, and I saw a flicker of pain in his face. But I knew a political mission had brought him.

"I come with a very important note for you," Father said. "I know you are the only person who can do this."

What, I wondered, could he have in mind now?

"The Americans are very worried," Father began. "They think something is seriously wrong. They can't reach Zhou Enlai. Communications have broken down for several months. A senior U.S. official sent someone to see me in Thailand. They want to talk with you."

"I think you should leave the matter to the Chinese and the Americans," I said.

He persisted. "You know that I believe that China and the United States must come to understand each other and learn to live in the same world with each other. But the Americans still do not understand how serious the Chinese are about the issue of Taiwan and some of the provisions of the Shanghai Communiqué that President Nixon and Premier Zhou signed in 1972. The Americans aren't sure how to talk with the Chinese, but they want to talk."

Father simply assumed that I would play my part.

I thought for a minute. "If I agree to do it, I will meet them only in Thailand." I had not seen my country for seventeen years, and technically I was still blacklisted there. Diplomatic relations between

China and Thailand had yet to be achieved.

Three weeks later I flew to Bangkok as the guest of the American ambassador. For years I had tried not to think of Thailand. Now, as we came in for our landing, I watched the green rice fields below and felt overwhelmed by its beauty—and by a sense of loss at having been away for most of my life. Bangkok had greatly changed, I had been told, but I couldn't really tell. It felt like home.

The Americans were putting me up in the presidential suite of the luxurious Dusit Thani Hotel. I was returning home, I mused, very much my father's daughter. My world here was inseparable from the politics into which I had been born.

Three Americans from Washington, led by a senior government official, promptly came to see me. I said I was there to listen.

They spoke for some time. They made it clear that they knew my personal history relatively well. As I listened, their concerns became apparent. The United States and China had come together swiftly with Nixon's visit. But problems had developed in carrying out the Shanghai Communiqué. There was a "blockage," and in connection with that, they thought, China's U.N. Huang Hua, chief of the Liaison Office, had returned to China. Taiwan, they knew, was perhaps the most vital and critical issue. But just how important was it to the Chinese? How serious was the split between China and the Soviet Union? They were very worried, they implied, about whether Zhou was under attack. Was he in danger of losing his power? And what of the other leaders I knew—Liao Chengzhi, Liu Shaoqi, Peng Zhen? Were they coming back into power?

We talked for several days. I was restrained, correct, sometimes very blunt, as I had learned to be. Never underestimate the significance of Taiwan, I said. China had not in the past, nor would it in the future, give in on that question, the principles of which had been accepted by President Nixon in the Shanghai Communiqué. "China has its reasons for acting as it does. This is particularly the case with Taiwan. If you are having trouble over Taiwan, you had better look seriously at this issue again. On the principles involved, they will not compromise."

Directly or indirectly, the United States had opposed China for years. "But you have not won the military fight. The threat of force will not lead China to a change of principles. You need to understand what this means for the Chinese," I said.

I talked about Zhou. One of the U.S. officials had met him with Nixon. Yes, I agreed, he was charming. He was also at ease in great crises. They should have no doubt that Zhou was behind every step of the policy; ill or not, he orchestrated every step. If they wished to strengthen that policy, they must adhere strictly to the Shanghai Communiqué.

Who were Zhou's opponents? Who opposed the policy? they asked. "With your intelligence, you must know far better than me." I had no intention of speaking on internal political matters.

Afterward one of the Americans commented to my father, "Your daughter was direct and sharp. We had a useful meeting."

IN DECEMBER 1974 I returned to Beijing to see Zhou. His health, I knew, was bad. And the Gang of Four were escalating their attacks on him. I was six months pregnant. If I didn't go then, I wasn't sure I'd ever see him again.

Zhou's large hospital room smelled of fresh paint. His big bed was in the middle, a smaller one in the corner for his attendant. All around stood machines, ready for use in an emergency.

Zhou was alone, sitting up in his bed. The energetic and vigorous Zhou I knew was gone; his operation the week before had left him pale, thin, and exhausted. Various dark thoughts went through my mind. I knew how Laio had been denied his medical needs.

"Uncle, are you being treated well?" I asked. He knew, of course, what I meant. I shouldn't worry, he assured me. He was fine.

"I wish I was well enough to visit Thailand," he said with a forced smile, evidently in pain, "but Marx's invitation to me has arrived. There are many things I have not done, and there is little time left to do them."

Zhou spoke proudly of the fact that Thailand and China would soon establish diplomatic relations. With him, as with my father, politics was an inseparable part of our relationship. Yet he had always imbued those harsh political realities with a warmth and responsiveness toward me that had enabled me to survive—and to enter into the China of which he was so proud. I told him that if I had a boy, the child would be named Joe, after him. He moved his hands slowly, but with traces of his old gracefulness, as he touched mine.

In this room nothing could really be private. Zhou spoke with few specifics of the current bitterness and conflict. He could assume I knew essentially what had gone on and what was happening now. He leaned toward me, though, and said quietly, "Politics can involve dirty tricks—have no illusions." Then he pulled himself back and changed the subject. Zhou had spent his life trying to make it more than this: all his integrity had been directed toward that goal. I sensed enormous pain in his words.

In June 1975 my son Joe was born. On January 8, 1976, Premier Zhou died.

No international leaders were invited to Zhou's funeral: it was to be restricted to a small number of Chinese. The Gang of Four, even at his death, could not let up on their hostility to him. Zhou, who had done more than anyone else to restore China's international stature, who had so many international friends, was to be buried without any of them present.

I saw Liao in May of that year, shortly after a demonstration by thousands of Zhou's mourners had ended in mass arrests ordered by the Gang of Four. We are playing a lot of bridge these days, Liao said wryly one night when I saw him with Marshal Ye Jianying and Wang Zhen. This was how the leaders were able to get together inconspicuously and prepare for the aftermath of Mao's death. One way or another, something big was going to happen.

Mao Zedong died on September 9, 1976. Early on the morning of October 6, Liao called me in London. "I am relaxed and overjoyed," he said, indeed sounding in great spirits. "You'll soon hear the good news." Days later the BBC announced that the Gang of Four, including Mao's wife, had been arrested.

Things changed rapidly after the downfall of the Gang of Four. Wai and I organized a delegation of Thais, including Pibul's son, Admiral Prasong Pibulsongkram, to visit China. Deng Xiaoping rapidly consolidated his power, and Liao resumed his state and Party roles fully, often meeting with Thai guests in the Great Hall of the People.

In February 1978 Father, Mother, Wai, Joe, and I went to China as guests of Zhou's widow, Deng Yingchao. Father and Liao, who in all those years had never met, hit it off immediately. They became like old friends, joking, discussing politics, dining together several times during those two weeks. We went to see Deng Mama. As we met again, I handed Joe, now three, to her. She stroked him affectionately. "Old friends, old friends," she said.

I began to talk with Liao about my most painful experiences in the Cultural Revolution. "You were right to stay," he said gently. "Many people suffered in those years, and you were one of them. This has made you a child of China, and if you had left then, I doubt the situation could ever have been sorted out. You stayed, and we know what it cost you and what that decision meant."

Liao spoke of on his own special tormentor, Mao's wife. Why had she hated him so? I asked. "I knew her past," he replied. "She hated me for that, just as she hated all those who knew it. And so she went after each of us, one by one." She had had quite a reputation in her Shanghai days; Liao himself had rejected one of her advances. She wanted revenge.

"That 'haw,' " Liao said in accented English. "She loved Mao's power more than anything else. She bewitched Mao. Even Zhou was not spared by her."

Liao never found it easy to criticize Mao. He had once all but worshipped him. Like many of the other old leaders returning to power, he tried to understand why such havoc had been wreaked on China and on the party to which he had devoted his life. To Liao, someone who had grown up in a cosmopolitan family and was familiar with the capitalist world, it was China's feudal backwardness that had partly accounted for what had happened. Some of Mao's methods had been fostered by that peasant feudal mentality.

When Zhou had told me in 1970 that China had a dowager empress, I had barely grasped what he meant. To Zhou it was a familiar aspect of Chinese history. Imperial court politics had always been marked by plots and murderous intrigue. Often the empresses came from modest backgrounds; some, seeking power, sought to shape their checkered histories into more suitable forms. A powerful empress meant a weakened emperor, a court of intrigue even more bitter and deadly than usual, and enormous danger to the dynasty. This was the world Mao had brought back. He had thought he could use it to his own ends, but even he had not escaped its destructivness.

MY SECOND SON was born in May 1978. We named him Leo, after Papa Liao. Several months later, Father had a stroke. I knew then that my life was going to change again. My marriage, I felt, was at an end, and I left for Bangkok with Joe and Leo. I was never to return to live in England again.

I was welcomed warmly by Father's old Circle—former ministers and military leaders and Pibul's family, still headed by Madame Pibul, who lived in the old house of my early memories. Pibul's son, Admiral Prasong, lived in the same courtyard, and every year Madame Pibul's birthday was celebrated with great festivities intended to honor both her and the late prime minister.

If many of these people only vaguely remembered me as a child, most knew about Sang's daughter, "the girl who denounced her father on the radio."

"You are certainly worthy of being Sang's daughter," Admiral Prasong said one day. "Sang never did anything like the rest of us. He was special, and he had a special mind and quite different ways of figuring things out. None of us would ever have dreamed of sending our own children to China in the fifties. Well, Sang did, and he did it well."

Old Air Marshal Fuen Ruenapakart was especially interested in meeting me. "I knew of our policies toward China back then," he said. "I knew you had gone, but I closed my ears." The air force had been too closely tied to the United States at the time; the navy, led by his close friend Yudhasard Kosul, had not. Yudhasard was the admiral whom I had gone to see right before leaving for China. But they all knew.

In 1980 I flew to Guangzhou to celebrate Chinese New Year with Liao and his family. His heart was bothering him, and he asked that I accompany him to Stanford, California, where he would have surgery. Before we went, he wanted me to meet a particularly courageous man, Wu Nansheng, the vice party secretary of Guangdong province.

Wu came that night to urge Liao and, through him, the Central

Committee to support his plans for the economic opening of the Shenzhen area. The region's proximity to Hong Kong promised a great future, but more than investment funds was needed, he argued; such a project could succeed only if it had strong backing from Beijing to make the region a special economic zone free to develop with only minimal restrictions. They needed someone to help them in their contacts with Thailand and the West.

You might get involved, Liao suggested mildly after Wu left. Several months later, I visited what was then a neglected border town. The roads were in poor condition. Telecommunications were virtually nil. There was no decent hotel and only a few shops along the dusty streets. Wu worked out of one small room with a single writing table and a big cabinet for documents. But he and his team had a vibrant faith and determination that, however different, reminded me of the commitment I'd seen in China before the Cultural Revolution. They spoke of the future; they lived for it; they appeared dedicated to realizing it as fast as possible.

Liao had still more ideas for me, asking me to work as an intermediary on various economic problems between China and other countries. He suggested I meet with the director of a Chinese construction company involved in a project in Jordan. It was not a particularly large one, but it was one of the first in which China had sent workers and equipment abroad to earn hard currency. Something had gone wrong; they had not been paid for their work. Whom, the manager asked, should he talk with in Jordan about his problem? Could I help? Shortly thereafter I arrived in Jordan, a rather worried arbitrator out on her first job. I was thirty-three years old.

Through a friend of Father's I met Mr. Khouri, the chairman of the Housing Bank of Jordan. The matter was settled quickly, and as we got to know each other, he urged me to develop business contacts in Kuwait and Saudi Arabia. After a few years, I felt I had embarked on an enterprise well suited to my talents and background.

LIAO WAS IN VERY GOOD spirits in the spring of 1983 when he told me he would be named vice president of the People's Republic of China at the meeting of the National People's Congress in June. In recent years, while deeply involved in the growing relationship with Japan, a country no other Chinese leader knew as well, he had remained engaged in his work with the overseas Chinese community. The significance of his family's role in the Chinese revolution had been dramatically recalled in July 1982, when Liao was asked to write a public letter to Jiang Chingguo, the son of Generalissimo Jiang Jieshi and the head of the Taiwan government. He wrote of the need for China to remain one—a goal inseparable, to his generation, from the objectives of the revolution. Even with an archrival such as Jiang's son, he could appeal to a shared history of commitment to Chinese unity going back to the founder of the Guomindang, Sun Yatsen.

Liao's heart still caused him problems, and he often stayed at the hospital, as many other Chinese leaders did, emerging only to go to work. "I'm heartless," Liao joked in English.

A few months later, when I was back in Thailand, Wai came into my room carrying a Chinese paper with Liao's face prominently displayed. For a brief moment I felt joy for him. Then I saw Wai's stricken face and the black frame around Liao's picture. Liao was dead.

First Zhou, then Liao. I felt as though my own father had died; he was the closest thing I had had to one for all those years in China. Without him China would never be the same for me.

The Chinese ambassador to Thailand, Song Ping, asked me to meet him at the embassy in Bangkok, where he and his wife spoke movingly of Liao, "our leader, our vice president." A state funeral would be held in a week, as was customary. He invited me, "as Liao's daughter," to attend with Liao's family.

Liao was greatly respected outside China, and nowhere more so than in Japan. On June 21, a few weeks after his death, Emperor Hirohito awarded the Order of the Sun to Liao, the first foreigner in Japanese history to be so honored.

The funeral was held in the Great Hall of the People, where we were received by Wu Lanfu, recently named vice president of China in place of Liao. Deng Xiaoping and all the other top leaders were there. "Be brave and courageous," the leaders said as they filed past the family. "Take care of your mother," they said to Liao Hui, who stood solemn and erect next to his mother. He was the heir to the family name and, some months later, would succeed to his father's official role, just as his father had succeeded his own mother. Wreaths were everywhere. It was an unsettling experience, with television lights and bright camera flashes going off in the background. But it was an impressive one as well. Liao's relatives came from all over the globe—the United States, Hong Kong, Europe, and other Asian countries.

Li Xiannian, the president of China, delivered the official eulogy. "He was born on 25 September 1908 in Tokyo," I dimly heard him say. I thought of Liao's Japanese dolls and his lovely Japanese screen and of how he had counted in Japanese.

"Educated and influenced by Dr. Sun Yatsen, Madame Soong Qingling, and his parents, Mr. Liao Zhongkai and Madame He Xiangning . . ." I remembered the first image I had ever had of Liao—sitting in Sun Yatsen's lap. And I thought of the affectionate rapport between him and his mother, of Liao leaning over her paintings, mischievously adding one of his own touches.

He had indeed felt "bitter hatred" toward Jiang Qing, as President Li was saying, but there was also "Liao's witty and jolly conversation." That was the Liao I'd loved so well.

Crowds lined the streets as the car bearing the coffin proceeded to Ba Bao Shan for the cremation. Liao Hui and Jing Puchun followed in the next car, and the rest of us, all seven other children, in a van. The next day we returned to Ba Bao Shan to collect his ashes and store them in the burial room next to those of other party leaders.

I stayed only a week. Every day I went to see Liao's wife. The day before I left, I walked into Liao's room for the last time. Bending on my knees in front of his large empty bed, still covered with the foreign detective stories and the Chinese and Japanese classics he so loved, I kissed it and prayed for him to go to heaven.

B y 1984 MY FATHER'S HEALTH, already poor, was deteriorating, and he was in and out of the hospital frequently. Inevitably, when the two of us were alone, he talked of China. "Whatever China is to become, it will always be the most important country for us. Its smallest move will shake our world. Nobody can ignore it." He hoped that China would always have a special place in our family's history. His wish was that Joe and Leo could spend time there, continuing the family's tradition into the third generation. I was not utterly opposed to the idea. I only knew that they would never go alone, without parents, as Wai and I had.

The opportunity soon presented itself. In March 1985 Wai and I were asked by the National Assembly of Thailand to lead the welcoming committee for a Chinese delegation from the People's Political Consultative Congress, led by an old friend of Zhou Enlai, General Lu Zengchao, the master planner of China's railroads. He knew of my link with Zhou, and that seems to have made for immediate trust. Would I come to China and help develop its railways? "You and Wai, the last hostages of China," he joked.

The next morning, as we walked along the beach in Phuket in southern Thailand, I told General Lu that I wanted to have my children educated in China for several years but that I didn't know how to do so.

"Don't worry about anything," he replied. "Bring them over, and I'll make sure that no harm will ever come to them, not so long as I'm alive." He was eighty-one but a vigorous man. I knew then that a plan could be worked out.

Still, I worried. I did not foresee any drastic emergencies in China, but I had to consider them, as well as the best ways for Joe, Leo, and me to live. At times I would be traveling, and they would need a reliable family setting. There would be no fully staffed palatial residence for them. I knew I could leave them in General's Lu's care or with Liao's family, but I also knew the new environment would involve a difficult transition. I wanted them engaged in China but not totally so. The best solution, I decided, was for them to live with their adopted grandparents, Sol and Pat, while attending an all-Chinese school. In school they could make friends their own age, while mixing on weekends with those I knew from my old world.

One night shortly after our arrival, Joe, Leo, and I went to dinner with Liao's family—Liao Hui, his wife, and their two boys; Liao's daughter Du Du; and Liao's son Ping Ping and his wife, the daughter of Marshal He Lung. Though Liao Hui had assumed his father's old duties, he had not changed much. He still rode a bicycle to his office.

"Uncle will take care of you," he said to Joe and Leo as he playfully mussed their hair. "But you must study hard and next time speak to me in Chinese." I remembered when those words had once been said to me.

We decided on the Second Experimental School for Joe and Leo, and they became the first foreigners ever to attend it. It had been founded in the late Qing Dynasty and had in recent years become a prestigious school for the sons and daughters of prominent young leaders and the grandchildren of the old revolutionary leaders. The special privileges and security Zhou had insisted on for Wai and me were no longer necessary, so the school authorities agreed to my request: no car. Joe and Leo could go to school by bus; they would be treated the same as the other children and be able to join in all the school activities. I laughed when I later heard how many of the children now came by car.

As Joe and Leo attended school, General Lu and I talked about the development of a huge coal mine in the Shen Mu-Dong Sheng area in Shanxi province and Inner Mongolia, the region where he had been a commander during the war against Japan. It was a desperately poor region, and without railroads its estimated 20 billion tons of coal lay untapped.

Old Lu knew every inch of the region. He knew its problems and the local people. Old Lu felt indebted to those who lived there; like Zhou and so many of the other revolutionary leaders I knew, they remembered the people who had made the revolution possible. To repay them, he wanted to lift the burden of their terrible poverty.

I listened with growing interest. If something succeeds in China, it is often because the knowledge of those at the top is matched by their ability to work effectively with leaders at the local level. Otherwise, so much that is pronounced in far-reaching plans never gets done or done well.

I met with various officials from the State Planning Bureau; I traveled throughout the region, sometimes by helicopter into the most inaccessible parts. Peasants still carried 150-pound burdens on their backs; their income was less than 100 yuan, or $25, a year. This was the mountain Zhou so often spoke of having to move. I promised to do what I could to help arrange consortium funding for what is now the Huaneng Fine Coal Corporation.

I had one other project in mind during the two years I lived with

Joe and Leo in Beijing. Father had asked me to set up a business venture with China as well, an oil-storage depot built on his parents' land at the mouth of the Chao Pra Ya River, where he had spent his early years. It would take a year of negotiations, and then several more years, before the project was inaugurated in February 1988. Father, I knew, would have been pleased, but he had not lived to see more than the initial arrangements. He died in June 1986.

For seven days people came to mourn him. Politicians, journalists, army officers came to pay their respects. Old friends spoke of how he had committed himself to the great issues of his time. They spoke of his deep love of Thai independence. Hardly anyone failed to mention his persistent, single-minded, brave efforts to find an enduring basis for friendship between China and his country.

When my mother died three years later, a large gathering honored her as well. Her many "political sons" came to pay her tribute—and to recount how she had helped so many and borne so much. My father's commitment had been public and obvious, but it was Mother's that had allowed the family to bear the costs and go on.

DESPITE ALL that had happened in China, many people, myself included, could not bring themselves to hate Mao. His accomplishments were too great. In the early 1980s, when there was widespread contempt for Mao in China's intellectual community—and bitter detractors claimed the Gang of Four had actually been five—I could not join the tide of repudiation. I did not believe it would ever lead to a realistic appraisal of recent Chinese history. Some wanted to praise Zhou and condemn Mao, but I thought this folly as well. Zhou would have been the last to set himself apart in this way. He felt that Mao's contribution was basically positive, and this despite his knowledge of the darkest aspects of Mao's leadership.

Some of the children of the old leaders returned determined to restore the honor of their fathers, but the best of them were not motivated by revenge or hatred. There was Liu Yuan, the only son of President Liu Shaoqi and Wang Guangmei. His father had been denounced as the chief enemy of Chairman Mao and the Communist party, and as a teenager Liu Yuan had witnessed the Red Guards' humiliation and imprisonment of his parents. Liu Yuan had been sent to the far north, and when he had finally returned, he and his sisters had written to Mao, asking what had happened to their parents. Finally, they had received a short reply: "Your father is dead. But you may visit your mother." That was all.

His father's body had been buried in secret, and for years Liu Yuan had searched for it. Finally, it had been found buried in the name of a peasant in Kaifeng county. Liu Yuan had decided to begin anew where his father had died. Instead of working or studying overseas, he had asked to be assigned to that region. He stayed there for ten years, eventually rising to become vice governor of Henan province in the early 1980s.

What was true of some of the children was true as well for the old leaders. Few men had been attacked more than Peng Zhen. Publicly humiliated and vilified, jailed for nine years, he had ranked close behind Liu Shaoqi as an archvillain. More fortunate than Liu, though, he and his wife had been able to live an ascetic life for several years in a remote rural area with their youngest son, Fu Liang. Once, after watching Fu throw a remarkable variety of odd ingredients together to make a tasty meal, I had asked where he had learned to cook like that.

"I cooked for my father all those years in the country. It sometimes meant scavenging for whatever I could find—weeds, rough grain—and figuring out how to make meals out of it. I learned to use practically anything!" And he had laughed. Fu Liang did not seem filled with hatred. Nor did Peng Zhen, who still saw Mao as a great man in Chinese history, too much a part of his generation to simply be dismissed. "His contribution was immeasurable in Chinese history; his destruction was enormous," but the former was greater than the latter, he had once said.

The leaders' attitudes were shaped in part by what they knew and their children did not: the source of the vicious personal attacks on them. At the very beginning, the leaders never expected the Cultural Revolution and Chairman Mao to turn against them so ruthlessly. But when that happened, they knew full well the vast store of personal resentment and vengefulness built up through the Party's history—particularly as embodied in three key leaders of the Cultural Revolution: Jiang Qing, General Lin Biao, and Kang Sheng.

Liao had told me to "trust Chairman Mao" but to analyze the situation for myself. Many of the leaders said much the same to their children. When Liu Yuan had asked why his father was being attacked so mercilessly, Liu Shaoqi had said only, "Criticism by the people is not wrong." He had assured his children that he had done nothing fundamentally wrong, that he had tried his best to live by certain values and standards. "It is the people who write history," he had said, "and I have never gone against them or the Party." But he had known full well how much both Lin Biao and Jiang Qing were involved in isolating Mao from his old comrades.

Such explanations helped few of the leaders' children make sense of the ferocity of personal vindictiveness and savagery that tore apart the Chinese elite. Most of the children stood by their own parents; but for many it was all but impossible to withstand the merciless propaganda against other senior leaders. Mao was portrayed as fully in command, agreeing with the assessments—and condoning the attacks. I never believed what was said of Liao, but I was confused by the accusations against others. I was stunned to see Peng Zhen, Liu Shaoqi, Yang Shangkun, and Lu Dingyi excoriated during the initial months of the Cultural Revolution. Liao had not explained that these attacks involved a settling of old scores. He had not said, "It's Lin Biao who's behind this. It's Jiang Qing. It's Kang Sheng."

By early 1967 the old leaders knew something else as well. The center had divided. Power had slipped from Mao's hands into competing centers that now defined the world within which he had to maneuver.

Many of the leaders supported some of Mao's objectives in the cultural Revolution. Many were concerned about the spread of privilege and bureaucracy. Few thought that much had changed in the early days of the Cultural Revolution. Even though mass movements in the past had often exacted considerable suffering and violence, Mao had always demonstrated an exceptional capacity to wrap those campaigns up and to derive certain positive lessons from them.

"Our parents were confident," a friend said. "They didn't oppose Mao at first, and when they realized what was happening, it was too late." Mao's role had been diminished after the Great Leap Forward, yet in those years the Party had used the image of Mao to bolster itself. "It is as though we needed an emperor." In reality Mao seemed to be slipping into that imperial role, immersing himself in such beloved classics as *The Three Kingdoms*. During the 1960s I heard allusions to this. "If you read *The Three Kingdoms* once," one leader told me, "you are well informed about Chinese history. If you read it twice, then you are starting to get a little too clever. But if you see somebody reading it three times, don't make friends with that person."

During the years I lived in China in the mid-1980s, I joined many of the leaders' children in discussions of what had happened. "Mao thought he could control his wife and people like Lin Biao and Kang Sheng, but he could not," an old friend said. "Mao never envisioned quite what happened; he had wanted a Cultural Revolution but never one that risked breaking the center apart. I think he meant what he said in July 1967, when he explained his concept as a three-year program: first year, 1966, the opening of the movement; second year, reviewing the situation; third year, bringing it to an end. But even as he spoke, it was too late. He became more a symbol of China's unity than its reality."

Zhou had survived, barely. In the 1980s I heard much criticism of him for not breaking with Mao and doing whatever he could to stop the excesses of the Cultural Revolution. But given the world of power that then existed, Zhou had to bide his time, watching as even his closest friends were brutally assaulted or, like He Lung, killed.

The Zhou I came to understand was deeply loyal to Mao. The two of them had never been equal, but they were ultimately inseparable. Mao needed Zhou; Zhou never thought of operating apart from him. Like the virtuous official of the *Huang di*, the emperor—a comparison Zhou himself made—he protected Mao from his follies yet remained devoted to Mao's interests, trying to ensure that the center held while working to provide for an orderly succession. Unlike Liu, Peng, and many of the old generals, Zhou had no ready organizational base of comparable power. His informal network was never completely smashed, but his ability to act directly and forcefully was crippled.

At times Mao spoke of Zhou as the "tactician." There was a certain coolness in that description. Mao was the great strategic genius of the Chinese revolution, but Zhou was admired for both his tactical flair and his skills in dealing with people. Mao, some felt, had wished to have both.

"I only want to be Engels to China's Marx," Zhou once said. He never had any desire to be number one. He saw Engels as dedicating his life to the accomplishment of Marx's great work, subordinating his own concerns to support the other's talent and vision.

Zhou concluded that by the end of the Cultural Revolution China had no unifying core but Mao. Mao might have been reluctant to give up the cherished revolutionary beliefs he had sought to consolidate in the Cultural Revolution, but when it came to key decisions on future leaders, he, too, accepted this verdict. That is why he agreed to Deng Xiaoping's being brought back. And it was not to a member of the Gang of Four that Mao turned for a prime minister when Zhou died but to a relatively unknown transitional figure, Hua Guofeng, who Deng, Mao, and Zhou knew could play the arbitrator's role. Whatever Mao finally felt about Deng's actual commitment to the revolutionary vision, he knew the costs China would have to pay if the center he embodied were torn asunder when he died.

Zhou was determined to open China to the world, but it was not clear how that was to be done. The system of self-reliance was deeply shaken. When the old leaders returned after the Cultural Revolution, they knew the Party was no longer the same. Too much of the foundation had been destroyed to simply build on it again, and the once-powerful Party was now tired and deeply demoralized. Something bold and new had to be tried.

Liao, too, was unsure what China's course should be. He knew that China had to change and that external capital would have to play a significant role. "China cannot live in a snail's shell," he said. But he watched uneasily as various leaders cast around for models to follow. Was it to be Yugoslavia, as one delegation that returned from there proclaimed? Or Japan? Or the United States itself, long the archenemy? On one thing the old leaders agreed: there would be an explosion against Communist rule unless the enormous energies of the people could be channeled into economic productivity.

By the early eighties, economic development, the market, and the United States had all become wildly popular. Once, shortly before he died, Father asked, "What really is happening with China's development?" The country seemed confused by the sudden discovery of the wealth of the outside world. Father had long respected China's independence; he did not wish to see this lost.

In its own way the economic reform was a kind of mass movement, different from but still comparable to those I had lived through, from the antirightist movement and the Great Leap Forward to the Cultural Revolution. I had known China as a country that swung from one extreme policy to another. The economic boom of the 1980s in some ways represented such a swing, although in slow motion. The Chinese were bewildered by the rapidity of the changes; they wanted economic development but were disoriented by the enormous corruption accompanying it.

Among some of the old leaders, enthusiasm for the United States was often ambivalent and limited. "Our American friends, American imperialists," they'd sometimes say privately. Many knew how contradictory aspects of the policy really were. Others plunged in without reservation, many forgetting that China had to do anything other than simply follow a foreign model.

Nowhere was this attitude more prevalent than among Chinese intellectuals. Many spoke of wholesale Westernization and adoption of U.S. ways, idealizing as they did both the United States and its wealth. Mao had turned on them repeatedly and had never trusted them enough to let them use their full talents; now it was often their resentment that fueled their idealization.

Zhou had sympathized with the intellectuals, but as much as he was aware of Mao's hostility toward them, he knew the problem ultimately stemmed from their own weak roots among the peasants and workers of China. The intellectuals looked up to power; historically they had served the emperor, or, if they went into internal exile, they withdrew to tend their own gardens and thoughts. Under the Guomintang the intellectuals had never emerged as a force to be reckoned with; they had not been strong enough to lead a revolution.

Zhou moved easily among these people; Mao never did. At first this seemed odd to me: with his love of the classics and of Chinese history, Mao seemed very much a Chinese intellectual; certainly the most highly educated, albeit self-taught, Chinese leader of his time. Part of the difference, Zhou said, lay in Mao's remarkable intuitive grasp of the peasants, without which, he felt, the Chinese revolution would not have succeeded. According to Zhou, Mao had an unsurpassed ability to communicate with China's peasants through his slogans. His aphorisms and pungent statements were deceptively simple: direct and subtle, they carried various connotations that made sense to the peasants. Mao had successfully appropriated forms of classical thought, once the exclusive preserve of scholars and officials, to mobilize the peasants. In so doing Mao challenged the traditional role of the Chinese intellectuals, who never quite recovered from the blow to their status in Chinese society.

Many intellectuals went abroad, feeling fortunate to get out of China and pursue their own interests. Others lauded Western ways to such an extent that they cut themselves off from the world of China's peasants and workers. That separation, Zhou often said, made it hard for them either to find their own identity or to create a new role for themselves within China. In such a divided world there can be no inner balance or any conviction that China can creatively find its own way to deal with the modern world.

The Chinese word for "China" includes the character *zhong*, meaning middle, center. As Zhou frequently observed, *zhong* also implies balance. For him it was the opposite of *luan*—chaos, loss of direction, loss of balance, with all the attendant disorder.

As I watched China dive headlong into this new economic world, I thought of the story Zhou had told me about how many of his own people sometimes lost perspective.

"A man was on a long journey," Zhou said, "and after a time he ran out of food. He struggled on, but there was nothing to eat, and he was becoming desperate. Finally he met a family on the road, and he asked them for some bread. The old lady in the family gave him three mantou, which was all she had. The man was still hungry, though, and when he passed a house by the road, he went in and asked for food. The people there gave him half of a bun. Now he was full and felt satisfied for the first time in a long while. That half bun saved his life, he said, thanking the family profusely."

Zhou never forgot his history. He knew how much the latest policies built on the contributions of the past. He remembered those who had sacrificed to build the revolution. China had found its own revolutionary ways at great cost; he ardently believed it could—and must—do so in the era it was entering as well.

Zhou had a deep inner confidence about himself and about China. Because he criticized so many of China's old ways, his pride in China and its accomplishments is sometimes overlooked. He was an intense patriot, an earnest proponent of making a new China out of the old. He also knew more about the world than many of the other leaders did. Zhou wanted a prosperous China, open to the world but confident in its own ways. It was the loss of such confidence at the top that partly led, thirteen years after his death, to the events at Tiananmen Square on June 4, 1989.

As I watched the demonstrations on television in Paris and spoke to his friends in Beijing, I wondered why the leaders refused to meet with the students. If it had been Zhou, I thought, he would have invited them to talk as he had during even the worst days of the Cultural Revolution. The newscasts showed children kneeling in front of the Great Hall of the People to submit their letters of complaint, but no one came to take them.

Several days after the horrific ending, my second husband, Anton Smitsendonk, then the ambassador of the Netherlands to the OECD, and I held a reception at the official residence in Paris. The guests were aghast at what had happened in Tiananmen Square. Several of the Western ambassadors had already openly condemned China. Now they looked at me. "What is your explanation for this massacre?" I felt like a criminal placed in the court docket. I felt they expected me to both explain it and to join in their condemnation of China. I could not.

While I knew that what had happened was horribly wrong and that enormous government corruption had fueled the protests, the reaction of the West distressed me as well. Westerners had little sense of what it meant to feed a billion people and to live on the edge of survival for so long. They had lived too long, too comfortably amid their own wealth and power.

When I returned to China a few weeks later, I sensed the shame among some of the old leaders. They had been revolutionaries; they had lived their lives guided by the desire to change the China in which they had grown up. The curse of Chinese history, Zhu De often said, is that dynastic revolutionaries become, in time, the old system. Or as one general put it, permanently withdrawing into his house in a traditional form of protest, "I didn't fight all those years in the PLA to shoot the people."

IN THE EARLY 1990s I took a European delegation to meet with a senior Chinese official in Zhongnanhai. The meeting was to be held in the great throne room where Zhou had once taken my mother, brother, and me some twenty-five years before. Everything appeared much as it always had: the flowers, the willows, the orange carp in one pond, the prawns in another. As we walked in, though, I suddenly felt disoriented. The room was enormous but no longer beautiful. I had known this place only with Zhou. He had made it seem magnificent and yet a small room, barely able to contain him.

When I had been a little girl in Thailand, Father had lived in a large government house. He had worked with great power every day, but his tastes had been simple and his personal needs few. I had once become furious when Father told me he was planning to escape all the fuss and return to the fishing village where he had grown up. I wanted to dress up and enjoy the scene; he didn't want to think about it.

I had never viewed these traits of my father as a virtue until I met Zhou. "Why don't you live in a better place, Uncle Zhou?" I had asked him early in my days in China. His rooms were dark and damp. His wooden bed was covered with books and documents, and he used only one plain-colored padded blanket cover instead of the bright silk and cloth covers I saw in others' houses. He didn't even have a cupboard in his bedroom. He folded his clothes neatly on four chairs—two at the head of the wooden bed and two at the foot.

"And it's noisy, too." His pavilion was situated not far from the main street. Passing trucks sometimes shook the house.

"I even hear the voices of the people going by," Zhou said, laughing. "I like to be near them; it keeps me more in touch with daily life."

Liao recounted a story Chen Yi had told him about Zhou. Once while Zhou was away on a trip to the south of China, an administrator had ordered repairs to the house, replacing the brick floors with wood, adding various new conveniences, and bringing in objects to decorate it. Zhou had been furious when he returned. He had insisted on paying for everything himself, but his personal savings could hardly cover the bill. "What will I say when members of the cabinet wish to repair their homes?" he had asked Chen Yi. "The others will want to. How can I possibly justify this when our country is still so poor and in such difficulties?" Zhou had refused to return to his house. Eventually, all the luxury items had been taken away, and with Chen Yi offering some friendly persuasion, Zhou had returned.

My father had said that he wanted only to be like the lotus; though its roots are in the mud, its flowers are of rare beauty. He wished to remain pure in his commitments in a corrupt world. He wished to accomplish deeds that often had little to do with his self-interest or that of his family.

With him, as with Zhou, power and privilege were rooted in a deep sense of responsibility and a personal distancing from the trappings of luxury. I came to China with no real understanding of this aspect of my father's character. That I learned from Zhou. Neither of them was naive about the world of power. They sought to lessen its cruelty and harshness when they could, but they could not simply turn away from it either: their commitments could be realized only within it. "Life is a negotiation," Zhou often said to me. It was tantamount to a precept for him, determining how he lived and dictating that he tie his own sense of responsibility to the demands of his world.

"It is easier to gain power than to hold it." More than anyone else, he maneuvered to enable China to have a period of stability after Mao's death. He also encouraged China's decisive, and now irreversible, opening to the world. But he knew that China's inner balance comes from a deep confidence in itself and its ability to cope with its enormous problems. "Hold your head high and use it" were his last words to me.

To China, I remain partly a "hostage."

Zhou wanted me to be independent and to move between worlds. It is what I have tried to do. But the result has been a hard-won, uneasy resolution. If I am a bridge between worlds, I'm all too aware now of the chasm that bridge must cross. Indeed, both to span and to reveal that chasm is the commitment I have made.

It is, after all, what I was trained to do.